DICTIONARY
of
DREAMS

HINKLER
BOOKS

Dictionary of Dreams
First published in 2002 by Hinkler Books Pty Ltd
45-55 Fairchild street
Heatherton VIC 3202 Australia
www.hinklerbooks.com

43 42 41 40 39 38
14 13 12 11 10

ISBN 978 1 8651 5568 5

Text: Rose Inserra
Design: Adam McCrow
Editorial: Bridget Blair, Alison Glenny & Lucy Treloar
Printed & bound in China

To my dream girls—Melinda and Andrea—who encouraged me to make my dreams come true.

Contents

Preface

Vanessa woke clutching her stomach, her heart pounding. It was the same dream. For five nights she had dreamed that she was standing barefoot on grass when she felt something cold on her feet. Looking down, a snake passed over her toes and moved on. Within moments, she felt pain and a miscarriage began. But when she woke up the baby seemed fine.

Was something wrong with the baby? Was this an omen? Or, as her husband suggested, was it just her subconscious fears expressed through her dreams?

Can dreams tell us something about the future? Are some dreams more significant than others? Is it possible to learn the language of dreams and unlock their messages?

Dreams offer useful information about our unconscious mind. For centuries people have believed in the power of dreams to heal, offer spiritual insight, foretell the future and solve problems and daily dilemmas. The emphasis in this book is on trying to unlock the code to the messages that our dreams beam to us through images. In dreaming, our unconscious minds are aware of aspects of our personalities that our conscious minds do not want to acknowledge. Dreams are a way of bringing up issues that our waking selves would otherwise continue to ignore at the risk of our emotional and physical health.

Interpreting dreams can, therefore, help us better understand ourselves through learning more about our true feelings, thoughts, behaviour, motivations and values. It can also help us to solve problems. People in creative fields, such as artists, writers, actors and inventors, often get their ideas from dreams. The most important things to keep in mind are that dreams reflect our innermost thoughts and feelings, and that all events that happen in our dreams are personal to us.

Aknowledgements

I wish to acknowledge the help that I received from various people. Firstly, I wish to thank Alison Glenny who has done a large portion of research and editing. Without the help and advice of Jen Roberts, I would have been unable to authenticate dream definitions, or unravel the mysteries of Freudian and Jungian theory. I would also like to acknowledge the assistance of Lucy Treloar, who helped me greatly with the editing and fine tuning of this book.

Every attempt has been made to list references used in this text in the bibliography section.

Introduction

There are three main theories explaining why we dream.

❖ Sigmund Freud said that the function of dreams was to preserve sleep; but that theory is contradicted by modern studies
showing that dreams happen very regularly—at least four to
five times per night during the most active part of sleep,
known as REM (rapid eye movement) sleep.

❖ Carl Jung, another famous dream theorist claimed that the
reason we dream is to compensate for those parts of the psyche
or total personality that are underdeveloped in waking life.

❖ Other dream theorists tell us that dreams have a problem-
solving purpose. Dreams are supposed to deal with problems
we can't solve in waking life and to offer some kind of solution.

Technically speaking, a dream is a hallucination. A dream is
also a fantasy journey in our sleep that either reduces our
stress or tries to live out our greatest fears in the safety of
sleep. When we sleep, we get rest and relief from our
waking days. In this sense, dreams are a way of relaxing and
letting our minds drift away into distant worlds. In this state
we can interact in a non-physical sense with people, places
and both living and non-living things. How many of us are
sad when we wake up from a beautiful dream?

INTRODUCTION

When we are in tune with our waking lives, dreams can help us to understand ourselves better. If we interpret them correctly, we can find a treasure trove of hidden secrets. Who do we wish would 'vanish into thin air?' Who or what are we running away from in a chase scenario? If our teeth are falling out, should we be paying the dentist a visit or is it all to do with losing our grip on things? These are common images and scenes that are locked in our subconscious. Isn't it about time you unlocked the message of your dreams?

Unlocking the Messages

The land of make-believe

Some people can actually control what happens in their dreams. This state or ability is called 'lucid dreaming'. A lucid dream is where the unreality of the dream makes the dreamer realise that it can't be real. For example, if you are breathing underwater without the help of oxygen or dancing in mid air, you know it can't be true. The dreamer not only knows that a dream is taking place, but also can somehow control the dream and maintain this empowering state for some time.

The strange fact is that the dreamer is in a rational state and can act voluntarily in the dream while still remaining sound asleep in an incredibly real dream world. Lucid dreaming can occur during the end of a nightmare, when the dreamer realises that it is only a dream and decides to see it through till the end, as one does in a horror movie.

Have you ever had a dream where you said,
'This isn't real, so I'm not going to run away and be scared'?
If you have, it was a lucid dream.

Accounts of lucid dreaming date back to Aristotle, who recorded his experience and dismissed the whole thing as a sign of madness or a message from the gods. Researchers specialising in lucid dreams found that lucid dreamers can control parts, but not all, of their dreamscape. An experiment found that when subjects were asked to turn a light on in the dream, the light switch would either not work or the bulb would blow.

How long does a dream last?

Most dreams are in colour, but the images soon change into black and white and within about ten minutes the dream completely fades unless we conveniently wake up and make an effort to remember. That is why we tend to remember only the last dream we had before we wake up.

Some dreams can last up to half an hour, although they seem to go on forever in the dream. Oddly enough, within seconds of suddenly waking from a dream we are usually alert and responsive. However, if we are suddenly awoken from the deep stage of non-dreaming sleep, we can experience confusion and lack of coordination.

Can you feel emotions in dreams?

Do you ever get hurt in a dream and go through the motions of pain without experiencing any real pain? The reason the dreamer experiences an emotional detachment from events in the dream, and becomes more of an observer, is because parts of the brain controlling the emotions shut down during the dreaming sleep. That is lucky for the dreamer. Imagine the pain you would feel when attacked by a crocodile or falling down an abyss in a dream if you were to experience the actual sensation.

Sometimes when we wake from a nightmare we may be feeling physically shaky or sweaty, and this is a residue from the emotions felt in the dream. Nightmares are the end result of a frightening dream. Night terrors, on the other hand, suddenly appear out of deep, non-dreaming sleep. In a night terror, the dreamer sits up and suddenly screams, often experiencing some kind of horrifying experience. The terror and sense of panic can last for up to ten minutes and is a grave concern to parents whose children suffer this state of fear. Unlike their parents, however, children will have little if any recollection of this experience the next morning on waking up.

Understanding sleep

Nearly every animal sleeps in some way. It is evident that sleep performs some important function for the nervous system. Many theories have been suggested, but the most practical seems to be the one put forward by Nobel Prize winner Francis Crick. He claims that the purpose of sleep is to allow the brain to 'take out trash'—to undo daily events that don't need to be stored for long-term memory. Basically, as humans we need to get rid of unimportant mental items clogging our brains and recharge during sleep so that nerve cells can be re-engaged the next day to face a new set of tasks.

Experiments in sleep deprivation have shown that it is not lack of sleep that causes people to be disturbed, but 'dream' deprivation. Dreams are likely to be the result of the brain sorting through its short-term memory of the day's events, storing some in the long-term memory and getting rid of the rest.

Who dreams?

Science tells us that everyone dreams—even animals and birds. Some of us can dream in vibrant colours and recall every detail the next morning, while a few claim they never dream at all. There are also those of us who dream some of the time and can remember the dream in sketchy detail.

Did you know that we spend one third of our lives sleeping? Not only that, but we spend two to three hours per night dreaming. That means that by the time we're 75, we have slept for 25 years and dreamed for about 10!

So, when do we dream? There are four stages of sleep:

Stage 1 The first stage of sleep is a very light sleep. You can easily be woken and might deny having been asleep on awakening. Ever heard someone say, 'I wasn't asleep! I only had my eyes closed'?

That's because the brainwaves are going from a waking frequency (beta) to a more relaxed phase, known as alpha state. This is when the body temperature, heart and pulse rate drop slightly and eyes begin to roll. Drifting thoughts and floating sensations, as well as vivid pictures flow through the brain. Stage 1 may last for five to ten minutes.

Stage 2 In stage 2, the brainwaves keep on slowing down. This is a much deeper sleep than stage 1 and is when dreams start to brew. Although there are no clear images, thoughts and ideas float in and out of the sleeper's mind. The brain frequency has now reached a level called theta.

Snoring is common at this stage and there's a decreased heart rate, pulse, blood pressure and temperature. Breathing can be shallow and irregular. Ever had that twitch or jerk but still felt unable to shake yourself awake? This is the stage at which it happens.

More importantly, the eyes now move back and forth rapidly beneath the closed eyelids. This is known as REM (rapid eye movement) sleep, and lasts for a few minutes the first time it occurs. If one wakes at this time, the dream can usually be remembered.

Stage 3 This is a deep sleep stage, with stage 4 being more intense than stage 3. These stages are known as slow-wave or delta sleep. These long, regular delta waves produce a deep dreamless sleep. The sleeper's muscles are totally relaxed and the heart rate and blood pressure has slowed down. Breathing is steady and even, and it's going to be very difficult to wake up. Delta waves can last up to an hour before the dreamer goes into the deeper sleep of stage 4.

Stage 4 This is the deepest sleep. It is virtually impossible to wake up from this stage of sleep. The sleeper's blood pressure and heart rate fluctuate. There is an increased secretion of growth hormone (this is to restore body tissues). That is why it is so important for infants and children to get as much of this sleep as possible.

This is the stage when dreams occur and REM is at its best because the brain is in an active state. The first REM period will last approximately ten minutes. After that, the sleeper goes back into a deep stage 4 sleep. Then it's back into REM stage after a short time and the cycle is repeated until the sleeper wakes up. The final REM stage lasts about one hour.

These four phases of sleep repeat four or five times during the night, approximately every 90 to 120 minutes. So a person may complete up to five cycles in a typical night's sleep. The REM stage lasts longer, the more one sleeps. The longest uninterrupted period of dreaming occurs in the early morning and may last up to one hour. That's why you remember dreams most vividly on awakening.

What happens
when we sleep?

The discovery of REM sleep proved that sleep is not a dormant state for the body, but a mentally active period during which dreaming occurs. During REM sleep there is intense activity in the brain and rapid bursts of eye movement under the eyelids. Your body is still during this stage but your brain is very active. Scientists also discovered that the body is paralysed during REM sleep and the brain at its most active. To imagine this paralysis when one is not dreaming is a horrible notion, since in many cases dreams can be violent and active.

Interestingly, the paralysis is absent during non-dreaming sleep. Here, sleepwalking and sleep talking can take place usually in the deepest stage of non-dreaming sleep. Have you ever tried to wake a sleepwalker or make sense of what they are saying? Sleepwalkers are difficult to arouse, even more than dreamers in REM sleep are. The best course of action is simply to usher them back to bed without trying to wake them. They will feel disoriented and confused. They may sometimes act in a violent manner. Be warned.

While we sleep, our senses of hearing, touch, taste, sight and sound no longer function in the same manner as when we are awake. We are only able to utilise these senses in an emergency. For example, you may be able to smell the toast burning or you'll hear a loud thunderstorm. Generally, while we sleep our sleeping systems are working free of input from the outside world. And amazingly, people have vivid dreams—many of which involve all the senses.

So why can't you sleep?

From research on brain patterns during sleep, scientists have begun to understand and develop treatments for sleep disorders. Sleep disorders affect the quality and duration of sleep. Change of sleep schedule, stress, environment and illness can all affect the sleep cycle. Medical and psychological conditions such as depression shorten the duration of REM.

You can increase REM sleep naturally by doing the following just before going to bed:

❖ Eating foods that contain amino acid tryptophan such as turkey, milk, bananas and cheese

❖ Having a warm bath

❖ Not doing strenuous activities

❖ Meditating or relaxing

Did you know that the frequency of REM sleep is highest during early childhood years? It drops during adolescence and young adulthood and decreases in old age. Total sleep time becomes shorter during childhood and increases in adolescence. Older people get less total sleep but a lengthening of REM stage.

What the dream experts say

Dream analysts believe that in dreams our unconscious minds are providing clues to help us understand ourselves better and provide solutions to our problems. Not many of us realise that we are being productive while we sleep. The problem is remembering the dream vividly so that you can unlock its message and apply it to whatever is affecting you in waking life.

The earliest examples of dream interpretation come from the Bible. The most famous biblical dream is Pharaoh's dream about the seven fat and thin cattle and the seven fat and thin ears of corn, which Joseph interpreted as a prophecy of seven years of abundance and seven years of famine. Joseph's interpretation had a huge impact not only on Egypt but also on the future of dream analysis.

Greek philosophers improved on the early theories of dream interpretation. Plato called dreaming 'the between state', an actual place where the soul went to meet with the gods. Aristotle spoke of the illusion of 'sense-perception'. He suggested that the malfunctioning of the senses allowed dreams to occur and that dreams, therefore, were formed by these imbalances of the body.

Not until modern times did two of the greatest pioneers in dream analysis come along: Sigmund Freud and Carl Jung. Their dream theories contributed significantly to current explanations of dreams and their functions.

Sigmund Freud (1856-1939) is known as the 'father' of psycho-analysis. He believed that the analysis of dreams was a powerful tool in uncovering hidden thoughts and desires and, as a result, his work focused on finding the causes of dreams. Freud's psychoanalytical approach theorised that dreams are created by unconscious desires, especially sexual urges and hidden fears. He believed that our conscious minds are disgusted by our hidden desires and they repress these urges because we are ashamed or afraid of what others might think. He claimed that 'the purpose of dreams is to allow us to satisfy in fantasies the instinctual urges that society judges unacceptable'.

Freud created a method called 'free association' in which the patient describes thoughts and feelings as they come to mind. For example, if the therapist said 'blue', the dreamer would have to reply with the first word that came to mind. This method was used to discover the real issue behind the dreams. According to Freud, there was a repressed sexual motive behind most dreams. A snake, bird or pencil represented the male genitals while a wineglass, cave, glove or tunnel represented the female genitals. Flying, falling, ascending and descending stairways all represented sex.

Today, dream therapists do not strictly follow Freud's teachings. What are fascinating to analysts today are the revelations of the unconscious mind—thought to be more honest and representative of our true selves than our conscious mind.

While Freud was interested in finding the causes of dreams, his student, Carl Jung, looked to the purpose of dreams. Carl Jung (1875-1961) was a psychotherapist, a philosopher and a scholar of mythology. He believed in the 'collective unconscious'—archetypal images shared by people all around the world, regardless of their religions and cultures.

Learning about symbols and images: archetypes

'Archetypes' are universal symbols that are common to every-one because they represent something that relates to the universal principles of life, or themes lived by each one of us. Archetypal characters and symbols can come from religious teachings and images, myths, fairytales, folk tales and legends.

Here are some of Jung's most common archetypes that appear in dreams:

The Divine Child

The innocent, playful 'child' represents the true self. If you dream of a baby or young child, you may be starting a new activity or a new beginning. Perhaps you are looking for more childlike qualities to apply to your life, such as spontaneity, a new perspective, more trust and playfulness.

The Divine/Earth Mother

The nurturing, loving female represents growth, generosity and wisdom. Dreaming of a mother figure can mean that there are areas in life you need to nurture.

The Shadow

The 'shadow' represents those parts of you that are deeply buried because they are seen as bad and rejected by your conscious. These parts scare you or trigger unpleasant emotions and are usually the opposites of what you consciously project. Paying attention to the shadow means having to accept the 'dark side' of your personality and dealing with the issues involved.

The Anima and Animus

The 'anima' is the hidden feminine part of a man's personality—the feminine side. The 'animus' is the masculine part of a woman's personality. When you lose touch with these personalities, your life is not in a state of perfect balance. It would make sense, therefore, to take note of them in your dreams and apply their symbolic meaning to your everyday life.

The Wise Old Man

The 'wise old man' can be represented by any authority figure whom you respect. It could be a king, judge, priest or an older person, whom you wish to take advice from—whether the advice you get is encouraging or disapproving.

The Hero and the Hero's journey or quest

As in any hero story or epic, the 'hero' must encounter challenges, hardships, villains, temptations and danger. To begin the hero's journey, you must first be cut off from your roots and be mistreated or misunderstood. Then you can begin the adventure and discover your true self, which only comes after encounters with all the challenges listed above. Finally, you experience an understanding and acceptance of your heroic self and reach your goal. It is time, then, to go back to the past—back to the time when you were misunderstood or mistreated—and enlighten those who caused you to feel this way. This process is one of spiritual growth and essential for development and enlightenment.

The Fool or Seeker

If you see yourself as the 'fool', or not efficient, in your dreams, the dream is suggesting that you have an important lesson to learn. The 'seeker' is looking for knowledge and experience and if the dreamer feels immature or naïve, it shows that he or she is unprepared and needs to gain knowledge.

Monsters

Monsters represent your worst fears or the parts of your personality that are usually kept hidden away. The best way to deal with these monsters is to face them and ask them what they want from you. This method helps you to deal with issues that are too scary for you to deal with in normal life.

Death and rebirth

Myths and legends describe heroes and creatures that die and come back to life. Even the Bible tells us of Jesus Christ who comes back from the dead. And nature gives us examples of this, such as the caterpillar that hides in its cocoon and emerges as a butterfly. When you dream of death, it is usually an indication of personal growth and suggests that after death there is rebirth and transformation. It is a positive dream you should embrace.

Typical dreams

Myth: *If you dream that you hit the bottom in a falling dream it means that you will have died in your sleep.*

Falling

Many people have dreamed that they have hit bottom in a fall and they are still alive to tell the story! Falling is a common theme, which often indicates that in your real life you are feeling a little out of control and insecure. You may be experiencing a lack of support and grounding. In your waking life you may be feeling unsupported, unsafe or weighed down. The circumstances of the fall in the dream are important to notice. Were you pushed or did you jump willingly? Could it point to a situation in real life where you are trying to escape something, someone or a situation that you either cannot cope with or don't wish to face?

The place of falling is also important. If you are in a falling dream, do you clutch onto something to break your fall or do you close your eyes and fall directly below? If you can control your landing in a fall and perhaps have a soft landing, it could mean that your crisis in real life might not be as difficult as you imagined.

Flying

Sigmund Freud claimed that flying represented dreams of a sexual nature. Most likely they are dreams of a longing for freedom or of letting go, as well as dreams of journeying. You need to pay attention to the details in your flying dreams so that you can interpret correctly the way in which you see yourself journeying through life. When you fall in a dream, you experience a lack of support and grounding. In real life you may be feeling unsupported, unsafe, or heavily burdened with a wish to be freer and lighter.

Naked in public

It can be a nightmare to feel embarrassed in a recurring anxiety dream where you are the only one naked. Ask yourself in which areas of your life you feel embarrassed, incompetent or lacking in confidence. Generally, being naked in front of others represents a fear of being exposed in waking life.

Driving

Driving was another of Freud's famous dream images. He believed driving fast in a dream was associated with sexual prowess and power. It may well be that sex is a 'driving' force in your life; however, it can also represent the desire for power or success. Losing control when driving, or being on the wrong side of the road, suggest that you may not be in control of your real life. Perhaps life is too hectic, so slowing down and not being so controlling are reflections of real-life needs.

It's important to notice the scenery and other persons in the car or around you in the dream so that you can explore your life in more detail and take control of situations. If you are a passenger, perhaps you should ask yourself why you're not the driver and who has control of the car. Driving can also represent a personal journey. Problems such as loss of control can be indicative of the obstacles or struggles experienced during that journey. The other symbols in the dream will give clues about the reason for the journey.

Swimming or drowning

Water is a symbol of emotion and your spiritual life. If you are swimming in a dream, the surrounding circumstances could tell you about your emotional and spiritual state of being. You may be in a vast sea or lake, trapped in a pond or being swept downstream by a fast flowing river. How you cope in these situations may indicate your real-life drama. Can you swim safely to shore? If so, it's a positive sign that you're going to overcome your emotional ups and downs and reach your goal.

If you're feeling overwhelmed, and begin to drown, then emotions are too strong for you and you're unable to cope. Dark, muddy water is also pointing out that you are stuck or are confused about an emotional issue.

Stuck in slow motion

Of all nightmarish dreams this one can be the most frustrating of all, particularly if you dream of being chased and can't get away. This could well indicate that you are stuck in real life, unable to get anywhere fast enough, or to voice your true feelings.

Being injured

If part of your body is being dismembered and you are feeling pain, it may well be that you are neglecting or mistreating aspects of yourself in real life.

Being chased or attacked

This common dream is one of the most frightening and can be disturbing. You have to ask yourself who is chasing you and why. The person doing the chasing usually represents a major fear—your shadow, or hidden self—that has grown to a huge proportion and causes terror and a feeling of being a victim. To find out what this fear or aspect of yourself is, ask the pursuer in the nightmare why they are chasing you. By facing your fear, you are standing your ground. This can in turn help you to stand up for yourself in your conscious life and take charge.

What to do with recurring dreams, anxiety dreams and nightmares

Almost everyone has experienced dreams that contain anxiety or fear. These experiences can be traumatic and haunt us by recurring repeatedly

Typical nightmare themes include:

✤ falling

✤ being chased or attacked

✤ walking into a meeting or a class unprepared

✤ being stuck in slow motion

✤ being trapped and unable to move or scream

✤ drowning or choking

✤ being naked in public

Experiences of this sort are unpleasant and usually tell us that we are not making progress in solving our real-life conflicts. Some theorists believe that recurring dreams are due to lack of action in the dreamer's waking state. One of the reasons for dream interpretation is to solve these problems.

What is a nightmare?

A nightmare is a distressing dream, which can cause us to partially awake. How many of us have sat upright from a nightmare, our hearts thumping with fear and glad to be awake? Did you feel negative emotions in the nightmare such as guilt, sadness, anger and especially fear and anxiety? The most frightening and common nightmare is probably being chased. Anxiety is heightened when we can't move, are trapped in slow motion or are paralysed and keep falling down.

Nightmares are regarded as a warning about current behaviour patterns or imbalances that we need to solve if we don't want such unpleasant dreams to repeat themselves. Some people try to block nightmares and those who have recurring nightmares usually try to change the outcome. However, if we block them or ignore these messages from the subconscious for too long, the nightmare may begin to show up in our real life—not as in the dream but as accidents, illnesses and relationship difficulties.

What causes nightmares?

A number of factors may cause nightmares, including:

✤ medication

✤ illness

✤ suffering a traumatic event

❖ undergoing a great deal of stress in one's life, such as surgery, loss of a loved one, an accident, a divorce, moving house, change of job, pregnancy and concerns about financial or other matters

Young children tend to have nightmares as they struggle to learn about dealing with the usual childhood fears and insecurities. It is normal for the majority of children to have nightmares between the ages of three and eight.

Carl Jung observed that parts of an individual's whole personality may become 'disowned' and these are frequently projected outward in dreams. These take the form of devils, monsters, intimidating people or animals, or even natural events such as tidal waves, floods and tornadoes. These symbolic forms are what Carl Jung referred to as 'the shadow'. If we become any of these elements of our shadow through nightmares, then 'accepting' these disowned portions of ourselves will help us reveal the message of the nightmare.

On the positive side, nightmares provide a release for the psyche as they can bring us valuable insight into what is causing the most stress in our lives.

Resolving nightmares

What can be done about nightmares? Young children should be encouraged to discuss their nightmares with an adult if it is a recurring nightmare. Usually, children forget their nightmares soon after waking. Adults' nightmares offer the opportunity to understand what is going on in their waking lives. With practice you can learn to unlock the code of the symbolic language of the nightmare and see how it relates to your real-life fear. Usually the dream connects to your life, and sometimes to your past, by evoking a specific feeling.

If you are distressed about a recent nightmare, redesign a different ending to the dream. Choose something that leaves you feeling empowered, instead of helpless, as you did with your original nightmare outcome. Then apply this new happy outcome to areas in your life that you feel need attention.

What are night terrors?

Night terrors are sudden, dramatic interruptions in our sleep and are quite different to nightmares. Nightmares occur after several hours of sleep—the dream phase of REM sleep—and they wake up the sleeper with a vivid memory of the dream. Unlike night terrors, nightmares do not usually involve screaming, thrashing about or running around without a purpose. People usually remember nightmares, but sufferers of night terrors have no recollection of the dream.

Night terrors occur during the first hour or two of sleep—the deep non-REM sleep—and can last anywhere from ten to thirty minutes. They're most common in children, causing them to bolt out of bed, thrash around and scream or run wildly though the house. Their eyes may be wide open, but they are not awake; neither are they aware of anybody around them. Night terrors can also cause children to sleep-walk and/or to urinate in bed.

Symptoms of night terrors include sweating, sudden awakening, terror, screaming, rapid heart rate, confusion and inability to explain or recall the dream. Night terrors, sleepwalking and sleep talking are all disorders of arousal, called parasomnias. They are usually brought on by stress.

Extraordinary dreaming—who can do it?

There are have been countless numbers of accurate dreams predicting future events. These are known as precognitive dreams. It seems that we are able to pick up information through a faculty other than our five physical senses.

Famous prophetic dreams

❖ Several people predicted President Kennedy's assassination a few days before it took place.

❖ A few days before his assassination, President Abraham Lincoln dreamed of his own corpse, laid out in a room in the White House.

❖ Several passengers, having dreamed that the *Titanic* sank, decided to cancel their trip at the last minute and lived to tell the tale.

❖ Joan of Arc dreamed that God instructed her through dream visions to save France from the English.

Other less famous and well-known events have been predicted by people all over the world, but there seems to be no scientific explanation for why this is so. However, it is wise to listen to warnings and omens as they may be pointing to things that need fixing in our lives, such as our health and well-being.

Forecasting dreams

When the body consciousness senses an imbalance, a warning of disharmony sounds throughout the body. That warning signal works its way up though the brain as we sleep and registers in the conscious mind as a forecasting dream— that is, a dream that forecasts a potential physical problem.

If you dream of a specific part of your body that is at risk, pay particular attention to it. If you dream of problems such as your car radiator overheating, it may be something to do with your overactive emotional state. Cars and houses often symbolise your body. For example, if the brakes won't work you may be feeling out of control and stretched for time. If the car won't start, perhaps you're lacking energy and need to refuel. A house renovation indicates that major work needs to be done on the body— whether it's exercise, rest or a health-check. If your house is on fire, you may be feeling feverish or perhaps have too many blankets on.

Insects are also another good indication of what's going on in your body. Dreaming of insects in general denotes infection; while maggots, worms and moths suggest that there is some sickness or emotional state that's 'eating away at you'.

Creative dreaming

Writers, artists, musicians, dancers and inventors have all found inspiration and reached their full creative potential by having lucid dreams or 'dream incubation' (see below).

Lucid dreaming takes place when we are aware that we are dreaming while still asleep and in the dream. Have you ever said, 'Is this a dream?' while you were dreaming? Or perhaps you're familiar with the dream and decide to change the ending or sequence of the dream. This means that you are manipulating the dream so that you affect its outcome.

Famous creative dreams include the following:

❖ Mary Shelley wrote *Frankenstein* after she had a vivid dream.

❖ The novelist, Stephen King, is said to find inspiration for his novels in his nightmares.

❖ Robert Louis Stevenson got the idea for *Dr. Jekyll and Mr. Hyde* from a dream.

Other artists who credit dreams as a source of inspiration include Mozart, Beethoven, William Blake, screenwriter Ingmar Bergman and many others. Inventors are also highly inspired by their dreams. Otto Leowi's dream resulted in the chemical mediation of nerve impulses. Others include Elias Howe's discovery of the sewing machine and many of Thomas Edison's inventions.

Experiencing a lucid dream

Lucid dreams are the ultimate virtual realities where anything is possible and the dreamer has some element of control, masterminding adventure, science fiction, romance, or gravity-defying stunts with no physical limitations. We can perform amazing feats in which the boundaries of the imagination are the only limits. Tibetan monks use lucid dreaming as a spiritual tool on the path to enlightenment.

How many of us can fly with owls and birds, swim with dolphins and dive underwater like seals or climb like mountain goats on the giant slopes of the Himalayas? This feeling of exhilaration, or being able to do anything, can translate itself into a creative process and be a great tool for anyone in the creative field. Dreams offer the chance to have fun, adventure and to explore one's creativity, as well as being used for healing or gaining insight.

Sleep on it—dream incubation

Dream incubation involves consciously asking the dream for guidance in solving an actual problem in waking life. There is an old saying that if you have a decision to make, it is best to 'sleep on it' beforehand. That way, you'll find a solution that isn't based on emotion or just a gut reaction.

To incubate a dream you must, before you go to sleep, have your question or problem clearly in your mind and then ask yourself that question. For example, you may ask 'Is this relationship good for me?' In the morning, record the actual dream and your thoughts about it and try to work out the meaning.

Unlocking your subconscious images

These are some common elements in dreams that can help you with dream interpretation.

Mood

The mood of a dream can help you to interpret the meaning more accurately. It may be totally opposite to how you would feel if you were in a real-life situation. Are you feeling confident facing lions in the Colosseum when in real life you would be terrified? Make a note of the mood, the people and place and action to help you work out why you felt that mood or emotion. Perhaps the dream is telling you that you are more confident than you give yourself credit for.

Activity

Physical and mental activities in dreams can actually make you feel exhausted when you wake up. Perhaps your life needs more action or you should put yourself in an un-familiar situation where you can use skills that are presently underdeveloped.

Setting

The place you find yourself in a dream is also an important clue to the message of your dream. The scenery usually represents the inner self, while weather conditions can suggest your mood.

Buildings may be a setting for the story of the dream or may be important keys in themselves. School could mean you should study something carefully in real life; an office represents status; a bar reflects your social life; a train station is about direction and a bridge could mean that two aspects of your life need to be linked.

The house represents the dreamer's inner self. Each room within a house symbolises a particular part of self. A room high up in the house represents the spiritual self or higher states of consciousness. Basements represent the primal or the emotional self. The bedroom is indicative of passion and rest.

Mountains can represent your aspiring self—reaching for success or spiritual goals. Freud, however, saw mountain peaks as phallic symbols, representing sexual desires.

Water represents your emotions. Whether it's ocean, lake or river, the appearance of the water is significant in your dream. Clear water gently lapping against the shore is usually a good sign, while stormy waves engulfing the swimmer is a sign of the dreamer being overwhelmed by emotion. A murky pool, or being stuck in mud, is also a reflection of being emotionally stagnant in your waking life.

Characters

Sometimes you dream of people you know or have known, while other times they may be strangers or famous personalities. The people in your dream can represent different aspects of your own personality. It's important for you to question your reaction to how they behaved in the dream. Do you see uniforms? Is it because you're a rebel or that you wish to conform? Perhaps you have a meeting with the president. What does this suggest about your attitude to things or people in real life? Are you traditional in your view? Do you 'rule' people?

Animals can either represent themselves, people you know or even aspects of your own personality. Birds usually stand for freedom; cats are independent; dogs are loyal; farm animals are productive; bees are hard workers; spiders are creative.

Recalling and interpreting your dreams

Do you have problems remembering your dreams? The problem of dream recall and lucid dreaming is that waking and dreaming memory aren't connected very well. This means that as the dreamer you have to make a consistent effort to remember and record your dreams.

Here are some tips to help you remember your dreams.

* Before you fall asleep, remind yourself that you want to remember your dreams. This desire to remember will provide motivation for your memory to respond to in your waking hours.

* Keep pen and paper by your bedside. As you wake up, try not to think of the day's routine. Focus on your dreams and their images and jot them down. Any distractions will cause the memory of your dream to fade. If you can't remember the dream, record the last thing you remember, or even fragments of the dream. It may not make sense right away, but eventually it may form a pattern that you'll understand.

* Don't try too hard to remember dreams. Sometimes, the harder you try to remember the easier it seems to be to forget. Be patient and persistent and stick with it for at least a few days before expecting results.

Using a dream diary

When you have written down your dream, read it through. This will help you to remember more details and make it easier to interpret.

Record as many details as you can. What was the mood of the dream? Think about how you felt in the dream, your actions, decisions, the location, the characters, symbols, colours or anything that stood out as distinctive.

Write down anything that has been causing you anxiety, stress or joy in your waking life. Compare these emotions with those felt during your dream. Sometimes the relevance of the dream is not immediately obvious. Ask yourself what your unconscious is telling you with the help of a dream dictionary and your own intuition.

Dream interpretation

The most important factor when learning to understand the messages in dreams is that they are your dreams and that it is up to you to unlock that message. Dream interpretation is very general, as the same dream can have a different message for each individual dreamer. It is best to use the dictionary of dreams as a guide only.

Ideally, break down the dream into symbols, archetypes, common elements and images first and then work out the more specific details. Follow your own instinct, relating the dream to your conscious life and using all the information in this book, design your own individual guide to your dreams.

How to interpret a story dream

To interpret a dream that has a story-like structure with a beginning, middle and an end:

❖ Break down the dream into scenes, as you would with a movie. Write them down.

❖ Identify the main elements of each scene and pay attention to the characters. Are they authoritarian, passive, helpless or frightening? Is there a conflict or problem?

❖ Look for emotions, especially those that are easy to identify such as love and fear.

❖ Interpret the dream literally at first and try to make sense of its main purpose. How did the dream end? Was there a resolution?

❖ Link your dream to something that's happening in your waking life. Try to identify the characters from your dreams.

❖ Decide what you're going to do and how you're going to act on the dream's message.

Case study: A story dream about an icy adventure

The dreamer is a 40-year-old woman who is deciding whether or not to end her marriage.

I was on a large ship floating on ice. 'I wonder if the weight of the ship will break the ice?' I thought. I looked outside and saw no sign of life—just ice and icebergs. But then I saw something moving in the distance. There, all in a row, were tiny baby snow goslings. They were white and fluffy and had orange beaks with black edges. I called out to my brother excitedly, but he didn't believe me at first. Then, with time, he saw the goslings too. Soon someone sighted a whale circling the ship. Time slipped by and I was home again. My parents asked me where I'd been. I told them I'd been on a trip to a cold place far away, but I was now back.

There are a number of symbols in this dream:

Symbol	Meanings
Ice	Frozen emotions; the dreamer's lack of warm in the marriage; her present life.
Ship	The dreamer (a vessel); she questions whether she can hold out in the state she's in—that is, the marriage being like an inhospitable frozen sea, ready to break at any minute. Would the ship (dreamer) float (make it)?
Goslings	New beginnings; taking new chances.
Brother	Masculine side of the dreamer—the rational and logical; the voice of reason doubting the dreamer's instincts.
Whale	Large part of life—the future/the unknown waiting to embrace the dreamer.
Parents	Nurturing or conscious side of self.

Interpretation

The dream is reassuring the dreamer that there will be a new life for her despite her present state of indecisiveness. The future is bright and she will be able to cope well with whatever decision she makes. It is a positive dream, full of reassurance and hope.

Dream Dictionary A-Z

A

Abandonment

Dreaming of being abandoned suggests that you are experiencing feelings of being unloved, unwanted and emotionally isolated to the point where you have difficulty focusing on any future success in your life. If you abandon others in a dream it indicates your anxiety about overcoming difficult conditions involving other people and situations. Trouble and quarrels, loss of money and friends are all associated with abandonment dreams.

However, abandonment dreams can also be seen as expressing a need to 'let go' of people, tensions and conditions that have been causing you grief, confining you to a negative perspective. Try viewing abandonment dreams as a sign of release and your need to move forward in a positive manner.

Abbey *see also* Buildings

To dream of an abbey or church environment means peace of mind, comfort for the soul and freedom from anxiety and stress. This building symbolises a place of sanctuary where guidance and direction can be sought and a peaceful and positive resolution to your problems can be achieved.

Abbot and other religious figures

This dream may be warning you of negative vibes around

you, particularly those of judgement and criticism. Be aware of smooth talking and flattery and do not be taken in by it. To dream of becoming an abbot or monk suggests that you are longing for peace and time out to reflect on your present lifestyle.

Abdomen *see also* Body

If you dream of pain in this area, it's a good idea to have it checked out by your doctor. Sometimes our conscious minds may be concerned about parts of our bodies and this anxiety may come out in our dreams. It may also be a sign to trust your 'gut' instincts about people around you. Feeling the naked abdomen indicates a recovery of money according to traditional beliefs.

Abduction

Dreaming of abduction can have different meanings depending on the position and circumstances of the events surrounding the dreamer. If you are the abductor, the dream suggests that you have a desire for control and power over a person or situation. If you dream that you are being abducted, this shows that you are not in control of circumstances surrounding your life and that you feel yourself being carried away by the enormity of it all. Dreaming of being abducted also reveals that you could be experiencing trouble and unrest in present relationships and situations in your life. It suggests that others are setting the pace and calling the shots and that this is leaving you vulnerable to their actions.

Abortion

As the action suggests, abortion dreams are about the release and termination of anything that is not working or is

41

no longer wanted in your life. It also represents feelings of rejection, guilt, sensitivity and anxiety associated with starting new ventures. It should be viewed as a sign to overcome troublesome events in your life and get rid of those things that are hindering your progress.

Above

Dreams of an object or something hanging above you and about to fall on you suggest that some danger or mishap surrounding you is present. If an object falls, but lands near you rather than striking you, it suggests that you will escape whatever hazard was meant for you, but that you must exercise caution.

Abroad

This dream signifies that a change is needed in your life. You are feeling very unsettled and have a real desire to break the chains and be free of the confines of your present circumstances and environment. The idea of travelling to a foreign destination invites new prospects and changes in your present work, choice of lifestyle and people involved in your life.

Abscess

A dream about an abscess is a dream of contrary meanings. If you are presently ill, dreaming of illness actually signifies that you will enjoy good fortune, health, or a speedy recovery. These dreams can also reflect illnesses in various other parts of the body, in which case suggesting that your system is in need of attention or cleansing of impurities that will enable it to heal more quickly. On a symbolic level, dreaming of an abscess indicates the need to rid oneself of bad influences, particularly friends.

Absence

Dreams in which something is 'absent' suggest that there is a 'missing' element from the picture that prevents it from being whole. For example, if you are placed in a room that has no door, this can signify that there is 'no way out' of a situation, whereas an absent window may indicate a need for more 'openness' in a situation. These types of dreams can also have contradictory meanings. For example, if you dream that an absent friend dies, it means that a wedding is imminent, while if you are happy over the absence of friends, it means that you will soon be rid of people who are causing the problems in your life.

Abyss

Just as an abyss suggests a 'bottomless pit', to dream of one or any hollow space foretells of trouble and difficulties ahead. Confrontations, quarrels, threats, loss of control and failure are all associated with this type of dream. If you fall into an abyss, you can expect your fears and disappointments in any given life situation to be realised and be overcome only with a feeling of loss. However, if you manage to avoid falling into an abyss you will overcome your troubles and recognise your potential, which will lead to self-acceptance and success.

Accident

Interpretation of an accident dream varies according to the surroundings and circumstances of the dream. One interpretation views the dream as a premonition of an actual accident threatening the dreamer, so it may be a good idea to avoid any type of travel for a short while. Accident dreams in different settings such as at sea, on land or in a car suggest disappointments in your love affairs and concerns in your personal and business ventures. They also warn of unexpected circumstances that can be accompanied by feelings of anxiety and insecurity. Dreams about accidents may be drawing attention to issues such as safety and the need to take extra care in your daily life.

Accounts

Whether you are dealing with checking and adding up figures or having accounts presented to you for payment, 'accounting' dreams are a warning that you stand to lose your money if you are too free in giving credit to the wrong people or institutions. If the accounts balance, then it is a good indication that a profitable venture is coming your way. Psychologically, it can also imply that you are 'accountable' for your actions. Do you need to 'pay back' a favour or repay someone with kindness? Working on accounts can also mean you are avoiding the work needed to solve financial problems.

Ache

Depending on the circumstance, a non-threatening ache can be attributed to some physical experience and a sign of ill health. If the ache is intense, it suggests that an upcoming important event will be very beneficial to you personally. This is likely to be a reference to the saying, 'no pain, no gain'. Aches in specific body areas, such as the back, suggest a lack of support or a feeling of being 'exposed'; a headache relates to the unsettling of the mind and heartache denotes some kind of emotional distress.

Acid

Handling, observing or drinking acid has psychological overtones that suggest you have something weighing heavily on your mind and conscience. Feelings of anxiety, being placed in compromising situations and a sense that your general well-being is being 'eroded away' by external influences are all related symptoms. Although you may feel that these issues are eating away at you, there is the opportunity get rid of all 'poisonous' issues troubling you at the present time.

Acorn

An acorn dream is one that foretells good health, wealth and happiness. It signifies there are many pleasant things ahead and that you can expect good luck. The saying that the great oak tree grows from a small acorn is symbolic. You can expect huge growth in your personal life but patience is needed for the process to become complete. In Europe, where anything related to nature's goodwill is a favourable dream, acorns are regarded as a symbol of well-being. Planting an acorn and seeing it grow is symbolic of a wonderful life ahead.

Acquaintance

To dream of people you know is a good dream. However, the degree of your relationship with the acquaintance, and the manner in which you conduct yourself in the dream, determines what message your dream is sending you. For example, if you are having a pleasant conversation with the acquaintance, then you can expect your business affairs to run smoothly and your domestic life to be stable. If you are engaged in a heated and loud discussion with the acquaintance, then you can expect a series of humiliating and embarrassing events to surround you. Making a new acquaintance in a dream could indicate that a change in your life is about to occur.

Acquittal

To dream you are acquitted of a crime signifies that you are about to come into possession of valuable property and become wealthy. Others being acquitted will also experience prosperity in business. Guilty people being acquitted indicate a period of ups and downs in fortune.

Acrobat

To watch acrobats performing means that you must be careful or you are likely to have an accident. If the acrobat in your dream is unable to perform his or her act, this signifies that you will escape whatever misfortune was intended for you. If you are the acrobat, it means you will experience difficult times but you will eventually overcome the difficulty. If the acrobat has a mishap then the dreamer's plans may go astray.

Acting

Dreams of acting and giving a performance suggest many things. If you are acting, it means that you will need to work hard for your money and your plans may be delayed; but if you work hard and persevere, you will be pleasantly rewarded and everything will work out right in the end. Performing dreams may also relate to the act you put on in front of others in real life. Do you feel that you're giving a good performance? Is it draining to keep up appearances and act as if everything is fine even when this is not the case? Acting may also suggest that your self-confidence is low and your performance may not be as good as you/your boss/colleagues/family expect it to be. It may also mean that you are avoiding serious problems in your real life.

Actors

To dream of meeting with actors is an indication that trouble in the domestic sector of your life is likely. The meaning of the dream will depend on the character portrayed by the actor, and whether the performance is tragic or comic. If you dream of a comic performance, you are generally happy with your present life and will continue to be so. If, instead, you dream of a tragic performance it may indicate that tough times are ahead. Shakespeare's words—'all the world's a stage and men and women are merely players'—may well apply to your next 'stage' in life. From a psychological perspective being an actor can represent uneasiness about present situations in life.

Adam and Eve

It is a good omen if you see the first biblical parents, Adam and Eve. The creation story may be telling you that you'd like to be 'first' at some achievement and seeing Adam and Eve will make those plans come to fruition. It can also be symbolic of balance between feminine and masculine aspects of inner self—the coming together of the dark and light side of personality, which again represents balance.

Adder see Animals, Snake; Reptiles

Address

If you dream of an address that has significance to you, your dream is trying to draw your attention to, and make you deal with, a situation that happened in your past but is still troubling you in your present life. If the address evokes feelings of safety and happiness, then you can take your mind back to that period and see if something is missing. If the address evokes feelings of unhappiness, this signifies that you wish to escape from the past but are being reminded of how you behaved at the time and that you now have an opportunity to correct it. Writing down an address usually means luck and predicts that good news is coming. A new address indicates a major change. A negative association with an address may signify that there is a feeling of alienation or lack of belonging and thus a need to move on in reality.

Admiral

To dream of a high-ranking naval officer may be an indication that something of importance will be coming your way, perhaps elevating your own status. It might represent an important event outside one's control that will bring about significant personal change as well as change in lifestyle.

Admiration

Being admired in a dream suggests that you have made useful friendships and that you crave approval from your peers. To admire others means that you are looking for guidance in some area of your life.

Adoption

If you dream that someone adopts you or that you have adopted a child, it could mean that you will be taking on some family responsibility. It could also mean you have been searching for your ideas to be adopted or that you may need to do so.

Adultery/Affair

Dreaming of an affair can indicate your need for excitement and stimulation. To dream of your partner committing adultery brings out your own feelings of sexual inadequacy or insecurity with emotional commitment. It may also be making you aware of temptation in some area of your life

A

where 'cheating' or some other dishonest method can be employed to make your life more exciting. The dream in this case is warning you to resist this temptation and not to stray from your honest ways. An affair with a famous or powerful person signifies that it's fame or power that you crave in your life.

Adventure

Exciting adventures in dreams can be a release from our ordinary lives. The wild and thrilling action in our adventures, which dreamers crave and suppress, is the opposite of our mundane working lives. Ask yourself whether you feel restricted, burdened or unfulfilled in your present life and if you wish to escape.

Adversary *see also* Enemy

To see your opponent or adversary in a dream could indicate conflicting forces in your waking life. If it involves confrontation, you may be having some difficulties in getting your point across and people just don't support your views. By not giving up and trying hard you can overcome these problems. You may also need to face your opponents in life in order to move forward.

Advertisements

If you see an advertisement billboard in your dream, take notice. You may need to pay attention to something you've been ignoring or treating poorly in your life. Be prepared for unexpected changes coming your way. Watching TV advertisements may suggest that you are prone to believing everything you hear and so there's a need for you to be more discerning. If you are aware of advertisements featuring in your dream it may be telling you that you'd like to be publicly acknowledged for something or that you need to sell yourself better in order to achieve the recognition you crave and deserve.

Advice

Receiving advice from someone in your dreams, particularly if it is from a wise old man or woman, is an indication that you need to listen to what others are telling you. You may also need to listen to yourself and your intuition.

Aeroplane *see also* Journey

An aeroplane indicates a swift journey, transporting you from one location to another. If you fear air travel, dreaming of being a passenger can be pointing you to some fear involved in travel. Freud regarded flying as a sexual dream—one of wild abandonment and desire for freedom. If you feel that you have no control over the plane, then it may suggest that there are issues in your life's journey that need to be addressed. If you are at ease with flying in a plane, it may indicate that you wish to rise above the rest and find an escape. A pilot means that you are in control of where your life is heading.

To dream of an aeroplane crash may not be a prophetic dream telling you of what is to come, but it can be a dream that reveals your feeling of helplessness in the face of things beyond your control. As planes are associated with long distances, the crash may be telling you that there will be a major change in the distant future.

Affair *see* Adultery

Affliction *see also* Illness; Health

If something is bothering you, or isn't quite right with you, pay attention to the details. Any health issue should be heeded. Traditionally, dreaming of affliction suggested that success was approaching and change for the better was assured.

Afloat *see also* Floating; Water

If you are floating on calm and clear water and are very relaxed, it indicates trouble-free times ahead. If the water is rough, on the other hand, be ready for a bumpy ride to wherever you are heading in your waking life. It may also mean that you cannot simply 'float' in life, particularly when it comes to emotional issues, and must make some responsible and concrete decisions. A dreamer feeling afraid of being afloat can suggest feeling cut off and isolated from part of him or herself or from others.

Affluence *see* Wealth

Africa

Africa is associated with adventure, wild animals and dangerous landscapes. Dreaming of this ancient and complex continent suggests that you long for something with these qualities in your life. It may not be necessarily be restricted to travel but to parts of your life that lack excitement, urging you to expand your horizons and adopt a new perspective.

Age/The aged

To worry about your own age could mean that you are burdened and feeling older than you actually are. It is wise to consider seeking medical help or using relaxation methods to give you an energy boost and prevent you from getting ill. Seeing old people in your dreams suggests wisdom and it's a good sign. It may mean that you have achieved some sort of enlightenment or that through hard work you will achieve your goal.

Agony *see* Pain

Agreement *see* Contract

Air *see also* Sky

A dream about the open air may be interpreted in various ways, depending on the details. Clean air and blue skies is an indication that life is positive and optimistic for you. Cold air or a draught suggests that plans may not go the way you'd hoped and that emotions need to be kept in check. Beware of anyone giving you the 'cold shoulder' or 'icy look'—all these idioms can alert you to why you're dreaming of the image. If the air is foggy or misty, trouble may be lurking and it's best to postpone any plans or changes. Stormy or cloudy air could be warning you that an illness or an unforeseen event is on the horizon.

Airport

An airport is a symbol of transition. A busy airport represents your desire for escape and freedom, while an empty one indicates that your own plans may be delayed.

Alcohol

To dream of drinking alcohol to excess represents the need for escapism. It may signify the need for you to be more 'honest' and 'less uptight' about things, as consuming alcohol allows us to be more open and sociable. However, beware of the consequences of your actions. Drunkenness is a lack of self-control and excess in any form is not a desirable trait.

Alien

An alien is someone not belonging, something or someone that is foreign. To dream of aliens suggests that we need to face part of ourselves that 'alienates' us from others. Ask yourself whether your ideas or views are too strange or 'alien' for others around you to appreciate. If you dream that you're abducted by aliens, it may indicate a fear of changing and adapting to a new environment. Moving to a new job, interstate, overseas, a new home or a new status in relationships such as becoming widowed or divorced may induce these feelings.

Alley

The setting in a dream can give you an indication about your 'inner landscape' and where you're at. If the alley is clear and bright, then you have a reasonably easy road ahead, despite some 'narrow misses'. An alley way that is cluttered, dirty, with a dead end is a warning of conditions to come or how you're viewing your present circumstances, either in your private or working life. If the place seems familiar but in actual fact is unknown to you, perhaps you are not solving a recurring situation. Are you trapped? Are you lost? How you feel about being in the alley is a good indication of how you should interpret the dream.

Alligator *see* Animals

Almonds

The almond is traditionally considered a sacred symbol in the East, and to dream of eating one symbolises happiness and travel. If you eat a bitter almond be careful with your ventures. An almond tree, however, is a good omen of what is to come. Freud interpreted all trees as having an erotic significance in their phallic state. In some European cultures 'sugar almonds' are part of a wedding feast, where each guest is given a small quantity to eat. They symbolise good wishes for happiness, long life and fertility for the couple.

Altar

An altar can represent a dedication to some cause that is important to you. In olden times, sacrifices were carried out on altars and therefore may represent your craving to be acknowledged. To see someone getting married at the altar may be a 'giving up' of the individual to become a 'whole' new entity.

Ambulance

An ambulance is linked with urgency and speed. Attention should be given to whatever is troubling you so that your plans may come to fruition in the least possible time. If you wish to interpret it as a prophetic dream, it is wise to pay attention to your health and welfare.

America

America is mostly associated with material wealth, success and freedom of the individual. It may suggest that these qualities are missing in your life and that you may need to be more ambitious through your own effort and determination. An urban environment highlights the stress and the competitive edge that comes with city living, while a rural setting may indicate a desire for freedom and enterprise.

Ammonia

Ammonia is a potent liquid and therefore to dream of such a pungent smelling product is to be warned of potential risks.

Amputation

To dream of a limb being amputated is a dream of personal loss. It may be the loss of someone close, a friend, a family member or even finding yourself retrenched and having your livelihood taken away from you. There are many sayings related to amputation about cost (to cost an arm and a leg) and value (I'd give my right arm for that). Beware of giving away something valuable as it may cut you off from your sense of individuality.

Anaesthetic

To be anaesthetised is to feel nothing. This dream may be telling you that you are avoiding painful situations because of your fear of the outcome. Avoidance is not going to resolve the issue. Facing the consequences is a better option in the long run.

Anchor

Spiritually, the anchor represents hope and sanctuary. In everyday life it is a symbol of stability and safety. It may indicate that you need to remain 'grounded' in order to weather a storm or a difficult situation ahead. On the negative side, to be anchored means to remain stagnant in one place and be afraid of taking risks.

Angel

Throughout history, angels have been described as 'messengers' from a divine source. They represent goodness, protection and divine grace. To dream of angels is a good omen, forewarning you of some change in your situation. Their appearance could be a warning of things to come and to keep faith during trying times ahead.

Anger

Anger in a dream can be a release of hostility you actually have towards someone. At times we cannot express anger openly in our waking lives because we're afraid to hurt someone or they may be in a position of authority at work. In sleep, anger emerges because it can no longer be contained. Pay attention to this emotion as it may indicate your true feelings towards someone or some situation.

Animals

Dreams about animals can represent the animalistic side of the dreamer; that is, the dreamer's instinctive rather than intellectual nature. Animals often symbolise parts of ourselves or our personalities that are present in our waking lives. Freud attached a sexual significance to animal dreams, but many dream interpreters give various meanings depending on the type of animal. Usually a domestic animal symbolises harmony and happiness, but a wild animal represents an enemy or an uncontrollable force.

Alligator/Crocodile These animals symbolise a cunning enemy or obstacle to your progress. Being attacked by one means that you are insecure and have a fear of an impeding situation or people. If there are more than one of these reptiles in your dream, beware of new ventures or business dealings.

Antelope Antelopes are a sign of a financial gain or suggest that someone has sought your advice.

Ape/Monkey Dreaming of apes or monkeys is a warning that there are those among your friends or co-workers who are mischievous and will try to get you into trouble. It may also mean that your childish nature may prevent you from achieving your goals and that you need to pay attention to your work and less to 'monkeying around'.

A

Baby animals These suggest a need to be nurtured. Baby animals could represent new ideas or the immaturity of the dreamer.

Badger Badgers are traditionally associated with persistence—'badgering away' at something. Dreaming of a badger indicates that your perseverance will pay off and that success may be close at hand.

Bat Bats spell trouble for you in financial matters or in personal relationships. As these nocturnal creatures have been regarded with fear for centuries, they are a symbol of misfortune or upset plans when you least expect them. (*See also* Bats.)

Bear Bears can represent motherhood in general, whether it's the image of a possessive or a caring mother or someone who is overbearing. Fighting or killing a bear means that you will be successful in a present struggle. If you are attacked however, it means someone or some issue is after you with great ferocity. (*See also* Bear.)

Boar Trouble is ahead when you dream of wild animals and the boar is both wild and dangerous. If you chase or run away from a wild boar, it means that you will be disappointed as you may be escaping from an issue that you should be facing head on. Freud saw the boar as a symbol of power and oppression. In biblical terms, the boar is a sign of impurity. Killing a boar, however, means improved conditions in your life, particularly when dealing with authorities at work.

Bull To dream of a bull suggests negative and destructive emotions the dreamer may be experiencing in real life ('like a bull in a china shop'). Anger, aggression and impulsiveness ('like a bull at a gate'), as well as sexual passion, are all associated with the image of the bull. (*See also* Bull.)

Camel Camels are known as the 'ships of the desert' because of their stamina in hostile environments. They are a symbol of patience and perseverance. However, they are also submissive animals and therefore the dream may indicate that you are no longer willing to 'endure' your present situation and submit to others.

Cat These animals are independent and refined, yet powerful as predators. This duality in their nature often makes people wary of cats and reluctant to trust them. They have often been linked to the sensuous side of human nature—especially the feminine side. The dream is telling you to be aware of the cat's qualities that you may not be making use of, such as independence or intuition. To dream of a black cat has been traditionally associated with treachery and evil, but this may have been due to cultural superstitions.

Cattle In herds, cattle indicate prosperity and plenty. In biblical terms cattle are a symbol of success.

Cow A nurturer and mother figure, the cow represents warmth and nourishment. Dreaming of a cow may suggest that you are in need of emotional or physical sustenance.

A

Deer/Reindeer These animals are regarded as a symbol of hierarchy. The herd is organised with ranking in place and therefore the dream may suggest a questioning of your place in life—of where you fit into the scheme of things in general. Deer have also been depicted as innocent and as creatures able to move with grace and speed.

Dog Dogs are considered loyal, faithful and devoted companions. However, if they appear in your dreams as vicious, they may represent aggression. If they are friendly dogs, it may indicate either that you are faithful in friendship, or be representing someone in your life with these qualities. Expressions such as 'top dog' or 'underdog' can also express themselves in dreams. Jung and Freud classify dreams of being bitten by animals as erotic or sexual dreams.

Donkey/Ass These possess the qualities of obstinacy and humility. They can also suggest hard work and the need to be patient in your life.

Elephant It is said that an elephant never forgets so it is no surprise that dreaming of an elephant signifies memory as well as wisdom and patience. The Eastern belief is that the elephant signifies luck and prosperity.

Fox Dreaming of a fox signifies someone sly and cunning. It is a warning to watch out for this sort of person or behaviour in your life.

Frog Frogs are a symbol of transformation, usually from something insignificant to something of value (the frog turning into a prince).

A

Goat The goat is the symbol of perseverance. If you see one perched on a high cliff, it indicates that, with patience, you will overcome problems.

Hare Hares are nimble and resourceful animals. If you dream of a hare coming towards you, it may suggest that you will be experiencing a new venture in your life.

Hedgehog Are you about to handle a prickly situation? Hedgehogs in dreams indicate the need to make a difficult choice. (*See also* Hedgehog.)

Horse It is generally a good sign to see a horse in your dreams. It usually represents the dreamer's vitality ('as strong as a horse') and independence. As the horse was traditionally a mode of transport in the past, dreams of horses also relate to travel. The colour of the horse is important to interpreting the dream. A white horse is a symbol of your spiritual awareness; a brown one highlights the practical or earthy side of your personality; and a black horse is a sign of your 'dark' nature or the uncontrollable part of yourself. Dreaming of a black horse was traditionally a bad omen. If a woman is the dreamer and is kicked by horse, it may reflect her relationship with a man.

Hyena Hyenas are scavengers by nature, so to dream of one or more of these animals denotes deviousness.

Jackal For the ancient Egyptians, the jackal was a symbol of judgement and watchfulness. Over time, dreaming of jackals has become associated with death and their watchful place—the graveyard. Be mindful to watch those who are trying to discredit you in some way or who are trying to bring about the 'death' of your reputation.

Kangaroo Since a kangaroo is a wild animal, dreaming of one or more may mean unexpected and exciting travel. The kangaroo may also represent a subconscious need to unleash the wild side to your nature.

A

Leopard These animals usually represent aggression and tyranny. They are also a symbol of rivalry, so if you dream of one you should be aware of dangers and difficulties ahead.

Lion The lion is a symbol of strength, power and courage. If you dream of fighting with a lion and win without being either hurt or killed, you will be successful in your present struggle. A lion is also known as 'the king of the jungle' and as such, stands for the ego. The dream needs to be interpreted in the light of its outcome.

Lizard In dreams lizards indicate the qualities of single-mindedness and quick instinct.

Lynx The lynx is famous for its excellent and keen eyesight. Are you being watched carefully by someone or do you need to keep a keen eye on a situation or person?

Mole Moles are usually associated with darkness and blindness. Make sure that you go about your business with your eyes wide open.

Mouse Mice are an indication of trouble with family and friends. This stems from the fact that as rodents they scavenge and fight each other for their food. On the other hand, the mouse is known for its shyness and unobtrusive personality. The dream may be giving you a message about your lack of individuality.

Otter Otters work well as a team and thrive in complicated environments. Dreaming of an otter could indicate that you might be working in an environment that involves interacting and solving complex problems.

Pig The qualities associated with pigs are usually negative—greed, selfishness and filth. However, the fattened pig may stand for a healthy bank balance or satisfied home life ('as happy as a pig in mud').

Rabbit Rabbits are recognised as symbols of fertility and new life.

Ram Unlike sheep, rams are a sign of masculine power and authority. The message may be for you to stand up to authority.

Rat Rats are unpopular because of their association with spreading diseases. To call someone 'a rat' is to cast aspersions on their character, as rats are regarded as untrustworthy or devious. The dream could be a warning of impending disloyalty from someone around you.

Sheep Sheep are known for their innocence, lack of intelligence and flock instinct. In a dream these qualities need to be explored further before you can decide whether they apply to the dreamer or a situation.

Snake/Serpent Since the biblical story of the Garden of Eden, snakes have been associated with deceit and trickery, as well as temptation. In modern interpretation, the snake represents our suppressed sexual urges and uncontrollable passion. Freud regarded it as a phallic symbol. A snake

A

coiled around you means that you are enslaved to sexual passions. A snake in the grass, however, is telling you that there is disloyalty and trickery around you. Because snakes are poisonous, most people fear them and usually associate them with death. On the other hand, a snake coiled around a stick is a symbol of wisdom.

Squirrel In a dream squirrels indicate that you will get by in life if you work hard. They can also suggest an element of possessiveness in your personality.

Tiger This is an obstacle dream. The image of a tiger is that of a powerful and dignified predator. It has the power to create and destroy, and to get away from one in your dream means that escape from a destructive element in your life is on the horizon.

Tortoise/Turtle Take note of this dream, as in Aesop's fable 'The Hare and the Tortoise', slow and steady wins the race. It may be telling you that if you slow down, success will eventually be yours.

Weasel Weasels warn us of our devious nature or that of someone in our lives. This may have a negative impact on our present situation.

Whale As the largest mammal that lives in water but also breathes oxygen, the whale is a powerful image of the ability to handle difficult circumstances in life.

Wolf Hunting in packs is what we associate most with the wolf. The dream may suggest that you feel threatened on an individual level or as part of a group.

A

Zebra According to traditional gypsy interpretation, the zebra was a symbol of ingratitude and misplaced trust in friends. Its stripes denote a more modern meaning about the need to balance the positive and negative in your life.

Ankle *see* Body

Antelope *see* Animals

Antenna

Raising an antenna will mean better communication. The dream may be trying to tell you to listen more carefully to those around you so that you won't lose 'reception' with them, that is, that you will have an open channel of communication at all times.

Antiques

Antiques are a symbol of that which is old and valued. Buying antiques can mean that you need to embrace good old-fashioned standards and stick to your old tried and true solutions. It is also thought to be an omen that an inheritance is coming your way. Selling antiques means a loss of value, whether it's monetary or moral values. The mood and circumstances of the dream are important in interpreting this dream.

Antlers *see also* Horns

Antlers are traditionally associated with masculine superiority and power. In some cultures, powdered antler was thought to give one the power of the animal or enhance sexual prowess. The dream may suggest the desire for control and power over a situation.

Ants *see* Insects

Anvil

An anvil is a symbol of a primal force—a spark of new life. Traditionally it implies that good fortune is ahead despite some obstacles. It may relate to how you use your energy and whether it can be used more effectively.

Apartment *see also* House; Building

If the apartment is small, dingy and uncomfortable, it suggests that your financial situation is bleak and future prospects are not good. It also means that your family or partner is taking up 'too much space' in your life. However, if the apartment is spacious and lavish, there will be a substantial increase in your financial affairs and your family life will also improve. When interpreting this dream, try to recall as many vivid images as you can, so that the meaning of the dream can be more accurate. The state of the apartment may be reflective of the dreamer's self or emotional state.

Ape *see* Animals

Apostle

If an apostle speaks to you in your dream, it will contain a spiritual message. Pay attention to the details in the dream, as it may be trying to communicate to you that some area of your spiritual life needs to be attended to. Dreaming of an apostle indicates the dreamer's need for meaning in life, for something to believe in and a need for spiritual guidance.

Appetite *see also* Food

A lack of appetite indicates a diminishing of other drives in your life such as your libido or ambition to succeed. It may be a warning that your health is not as good as it should be. Feeling hungry or thirsty can be sexual desire or a need to consume what is around you—especially financially. Take care not to overspend and manage your money carefully.

Applause

Have you achieved something lately and want to be recognised for it? This is a wish-fulfilment dream. But beware that you are not vain, but genuinely wish to be appreciated or given approval.

Apple *see* Fruit

Apple tree

In biblical imagery, the apple is the tree of life. To see one in bloom or thriving is a good omen. A dead apple tree is indicating troubled times ahead.

Appointment

Time length in dreams is fluid and is rarely accurate. Having an appointment with a professional such as an accountant, dentist or lawyer may be an indication that you wish to use time more effectively. If you are on time for an appointment it means that whatever goal or project you have in mind will run on schedule. If you're frustrated and late with obstacles preventing you from getting you to the appointment, it may suggest that you need to be more efficient with your planning.

Apron

Are you tied to your mother's apron strings? Or perhaps you crave those times when you felt safe in your mother's arms. An apron can represent the need to be nurtured or that you need to connect to the nurturing side of your nature. It is also a sign of being domestic, so throwing away the apron can be telling you that you want to get away from domestic issues or the mundane.

Arab

To see an Arab in your dream suggests that you are concerned about your involvement in business transactions with someone outside your usual business clientele. Dreaming of being an Arab represents concerns about changing fortunes.

Arch

An arch in a dream is symbolic of distinction and gaining a new status. In Roman times, arches were erected after victories and named after Roman Emperors to mark the event. At some traditional weddings, the bride and groom walk under an arch together as a sign of a new status as a married couple. If you're about to take on new responsibilities or move into a new phase of your life, you may see an arch or doorway. Don't be afraid to go through, as your courage and effort will be rewarded.

Archbishop

As head of many Christian denominations, the archbishop is an important authority and spiritual figure. To be in the company of an archbishop could mean that you are holding onto religious beliefs of your childhood years. Your personal attitude and how the role of the archbishop was presented to you in your early years will determine the meaning of the dream. Are you struggling with a moral dilemma or a crisis of faith?

Archer/Archery *see* Arrow

Architect

If you see yourself as an architect, then you will be controlling your own plans. However, if you see an architect drawing plans it will mean changes in your business with possible financial loss.

Arena

As it is a place where games are held, an arena can indicate a need for release of tension. It is usually a place of conflict and competition and perhaps it is suggesting that you make a space in your life for these feelings. Arenas are also associated with ancient war games and battles. Do you feel that you have to prove your worth or courage?

Argument

Depending on whom you are arguing with, an argument can be considered to be a warning against a hasty decision. Are you arguing with yourself? Sometimes the person you are arguing with symbolises what you really are upset about. For example, arguing with a policeman could mean an argument against an authority figure in your life or a legal issue that you haven't resolved.

Ark

A positive dream filled with optimism about a new development in your life. Possessing an ark represents safety and protection.

Arm *see* Body

Armchair *see also* Furniture

An armchair is a place of comfort and familiarity. If you see someone else occupying the chair, it may be telling you that unexpected changes will be taking place.

Army

If you see a marching army it is a warning that a long journey is ahead of you, but with each victory there will be ultimate success. Fighting is an obstacle dream and it may be an expression of how you are feeling. If you see your life as a battle, it is a good idea to reassess what is making you feel this way. An army is often a symbol of discipline and obedience. Once again, you will need to think about where these qualities fit into your life.

Arrest

Being arrested by police in a dream means being caught out. It is a warning to choose your friends carefully and to be honest in all business dealings.

Arrow

An arrow signifies some strife or misfortune in your life. To dream of many arrows suggests that you see yourself surrounded by enemies. To break an arrow is symbolic of a failed relationship or business partnership.

Attic *see* Buildings, parts of

Autumn *see* Seasons

B

Baby

In dreams, babies usually represent something precious to the dreamer, such as a talent, relationship, or situation that needs protection and care. If the baby is sick or in distress, and you are unable to comfort it, it may be a sign that you are afraid of losing someone or something through your inability to nurture it adequately. A happy baby suggests a joyful sense of adventure or new beginnings. In dream lore babies are often identified with the dreamer's soul life, or 'inner child'. A healthy baby can also mean growth in a relationship or situation and the opposite if the baby is ill.

Baby animal *see* Animals

Back *see* Body

Backseat driver *see* Driving/Driver

Backstreets

Backstreets carry connotations of illicit activity or concealment. If your dream is accompanied by pleasurable feelings, it may suggest your sense of indulging in a secret or guilty pleasure. If the dream has anxious or threatening feelings, it is likely to indicate that you feel involved in something 'shady' and are fearful of the consequences should the activity become public knowledge. This type of dream indicates an inner desire to break loose, to explore the deviant side of self, particularly if the dreamer feels they are being good to others and not themselves in real life.

B

Badger *see* Animals

Bag/Basket

These are containers, and for that reason they serve as symbols of the dreamer's own consciousness. Is your bag or basket full or empty? This may tell you about your current emotional state. Are you having trouble finding things in it? Is it too full to carry comfortably? Perhaps you have too many commitments or responsibilities. The contents of bags or baskets can also stand for our 'emotional baggage'. Some interpreters claim that luggage represents our burdens: things in our life that need to be disposed of. If you are unpacking a bag, it may be a sign that you want to leave an unrewarding job or difficult relationship. Packing for a journey can forecast a new enterprise or adventure.

Baking

Are you baking in your dream? If it is a pleasant dream, the activity is likely to express your feelings of well-being, of being nourished, or of nurturing others. But if the dream includes feelings of anxiety, it is probably telling you that you feel overworked, or forced to take care of others at the expense of your own resources and well-being.

Balcony *see* Buildings, parts of

Ball

If in your dream you're watching a ball game without

joining in, it's a sign that you're standing on the sidelines of life; afraid to take the initiative because you think you may not have what it takes. In this case, your dream may be telling you that you need to place more confidence in yourself. But if you're right in the middle of the ball game, then it's a sign that you are a participant, who is confidently dealing with what comes your way. If you're throwing a ball to someone else, it could be a sign that you want to shift some responsibility onto another.

Balloon

If you dream of balloons, it could be a sign that you're longing for change. You're sick of your tired old routine and you want to rise up above the crowd and float off to new pastures. If the balloon is brightly coloured, expect a celebration in the near future. If the balloon is having trouble staying aloft, it's likely that you're feeling frustrated about your progress. To dream of balloons can also suggest that the dreamer has an inventive mind, which is not being used to its full potential.

Banishment

Being sent away from the company of others is one of the worst forms of punishment we can experience. Dreams of being banished usually draw on childhood experiences of ostracism or punishment. If you dream of being banished, it is likely that you are afraid of doing or having done something that will earn the disapproval of your friends or colleagues. However, it may also mean that you want time away from others because you are feeling socially pressured.

Banknotes

A dream with banknotes in it could be about your financial situation, but it could equally be about your creative or emotional life. If you're giving the banknotes away, it's probably a sign that you're feeling good about your current situation and the people around you. But if you're standing in front of a shop window full of beautiful things and your wallet is empty, it's more likely that you feel unsatisfied in your waking life. It's a good omen if someone in your dream is giving you money. But if you're borrowing money, then watch out that you're not over-extending your financial or emotional capital by getting involved in a dodgy business deal or relationship, or making an extravagant purchase. This could be a sign that you need to slow down and build up your resources. Giving away banknotes to relatives and friends may express an inner desire to help loved ones in times of financial troubles. This is a feel-good dream.

Baptism

Dreaming of a baptism suggests that you want the blessing of someone around you on a new project or activity. It may also suggest your desire for a new beginning or that you want recognition from your superiors of some special talent or property that you possess. In general, this is a positive dream that suggests you should move forward with confidence. It can also represent a cleansing or rebirth, being relieved of past transgressions and therefore able to move on without being hindered by the past.

Bar/Bar room

If you dream of being in a bar or a public house, it suggests that you need people around you for socialising. Perhaps you are feeling isolated in your private life and need to make new friends. Generally a dream about this public place is to do with how we relate to group situations.

Barriers

Dream barriers tend to symbolise our frustrations or the obstacles in the way of our progress, whether these come mainly from others, or ourselves. If you are struggling to cross a barrier in your dream, it suggests that your current situation requires effort and struggle. It may also suggest that you need to stop what you are doing and consider taking a different route towards your goals.

Basement *see* Buildings, parts of

Bath/Bathroom

As the Christian ritual of baptism suggests, bathing is a symbol of purification, regeneration and preparation for a new day. Water is also a symbol of our emotions; so if you dream of having a bath, it may be a sign that you need to pay more attention to your feelings. However, if you have trouble getting out of the bath, maybe you are too immersed in your emotions. Similarly, if the water is going cold, perhaps it's a sign that you are lingering too long over some activity or relationship. Dreams in which you are embarrassed about bathing in public suggest a fear of exposing your inner self and emotions to others.

Bats *see also* Animals

Bats are traditionally associated with night, caves, death and the underworld. For this reason they may symbolise the 'shadow' side of your personality or situation. Because they hang upside down to sleep, they also suggest reversal or opposition. The bats in your dream may be prompting you to take a contrary position, or look at things from a different perspective. This can be a warning that the dreamer is turning his or her back on what is important and taking the wrong path, seeking the more unworldly. Look back and don't run from present situations.

Battle

If you dream that you are involved in a battle or war it is likely to suggest that you are 'battling' difficulties, or striving to overcome opposing forces. Paying attention to the nature of your opponent in the battle may help you to identify what these forces are, so you can devise strategies for dealing with them.

Beach

If you dream that you are on a beach, chances are that you are overdue for a holiday and need to get away from it all. Dreaming of being on a beach can also signal that romance is headed your way. But if the beach is empty or threatening, then it's a sign that you feel rejected or lonely and want people to pay you the attention you deserve.

Beads

Beads suggest accumulation and order, and can symbolise material, spiritual or emotional wealth. If you are stringing beads in your dream, it may represent the need to be careful with something of value to you. If the beads are broken or spilled, it may signal your feeling that things are slipping out of your grasp.

Bear *see also* Animals

Bears are powerful animals that play an important part in the mythological beliefs and ancestor worship of cultures such as the Inuit and North American Indians. Because they walk upright like humans, they lend themselves to being made into symbols of human attributes. In Western cultures they are often taken as symbols of aggression and brute force. If your dream is menacing, it is probably a sign that you are feeling threatened by some situation or individual. However, because mother bears are known for protecting their young, the bear can also symbolise protectiveness and caring. A 'bear hug' can be reassuring, as well as frightening, and it may signal ambivalence towards a powerful person or figure in your life. Alternatively, you may be frightened of the strength of your own emotions.

Bed *see also* House; Furniture

Beds are symbols of rest, comfort and security. They are also associated with intimacy and relationships. If the bed is in an uncomfortable or dangerous situation (on top of a cliff, for example, or in a place where people are watching you) your dream could be telling you that you feel vulnerable or 'exposed' in your relationships with others. If you feel protected and happy in the dream environment, it is more likely to suggest your desire for an emotional or sexually fulfilling experience or relationship. If, in your dream, you are frightened by something under the bed, the dream may be trying to draw your attention to something that has been unconsciously threatening your relationship with another, or with yourself. Traditionally, dreaming of making a bed was interpreted as a sign to expect visitors.

Bedroom *see* Buildings, parts of

Bells

Bells in your dream signal the approach of an important event. If the bells are cheerful, it's likely to be a celebration. If they are mournful, you should be prepared for difficulties or sadness.

Betrayal

Dreams of betrayal suggest a fear of being disappointed by a thing or person. Perhaps you are worrying about a purchase or decision you have made. The dream may also be warning you that you have misgivings about a friend, associate or family member, or that you need to think about the advice others are giving you.

Bicycle

Cycling symbolises the dreamer's personal projects or aspirations. If you are riding your bicycle in the air, for example, it may suggest your desire to gain a larger perspective on your life and surroundings. Like all dreams with movement in them, dreams in which you are riding a bike tend to reflect how you feel about your progress in life. Take note of the surroundings through which you are cycling. Are you passing through attractive countryside, or are you lost in difficult terrain? Is your progress easy or an uphill struggle all the way? If your present progress is difficult, but you can see something attractive ahead, your dream could be reminding you that even if you are finding your life difficult at the moment, something better may be just over the horizon.

Birds

Like angels, which share their power of flight, birds are often interpreted as symbols of the dreamer's soul or spiritual aspirations. However, just as there are many different kinds of birds, so there are many possible meanings for this kind of dream.

Bird's nest If you dream of finding a nest full of eggs, good luck in business or a sudden windfall may be near. Dreaming of an empty nest, however, suggests disappointment.

B

Birds of prey Hawks, falcons, buzzards and other birds of prey represent our hunting instincts and our wish to dominate or be in control of our environment. These birds all have excellent vision and, together with their hunting skill, this makes them a formidable group.

Blackbird These common birds symbolise domestic happiness and the protection of your home. Dreaming of one could mean that you want to settle down. It could also signal your anxiety about the well-being or security of your family.

Caged birds These symbolise frustration, unhappiness and your desire for expansion and release.

Canary/Singing birds These birds are symbols of happiness and contentment.

Chickens Symbols of family life, chickens are possibly a sign that the dreamer wants to be a 'mother hen'. If in the dream you're having trouble keeping the chickens together, it could indicate anxiety about your children.

Crow/Raven Traditionally regarded as an omen of death; this bird is more likely to be interpreted today as a sign of change or renewal.

Dove This bird symbolises your desire for a peaceful resolution of a conflict. A dove is also a symbol of pure love.

Duck In Chinese dream interpretation, a traditional symbol of good fortune.

Eagle This majestic bird represents aspiration, vigilance, and authority. Its appearance in a dream is a positive sign in business or romance.

Flocks of birds Flocks suggest that the dream is about your relationships with others.

Flying birds Birds in flight suggest a desire for freedom, expansion and independence. Perhaps the flying birds in your dream represent your desire to escape from a situation which is 'holding you down'. Birds in flight are also associated with sexual desire and freedom.

Injured A bird that is injured or unable to fly suggests that some area of your life needs attending to before you will be able to move on.

Quail Traditionally, these small birds were regarded as a symbol of good luck. However, eating them was also thought to symbolise the risk of over-extravagance.

Raven *see* Crow

Stork This bird foretells change and is traditionally associated with the birth of a child.

Vulture This is a sign that you fear the evil nature in people.

Waterbirds Waterbirds such as ibises and swans connect with our emotional and subconscious natures.

Bird's nest *see* Birds

Birth

Giving birth in a dream is generally a positive image, suggesting new beginnings or the start of a project, in which you feel 'reborn'. If the birth is very difficult, it may reflect your fear of difficulties to be overcome.

Birthday

Dreaming about a birthday is likely to suggest pleasure, shared celebration and a sense that you feel appreciated. If the dream is anxious, however, it may be a sign that you worry about ageing and the passage of time. If you are being given gifts in a dream, your response to the gift may provide clues to how you feel about your friends. Dreaming of someone else's birthday could be a sign that you feel undervalued or forced to give your attention to others.

Black *see* Colour

Blackbird *see* Birds

Blackboard

Blackboards symbolise instruction: the desire to learn or remember something. They may also suggest that you are seeing the world too simplistically, in black and white. Or, you may feel anxious that something of value is in danger of being 'erased'. The dreamer may not be taking note of the lessons concerning them. Ask yourself what you have learnt.

Bladder *see* Body

Blindness

Being unable to see can be a frightening dream experience signalling the dreamer's sense of helplessness or inability to know or perceive something. Perhaps you are 'in the dark' about a matter affecting you. You may even be deliberately closing your eyes to an aspect of a situation or person which you find it difficult to acknowledge. However, blindness can also make us more aware of the information we obtain through our other senses. In classical mythology blindness is a characteristic of those gifted with the powers of inner vision and prophecy.

Blood

Because blood is a precious life substance, it is sometimes taken as a symbol of the life force itself. If in a dream you are losing blood, it may suggest that you fear weakness or being disempowered. Because of its bright red colour it is also associated with passionate feelings, such as love or anger towards another. Dreaming of blood may also indicate that you feel called upon to make a sacrifice.

Blossom

Blossom signifies new growth, change, and renewal. It may suggest that you're about to embark on a new activity or phase. In general, it suggests hopefulness about the future. Things are going to get easier, or you will begin to reap the rewards for previous actions.

Blushing

If you are blushing in your dream, it is probably an indication that you feel self-conscious, embarrassed, or uncomfortable about some situation or person. It might be a sign that you feel unfairly accused, or put in a humiliating situation by others, or that you fear that they will see through your defences. Blushing can also be a sign of sexual passion. Perhaps your blushing tells you that you are romantically interested in somebody, but afraid of embarrassment if your feelings became known.

B

Boar *see* Animals

Boat

Of all modes of transport, boats are one of the most suggestive. Perhaps this is because they carry us through water, a symbol of the emotions. The boat in your dream may be a symbol of your hopes and fears for the immediate future. Pay attention to the water surrounding you in your dream. Is it still and reflective, or are you buffeted by storms, or even afraid of falling overboard and being drowned? These details may be forecasting the emotional 'weather' you are currently experiencing in your journey through life. If the boat is drifting it may be a sign that you worry about not being in control of your life. If it is in danger of capsizing, you may need to act decisively to avoid a bad situation.

To dream of a boat is also symbolic of significant emotional change from negative to more positive emotion, particularly if the boat is moving through calm waters. If the weather and water are stormy then it's a warning of conflict or emotional turmoil to come.

Body

The human body is made up of many different parts, and one or more of these may figure strongly in a dream. If a particular aspect of your or another's body features strongly in a dream, the following interpretations will help you make sense of the message the dream is sending you.

Ankle The ankle is both a support or foundation for the body, and a possible source of weakness. If you dream of ankles, chances are that these associations will be present in the dream. For example, if the dream is anxious, it could be signalling that the foundations of a certain matter aren't sufficiently strongly laid. But if you feel strong and happy in the dream, it is more likely to be a positive message about your strength and confidence.

B

Arms To dream of arms suggests an emphasis on striving if the context is business or adventure, and nurturing, if the context is romance or family life. If you dream that your arm is cut off, it suggests that you are anxious about losing someone close to you. A broken arm signals a fear of difficulties ahead.

Back Back problems are a common injury, so a dream about a bad back could simply be warning you about your health. But if your dream is of people turning their backs on you, it is a sign that you fear the jealousy or disapproval of those around you. In general, the backbone symbolises strength of character and firmness.

Bladder If you are conscious of your bladder while dreaming it's probably just your unconscious registering an actual pressure on this part of the body. Symbolically however, it may suggest 'pressure' on your general health or well-being.

Bones To see bones in a dream is a sign that you haven't gone deep enough towards the heart of a matter.

Breast Because female breasts have both erotic and nurturing associations, they tend to symbolise contentment, plenty, and gratification. They could also be drawing attention to the dreamer's relationship with his or her mother, or with the person from whom he or she expects nourishment and understanding. If a woman dreams that her breasts can be seen through her clothes, it may signal her sense that she is admired by someone.

Buttocks Usually a sensuous dream; they can be a sign either of erotic satisfaction, or financial prosperity. Buttocks are also associated with redecorating, especially furnishings.

Constipation This is a symbol of the dreamer's inability to let go of attachments or forms of behaviour that are no longer relevant.

Eyes As organs of vision, our eyes symbolise our qualities of perception and intuition. To dream of being blind suggests a disorder in these faculties, while dreaming of the eyes of another signals a fear of being observed or 'found out'.

Face Your own face seen in a mirror provides a clue to your current state of mind. If it's happy and smiling, things may be better than you think. If mournful or worried, it is a sign that you need to explore an issue that is giving you problems.

Finger A finger usually occurs in dreams as a symbol of our fear of losing something.

Hair Hair is a symbol of virility and also of our attractiveness to others. Dreaming of losing your hair symbolises anxiety about these matters. If you dream of long, luxuriant hair, it could be a sign of sexual fulfilment or the start of a new affair. If you're trying to untangle your hair, it is a sign

of your need to pay attention to a 'knotty' problem or difficulty in your waking life.

Hands Hands are associated with our creative powers and
general ability to make things happen. Hands that are gestur-
ing or using sign language indicate frustrated communication.

Head The head usually symbolises the whole person: personality, hopes and fears. A disembodied head signifies
imbalance in your life.

Heart To go to the heart of a matter is to explore its very
core. To dream of your heart is therefore a positive sign of
self-knowledge.

Intestines 'Having guts' or being a 'gutsy' person means
you are unafraid to do something. To dream of 'guts' may,
therefore, be a sign that you wish you were 'gutsy'.

Knees Traditionally, gypsies interpreted dreams of falling
on your knees as a sign of the dreamer's need for help.

Kidneys These symbolise a need for cleansing and renewal.

Legs Legs represent our support and 'drive'—that is, what
motivates us. Legs carry us forward and support our whole
movement. If you are dreaming that your legs are weak or
paralysed, consider whether you have lost your confidence
in some aspect of your life, or whether your motivation is
not as strong as you wish it to be.

Mouth This part of the body symbolises our most basic
needs, and tells us whether or not they are being fulfilled.

B

Nose The nose is associated with breath, and therefore with the dreamer's soul or essential qualities. To dream of a blocked nose can be an indication of spiritual or emotional problems. If your nose is a source of embarrassment, the dream implies your self-consciousness about a current aspect of your personality or your situation.

Penis If you are a woman and dream of having a penis, the dream probably suggests your desire to behave more assertively or have more authority or confidence, qualities that are considered to be masculine. This dream could also be a result of the subconscious's desire to freely explore or imagine other roles and identities. For men, this dream is most likely to take the form of a threat or anxiety about castration, in which case it indicates lack of confidence or a fear of punishment by an authority figure.

Stomach/Belly The stomach is connected to your 'gut' reactions and instincts. Dreaming of the stomach could be a sign of the need to examine a matter or emotion that you have been avoiding.

Teeth The teeth are traditional symbols of aggression and appetite. Dreaming of dental problems or of losing your teeth is very common, and signifies fear of impotence or reduced authority.

Vagina The vagina is associated with the dreamer's femaleness and sexuality. It may represent the confidence and self-image of womanhood, and the desire to create—either socially, reproductively or artistically. In a man's dream, it may suggest his desire for sexual expression.

Weight loss or gain To dream that your body shape and size changes radically tends to indicate your difficulty in accepting a major change in your circumstances or personality.

B

Wrist Like the ankle the wrist is both strong and delicate. It indicates a need for balance or coordination of opposites. It is also a symbol of connection or joining.

Bomb *see also* Explosion

Dreaming of a bomb suggests that you may be feeling 'explosive' at the moment. Are your emotions in check? What explosive situation are you dealing with? It may have to do with a relationship or with matters at work. If the bomb explodes in your dreams, it indicates that a sudden and unexpected event will take place as a result of deep feelings that have been brewing. We refer to people being 'walking time bombs' when their emotional and psychological states of mind are not balanced. On a deeper level, it is generally believed that a bomb represents your fear of death.

Bones *see* Body

Books

Books can symbolise your accomplishments; the wisdom or success you have accumulated during your life. Reading books in a dream suggests a desire to find something out, to acquire knowledge, power or public recognition. Turning pages in a book could represent your desire to 'turn over a new leaf'. Looking for something in a book may also suggest that you are trying to remember an earlier event, or need to review an aspect of your past. Dreaming of books may also suggest your fear that some hidden aspect of yourself is about to be made known or 'published'.

Boss

The boss in your dream may be standing in for anyone with authority in your life, such as your parents, or your own inner sense of duty or obligation. This dream is likely to suggest attitudes towards power: either yours or that of others.

Box

Traditionally associated with the feminine aspects of the personality, especially in its physical aspects. Boxes suggest containment, but also the desire for expansion. If the box in your dreams is empty, it's a sign that something is missing from your waking life. This dream could be warning you to mistrust the promises that someone has been making to you—whether in business or your romantic life. If you're struggling to open a box in your dream, it suggests that you've become bogged down in the pursuit of your goals, and need to think about adopting a different approach. If the box contains something frightening, it's a sign that you need to face up to some problem that you may have been trying to ignore.

Boyfriend *see also* Girlfriend

Dreaming of a boyfriend or ex-boyfriend generally indicates your feelings about attachment and romance towards this person. If you dream of someone who is the least likely person that you'd be romantically involved with as a boyfriend, this suggests that you need to be more open in your relationships to men in general and that there is no ideal lover.

Branch

If branches are blocking your progress in your dream, then you need to take a look at the obstacles in your waking life.

Perhaps you've lost the ability 'to see the wood for the trees'. Branches that snap off in your hand suggest incompleteness, or frustration at work or in your relationships. They may suggest that you're having trouble finishing something you've started. If the branches are swaying in the wind, get ready for change to come your way.

B

Breast *see* Body

Bride/Bridegroom

In general, dreaming of a bride or bridegroom suggests your desire for harmony and union in some aspect of your life. If you are a woman and your dream contains a bridegroom, it may suggest that you need to listen to the 'masculine' side of your personality, and vice versa. If your current partner is the bride or bridegroom, and in the dream he or she is walking down the aisle with somebody else, then it's a sign that you have a real or imaginary rival, or that you don't trust your partner. Either way, the dream could be telling you to take a look at your relationship, and to come to grips with your feelings of jealousy and insecurity.

Bridesmaid

If you dream of being a bridesmaid, it may suggest that you're jealous of someone who's getting more attention than you are. But if you feel comfortable in the dream, it could be a sign that you're happy to take a supporting or background role in some activity or venture.

Bridge

These structures are symbols of the power of human ingenuity to overcome obstacles and forge connections. Crossing a bridge suggests progress from one state to another. This progress has the potential to be both dangerous and exhilarating. For example, if you fear losing your balance and fall off the bridge, it is a sign that you doubt the power of your own abilities to carry you successfully through a project or undertaking. If you are exhilarated in your dream, it suggests that you are anticipating a new challenge and are prepared for risk and adventure.

Broom

If you're sweeping the floor in your dream, it's likely that your life has become cluttered with obstacles and you need to get rid of them in order to move on. Perhaps you've become emotionally attached to someone who's making demands on your time and energy, or you've taken on too many commitments at work. This dream could also signal that you're being held back by outdated emotions from the past and that it's time to 'take out the trash'. Of course, it could just mean that you need to clean your house!

Buildings *see also* Buildings, parts of

In dream lore buildings are said to represent the dreamer's self in relation to his or her current environment. Some interpreters even claim that the different rooms in a house symbolise different aspects of the dreamer's personality. Examples of different types of buildings that might occur in your dreams are as follows:

Castle/Fortress Do you regard your house as a fortress? To dream of a castle can suggest either the desire for a protected space, defended against things that threaten us from the outside world, or a sense of imprisonment within a home where security has become claustrophobic.

Church/Temple etc. These sacred or religious buildings help us either to reflect on the things that are most 'sacred' to us, or to assess the state of the spiritual aspects of our lives. Churches also carry traditional associations of refuge or sanctuary from problems or issues that may be pursuing us.

B

Falling buildings Not surprisingly, dreams of falling buildings suggest that the dreamer is at risk of being overwhelmed by problems or responsibilities.

Hotel/Motel These forms of temporary residence may suggest either a sense of insecurity, or our desire to take a holiday or make a change in our living situation.

House/Home This building says something about your private life and emotions. To help you interpret these you should pay attention to where it is situated. Is it in a location you feel happy, dissatisfied, secure or unsafe in? What can you see out the windows? These details may provide clues about where you feel you are in your present life, and where you would like to be.

Public building (e.g. museum or library) These buildings are likely to tell you about your social or work relationships.

Pyramid The triangular shape of the pyramid is traditionally believed to focus energy. Pyramids also carry strong connotations of death and the afterlife of the spirit.

Tower/Lighthouse Like castles, these buildings or monuments suggest a desire for protection and security.

Warehouse To dream of a warehouse suggests a concern about your internal reserves of energy or resourcefulness. The amount of activity in the warehouse should help you decide whether to interpret this dream positively or negatively.

Buildings, parts of

Different parts of buildings can symbolise different things. Below is a list of building parts that may have significance in dreams.

Attic This room can stand either for your memory or intellectual life, or for matters that you have been trying to store away from your conscious mind.

Balcony Balconies are associated with the thrill and perils of romance. They also suggest aspiration: reaching for something desirable. If you are high up on a balcony with a good view, it may suggest your desire to be less involved and to take a more detached perspective on a matter or situation. If you are in danger of falling, the dream denotes anxiety about your hopes and aspirations.

Basement This is where you keep your most secret fears, or those parts of you that are still hidden or undeveloped.

Bedroom Likely to symbolise the way you feel about your emotional or sexual life. The bedroom is associated with privacy, relaxation and sensuality.

Chimney As a conductor of heat from inside to outside, the presence of a chimney in our dream can help us to assess the ways in which we deal emotionally with others.

Door If you are passing through a door in your dream, it's a sign that you are ready to tackle your inhibitions, or make progress in respect to a certain area of your life. Closed doors, on the other hand, suggest either that someone is shutting you out, or you are not ready to explore your own fears and desires.

B

Elevator/Lift A lift or elevator can suggest the aspect of ourselves we are most in tune with. If you are going up in a lift, it is likely that you are comfortable with the rational and intellectual side of your personality and thoughts. To go down in a lift, on the other hand, suggests a willingness or ability to explore your subconscious.

Kitchen This room represents your family life, the heart of the matter, and the place where your emotions are most at home.

Outside The outside or exterior of your dream house tells you how you feel about appearances; the side of you that you present to others. Being outside, looking in on a building with no means of entering, indicates the dreamer feels if he or she is an onlooker in his or her own life. Empower yourself and take control.

Passages/Corridors As conduits between the different parts of a house, these spaces tend to symbolise the transitions we make between different aspects of our personality, or contrasting life stages.

Stairs These symbolise the efforts we must take to achieve a certain goal or reach a state of greater enlightenment.

Walls Walls symbolise our ability to construct our lives, and to make sense of the world by erecting divisions between our different activities. But as structures that divide and impede vision, they can also suggest the things that frustrate us or stand in the way of our desire for an uninterrupted space or view. The dreamer may be feeling vulnerable and the walls in the dream may reflect the boundaries constructed in life as a self-protective mechanism. Sometimes such a dream suggests it is time to pull down some of these boundaries so that you can obtain what you presently desire.

Windows Windows are about your view or perspective on what is going on around you. Opening a window reflects your wish to let other people come into your life or influence you in some way. If you are on a high floor, you are looking at life from up high: that is, you are objective and think rationally about the view or situation. A window in the basement is looking at your primal self and therefore you're exploring your emotions about an issue. If you are climbing out of a window you are possibly trying to avoid emotional commitment.

Bull *see also* Animals

If the bull in your dreams is attacking you, it's a sign that you feel insecure about a person or situation. You may also feel as if your own aggressive impulses are out of control and likely to inflict damage on those around you, like a bull in a china shop. If you manage to tame the bull in your dream, take it as a positive sign of your ability to integrate these destructive aspects into your personality. It may also signify your ability to handle a potentially damaging person or situation, or to overcome a source of threat that lies in your past.

A bull is also a symbol of stubbornness. To dream of a bull may be depicting how you are handling situations in your own life. Are you willing to see others' perspectives or are you stubbornly hanging on to your own beliefs whether they be right or wrong?

Burglar

If you dream of being burgled, it's a sign that someone is trying to take something away from you. The dream could be telling you that you feel insecure or under threat in your business or personal life, and need to take precautions. If, on the other hand, you are the burglar, chances are you feel as if you have or are about to do something underhand. If in the dream you feel frightened about being caught, it probably means that you feel guilty about the methods you've used to obtain something. But the dream could also be telling you that getting what you want would require deviousness or cunning.

Buried alive

The dream of being buried alive is one of the most terrifying dreams we can experience. However, this dream can be positive if, by indicating that you feel trapped, or that others are disregarding your needs, it prompts you to take action. If you are observing someone else's burial, the dream may indicate your relief that a worrying issue or matter has been successfully laid to rest.

Bus

The bus journey in your dream may suggest how quickly or directly you are moving towards your goals. It makes a difference whether you are a passenger or the driver. If you are a passenger, it could be a sign that you don't feel you are in

B

control of your life. If you are enjoying the ride, however, it may suggest that you would like to enjoy the freedom of being without responsibilities. If you are driving the bus, you probably feel responsible for others, perhaps at work or in your family.

Butterfly *see also* Insects

Because of their life cycle, butterflies are traditional symbols of rebirth and transformation. However, they also suggest a fragile, short-lived beauty or happiness. The butterfly's erratic, flitting progress could also be warning you that you need to settle down and stop 'flitting' from one person or situation to another.

Button

If you dream of a button or buttons, it may be a sign that you or someone close to you is afraid of rejection or of being left behind or 'mislaid' in some way. On the other hand, if in the dream you are sewing a button it could be a sign that you are trying to communicate with somebody, or bring some person or experience into your life.

Buzzard *see* Birds, Birds of prey

C

Cab/Taxi

The way in which you travel in your dreams reflects the course you are taking in life. As it is a means of transport, dreaming of being in a cab or taxi indicates going places or being taken somewhere. Just make sure that you aren't being taken for a ride!

You could be worried about the meter ticking over (can you afford your current lifestyle?) or anxious to reach your destination (will you ever arrive?). To help you interpret this dream it's important to take note of the state of the car, the nature of the journey or the driver, and how you felt during the trip. A taxi represents help that you receive but have to pay for.

Cabbage *see also* Food

This vegetable is a basic symbol of nourishment; perhaps a type of nourishment we didn't enjoy very much as children. But the complexity of a cabbage when cut in half suggests the complex layers of our emotions. We can think of it in terms of layers that grow as we ourselves grow and mature over time. In this context, the emotions that accompany the dream may provide the clue to its meaning.

Cabin

Whether a ship's cabin or a cabin in the woods, this is a

symbol of refuge and comfort set in the wildness of nature. As a result, it serves as a symbol for feelings of security in which excitement is never far away. Taking the opposite view, to dream of a cabin can also be indicative of feelings of being closed in, similar to symptoms of 'cabin fever'. Again, it's up to the dreamer to interpret the symbolism that relates most closely to his or her experiences.

Cabinet

Like most enclosed spaces, cabinets represent the inner aspects of your personality. In the case of the cabinet, which is associated with the collection of valuable or unusual objects, the association is with memory.

Cable

A dream with cables suggests a desire for emotional security. This dream warns you to take steps to ensure that your life is properly 'anchored'. Don't take too many risks with your emotions.

Cactus

To dream of a cactus suggests that the dreamer is a real survivor and will flourish despite the barren and arid circumstances in his or her life. If the cactus is in a desert, it is a sign that you or someone close to you is struggling to stay on track in an inhospitable environment. If the cactus is in a pot, it may symbolise your attempt to nourish a relationship with somebody who is prickly or defensive. How you react to this plant in your dream may tell you whether or not the relationship is worth persevering with.

Caddy

If a caddy is following you in your dream, it may be a sign

C

that a friend or work associate is acting in a subservient role to your ambitions or personality. They may be looking up to you for leadership and guidance. If you are the caddy, the dream may suggest that you are feeling unhappy with your status as 'helper' in which you play a secondary role.

Cage/Cell

Dreams of caging a wild animal suggest the desire to overcome threatening obstacles, whether they come from others or from within yourself. If you are the one who is caged in the dream, be alert for a potentially negative situation at work or in your emotional life. Feeling 'caged in' and wanting to 'break out' are reflections of frustration coming from different areas in your life.

Caged birds *see* Birds

Cake *see also* Food

Dreaming of eating cake is usually a positive dream; a sign that you'd like to feel indulged or approved of by others. It could be a sign that you feel a particular need to be pampered or nourished, especially if you've deprived yourself of the 'sweet' things or 'extras' in your waking life.

Calculator

To see someone in your dream using a calculator suggests that you feel somebody around you may be untrustworthy. If you are using a calculator, chances are that a current situation is forcing you to behave more rationally or coldly towards your friends than you would like. This dream can also reveal money or business worries. If you can't find the answer to your sums, something in your life is not adding up.

Calendar

A calendar in your dream may be prompting you to remember something, either in the future or the past. Do you need to remember an anniversary or birthday? If you are putting up a calendar, it's a sign to be prepared for an event or change in your life. Marking a calendar in a dream indicates impatience for a particular date or event to arrive.

Calf *see* Animals; Baby Animals

Calling *see also* Name

If you dream that someone is calling you by name, it may be a sign that a friend or someone close to you needs your help. This dream may also be reminding you to take care of a matter you have been trying to ignore or put off. If the person calling your name comes from your past, the dream is a sign that your emotions are still too engaged with this person, and that it's time to move on.

Calmness

If your dream radiates calmness and reassurance, it may be telling you that the foundations of a particular matter are firmer and more positive than you think. This dream may also be encouraging you to relax, slow down, and learn to appreciate some peace and quiet in your life.

Camel *see* Animals

Camera

To dream that someone is taking your photograph suggests an anxiety about being noticed or put on show. But if in the dream it's you who are taking pictures of others, the dream suggests either a desire to remember, or difficulty retaining information. Taking pictures with a camera may also suggest that you are not interested in knowing or understanding the objects of your focus, whether they are people, objects or action shots. You'd prefer to reflect on the image that you created. In other words, your perspective is what attracts your attention.

Camp

A camping ground offers us a temporary refuge or stopping place in a longer journey. If you dream of such a place, it may symbolise your desire to take some time out to gather your strength. But it is also a reminder that you can't afford to relax for too long, because a longer process or journey demands your attention. Dreams of camping also reflect the desire for adventure—getting away from the hustle and bustle of city life and living with nature's challenges.

Can

If you are struggling to open a can in your dream, it may represent an actual goal that you are striving to reach in your waking life. The difficulty or ease with which you unlock the contents of the can tells you how close you are to reaching your goal. If you can't reach the contents at all, it may be worth thinking of a different strategy.

Canal *see also* Water

These slow-moving passages of water are symbols of communication, calmness and reflection. Their appearance in a dream is a sign that you need to be willing to slow down and even drift for a while so that you can reflect more deeply upon your life and progress. It can also be an indication that different aspects of your self—such as your business and romantic sides—need to be in better touch with each other.

Canary *see* Birds

Cancer

Unless we are actually ill, a dream in which we have cancer is unlikely to reflect a genuine illness. Rather, it suggests that you have not sufficiently come to terms with a major source of anxiety or insecurity, and that this is eating away at you from within. If someone else in your dream has cancer, the dream represents your concern for his or her well-being.

Candles *see also* Light

These can symbolise both celebration, and the exploration of your spiritual side. If the candles are on a birthday cake, this may be a reminder of an important date or anniversary.

Candlestick

As a device that holds a light, the candlestick in your dream suggests the basis of an insight or investigation. What's the reason for that spark of light? If you are carrying the candlestick, it could be a sign that you are ready to explore a previously hidden part of yourself.

Candy *see* Sugar

Cannibals/Cannibalism

These primitive symbols of fear tell us that something is 'eating us'—either from within, or from something threatening in our environment. If your dream features cannibalism, you may need to face up to a situation or emotion that you have been avoiding. It may be that your work environment is one that embodies the term 'dog eat dog'.

Cannon

A symbol of extreme aggression, and often a sign that someone is threatening you in a rather exaggerated or obvious way. A cannon in a dream could also be a sign that you are overreacting to a perceived threat and are at risk of making yourself look ridiculous.

C

Canoe

To be 'paddling your own canoe' is a symbol of independence and your ability to manage your own affairs. If you share the canoe with another, it suggests that you and a romantic or business partner need to 'pull together' if you are to reach your goals.

Canopy

This ancient form of covering suggests mystery, formality and power. Perhaps a sign that, for better or worse, you are currently surrounded or protected by traditional, ritual forms of behaviour. Usually a canopy is part of a celebratory ritual. Therefore, it is a good sign that there will be something to celebrate or that the dreamer will overcome current problems.

Cap *see also* Clothes

If you are doffing your cap in a dream, it implies a sense of inferiority. In olden days it was customary to do this to those in authority. But putting on a cap can also signal your desire to be prepared for and protected against any unexpected event or circumstance that may arise.

Captain

If you play the part of a captain in a dream, it is an indication of your willingness to take on the role of authority. You may feel that you are already occupying this role in waking life. If someone else is ordering you around, however, the dream suggests that you are unhappy with authority figures.

C

Captivity *see also* Cage; Trap

Not surprisingly, captivity dreams express our fears and feelings of being trapped. The nature of your prison in the dream will help you to interpret the matter or the circumstances that are holding you back. If you succeed in breaking out of your dream prison, it is a sign that these obstacles can be overcome.

Car *see also* Journey; Travel; Driving

Like other forms of transport, cars are a symbol of where we are going on our life journey. Think about the circumstances of the dream. Are you in control of the car or are you a passenger? Are you clear about where you are going, or does the car seem to be driving you? Do you have passengers, or are you alone? Are you travelling fast or slow? These factors can help you to assess the current state of your 'drive' and confidence. A dream in which you are driving, especially long distance, may also be telling you of your desire to be somewhere else.

Caravan

A caravan represents adventure and travel, not necessarily physical, but also in the mind or imagination. Take this as an indication that it's time to consider either a holiday or a new approach to a familiar situation.

Cards *see also* Gambling; Games

Depending on the context of the dream, cards are symbols of either risk, or sociability. If you have a winning hand, it is a sign of confidence in your ability to achieve a particular goal. If your are losing, it is a warning to proceed with caution, whether in business or romance.

Caress *see also* Kissing

This dream is a symptom of our need for basic reassurance and affection. If you dream of being caressed, the dream may be reflecting your desire for being nurtured and simple physical affection. If you can't find this kind of affection from humans around you, domestic pets such as cats and dogs make a suitable alternative.

Carols

To hear or sing carols in a dream foretells either the approach of a holiday (usually Christmas), or your desire to express yourself spiritually.

Carpenter

If you are doing carpentry in your dream or watching someone else doing it, it is a sign that some part of your life needs work or repairing. It may also signal that the overall structure of your life requires attention. Alternatively, you may have been watching too many home renovation shows on television.

Carpet

The pattern and colour of the carpet will help you interpret this dream. If it is plain and ordinary, it may reflect your sense that your current life is dull and lacking in contrast, whereas a highly patterned carpet denotes a life that is eventful and passionate.

Carriage *see also* Journey; Travel

This traditional and romantic form of transport suggests

either romance (whether of the 'runaway' or the more sedate variety) or a desire for a traditional marriage.

Carrot *see also* Food

To dream of this bright orange vegetable may be a sign that you need to take better care of your health, especially where vitamins are concerned.

Carrying

If you're carrying a heavy weight in a dream, it may be because you are presently feeling burdened. The nature of the load will help you identify the matter that's weighing you down in your waking life. Is it a load of paper? If so, upgrade your filing system or clean up your in-tray.

Carving

A dream that denotes emergence and creativity. If you are carving something in your dream, this activity probably reflects your desire to give shape to your life and to bring order and focus to a particular event or circumstance. Paying attention to the shape you are trying to carve, whether the surface is soft or hard, and the ease or difficulty with which it emerges, will help you to interpret the current state of your progress. Idioms such as 'carving a niche' highlight our need to make our lives fit in with our talents.

Cashier

Not surprisingly, the appearance of a cashier in a dream tends to reflect money worries, or anxieties about your business transactions. To help you interpret these you should pay attention to the attitude of the cashier, whether he or she is friendly or hostile, what you are purchasing, and whether the price demanded seems reasonable or too high.

Castle *see* Buildings

Castration

A classic male anxiety dream. Like dreams of losing one's teeth, a castration dream indicates a fear of impotence and loss of authority. Perhaps it is a sign that you feel threatened, whether by someone around you or by an attitude or person from the past, such as your parents' refusal to take you seriously as a child.

Caterpillar *see* Insects

Cats *see* Animals

Cathedral *see* Buildings

Cattle *see* Animals

Cauliflower *see* Food

Cave

Like cellars, caves are usually interpreted as a symbol of the unconscious. If your dream involves entering a cave, it is a sign that you need to explore some hidden matter or emotion. For male dreamers, this dream may also be an indication either of frustrated sexual desire, or of the need to get in touch with their more 'feminine' side. What is being explored in this dream is the primal self—deep, dark emotions and sexual desires.

Ceiling *see also* Buildings

A ceiling represents what is above you, the horizon or limit of a particular matter. If the ceiling is peeling or leaking, it is a sign that your life lacks security or that some part of it requires urgent attention. If it is high and lofty, this should be taken as a positive indication of your capacity to think or express yourself freely. If it is made out of glass and you're a woman, consider the expression 'breaking the glass ceiling'. If you are unfamiliar with this term, it is an expression that describes women's feelings of frustration at being able to see the possibilities for success in a working environment, but being unable to achieve them due to a variety of factors. When a woman breaks the glass ceiling, it means that she has broken through opposition and sexism and achieved success.

C

Celebrity

If you dream of being a celebrity, the dream suggests either your feeling that others don't appreciate you enough, or an anxiety that you are drawing too much attention to yourself. If celebrities appear in your dream, they should be interpreted as aspects of yourself in relation to your current life and activities. You want to be recognised and validated for your efforts or talent.

Cell *see* Cage

Cellar *see* Buildings

Cement

Unless you work in the building industry, a dream in which you are laying cement is likely to signal your attempt to cover something over. If the cement won't cover the surface it's intended for, or the work is very hard and exhausting, you should take it as a sign that the matter you are attempting to hide won't go away easily. If the cement goes on easily, it is a sign that you are prepared to move on.

Cemetery

Dreaming of a cemetery may indicate your desire to take a rest or time out. But this dream may also be a warning that some part of you, whether a talent, emotion or activity, is at risk of 'dying' if you don't put it to use. To dream of a cemetery can also denote an awakening or a need to seek higher knowledge so that your talents and desires are realised.

C

Certificate

A dream in which you are given a certificate suggests your anxieties about your qualifications or confidence in performing a particular task. This dream may be trying to reassure you by giving you a positive message about your competence. If the certificate is illegible, however, or you have trouble unfolding or reading it, you may need to do more preparation before you complete a task successfully.

Chains

Like cages or prisons, these are symbols of the forces that prevent us from making the progress we aspire to.

Chair *see also* Furniture

The chair in your dream is likely to symbolise how supported or unsupported you feel in your emotional or work life. You should pay attention to how comfortable the chair is, whether it is adequate to the task of holding your weight, and whether you feel content sitting in it or not.

Champagne

This sparkling and bubbly drink is associated with your own social personality and how you act in the company of others. To dream that you are drinking it signals an active social life.

Chandelier

A symbol both of prosperity and brilliance. However, if in the dream you are worried about the chandelier falling on you, it is a sign that you feel potentially overwhelmed by your current lifestyle.

Charity

To dream of giving money to a charity suggests that people are making too many demands on you. It could also be a warning that you don't give too much of yourself in real life.

Chased *see also* p.17 (Typical dreams)

Dream chases are typically both vivid and frightening, making it a relief to wake up. If you have a dream of being chased, it may pay to think about what you are afraid of in your waking life. Pay attention to who or what was chasing you, whether you were caught, and how the dream ended. These details can help you to unlock the meaning of this dream. Don't forget that the 'pursuer' can be a part of your own psyche, and not just an external person or persons.

Chasm

If you see a chasm in your dream, it refers to some basic source of anxiety that is taking place in your life right now. Something is not adding up, or some crucial foundation is absent. This makes you afraid to persevere with a particular project or plan.

Cheering

If people are cheering for you in your dream, it's a sign that you feel you don't get enough encouragement and support from your friends or work colleagues.

Cheese *see also* Food

Dreaming of cheese could be a sign that you have been overindulging in rich food or social events. You may need to take more care in your diet or lifestyle.

Chemist

To dream of a chemist usually signals your sense that some vital ingredient is missing from your life. What's the missing component? The nature of the substance that you are trying to obtain from the chemist may help you to discover what this is.

Cherries *see also* Fruit

These popular and richly coloured fruits are traditional symbols of romance and sensual enjoyment.

Chess *see also* Games

To dream of playing this game of skill and strategy denotes the need for careful thought in a business or financial matter.

Chest

The chest in your dream signals something that you are either shielding, or trying to conceal from others or yourself.

Chestnuts

To dream of these rich brown nuts may be a reminder to appreciate something valuable in your life that you have been taking for granted, or that you are in danger of throwing away.

Chicken *see* Birds

Children

Like babies, children usually stand for something precious to the dreamer, or symbolise his or her responsibilities. If the children are crying or badly behaved, it is a sign that you feel doubt about your capacities to deal with a current situation. It could also be that you are feeling resentful of duties at home or at work. If the children are happy, the dream is a positive indication of harmony in your emotional life.

Chimney *see* Buildings

China

To dream of china, particularly bone china, suggests the need to exercise great care and delicacy in a social matter.

Chocolates *see also* Food

Like cherries, chocolates are associated with romance and sensual pleasures. Dreaming of them may suggest your desire to be spoiled or indulged. It may also be reminding you of a special occasion coming up such as birthday or anniversary. Check your diary.

Choir

A choir is usually a symbol of your desire for spiritual insight or reassurance. Like all dreams involving music, this one also carries the message of your need for harmony.

Choking

This dream reflects your doubts concerning your ability to successfully complete an enterprise or undertaking.

Christ *see also* Religion

To dream of Christ signals your fear that you will be called upon to perform a superhuman task or to make a sacrifice. Christ is also the ultimate symbol of unconditional love, and maybe this is what's missing in your life.

Christening *see* Baptism

Christmas tree

This festive tree denotes the need to exercise special generosity or care in your dealings with significant persons in your life.

Chrysanthemum *see* Flowers

Church *see* Buildings

Cigar

Traditionally regarded as a symbol of the phallus, although as Freud is said to have once commented, 'Sometimes a cigar is only a cigar'. Cigars are associated with masculine power and prestige, so a dream of smoking one may suggest a desire for these personality traits.

Cigarette

Lighting a cigarette in a dream is often a sign of anxiety, possibly about a social event or situation. If you are a smoker and trying to give up, however, or the people in your dream are reacting negatively to your cigarette, the dream is likely to be a reflection of your desire to smoke, or guilt about not being able to stop.

Cliff *see also* p.17 (Typical dreams)

If you are walking on the edge of a cliff in your dream, it is a sign that you are engaged in a risky situation that demands all your attention and care. If you jump off the edge of a cliff, note whether you land softly or wake up instead. You may be taking a leap of faith or trying to get away from your responsibilities.

Climbing

If you feel as if a current situation is an uphill struggle, this dream symbolises the need to persist if you are to reach your goal.

Cloak

Mystery, adventure and concealment are all symbolised by the dream of a cloak. This dream can be a sign that you or someone close to you is deliberately or unconsciously attempting to hide something. Consider the term 'cloak and dagger', which has long been associated with secrecy, danger and undercover violence.

Clock

A sign that you are worried about deadlines or anxious that time is 'ticking away'. This dream may signal the need to make a start on some project. It is also common to dream of a clock before an important appointment. The alarm clock that goes off in your dream, however, may be telling you that it's time to 'wake up' to something you have been deliberately refusing to acknowledge.

Clothing

Having new clothes in a dream is a positive sign, suggesting that you are about to embark on a new period of self-expression and heightened self-esteem. To dream of getting dressed suggests that it's time for a change. If people are looking at you critically, however, or you are forced to dress in public, the dream suggests anxiety about your ability to perform adequately in a new role.

Clouds *see also* Sky

To see clouds in a dream is a sign that you are not paying

enough attention to practical details and realities, that is, that you 'have your head in the clouds'. The expression—'to cast a cloud over'—is to be sad about something, whereas 'to hang over someone like a cloud' is the same as a menacing presence. Dark clouds usually indicate tough times ahead, but if your 'cloud has a silver lining' things will work out for the best. It all depends on your nature—are you an optimist or a pessimist?

Clown

To see a clown in a dream or to dream of being one suggests a fear of not being taken seriously.

Coat

If you are wearing or putting on a coat in your dream, it is a sign that the next part of your life will be accompanied by protective influences. It also suggests a 'cover up' or that you are protecting yourself from the world or others around you. Think about how this fits in with your waking life situation.

Cobweb

A sign that something from your past is preventing you from moving forward. You will be able to overcome it, but the process may require you to confront something that is either unpleasant or that you have tried to brush out of sight. On a positive note, the cobweb is an intricate trap effective in catching prey. Perhaps you need to employ a new strategy to get what you want.

Coffin

An empty coffin can signify grief at the loss of a friendship, whether through death or some other cause. If sadness and anxiety accompany this dream, it suggests the need for you to work hard if you want to preserve a relationship that is on the verge of 'dying'. If your feelings are more detached or positive, it is a sign that you are ready to lay a matter or relationship to rest. This type of dream also denotes fear of failure.

C

Coin

Finding a coin in a dream symbolises good luck and foretells a boost in your confidence and self-esteem. But if you are looking for a lost coin, the dream signals a lack of confidence in yourself or another.

Cold

Experiencing cold in a dream is likely to be a reflection of your emotional rather than actual temperature. If you can't get warm, it is an indication that you need more protection or emotional support in some aspect of your life.

Collision

Dreaming of a collision is a warning to slow down and reflect more carefully on where you are going.

Colours *see also* p.2 (The land of make-believe)

Most dreams are in colour, although we are not aware of this because we may find it difficult to remember our dreams or because the colour is taken for granted—that is, the colour looks normal! Colours also have archetypal meanings, derived from ancient times and from various cultures. They can communicate emotion or states of energy. If the colour is unusual, this means it is there to draw your attention. If there are two or more clashing colours, these could denote aspects of your life that are out of balance or harmony. Therefore, you should take particular note if this shows up in a dream.

Black Black is devoid of all colour and light. It is not an actual colour but a shade, and can signal the need to explore the darker or deeper side of your nature—your subconscious mind. The blackness can represent depression or even death—not necessarily of a person, but of an idea, an aspiration, or a phase of your life. In olden times it was thought to represent the underworld, a deep space away from God where a person was said to be hiding. If you dream in this colour, it is a good idea to ask yourself if there is anything lacking warmth or colour in your life, or whether you are hiding something. In general, the colour black in dreams suggests uncertainty about an aspect of yourself or your situation. At its most serious, it can signify grief or mourning; that something has or is about to end. It can also suggest aspects of yourself which are undeveloped or hidden. This dream is positive if you use it as the basis for thinking about your own development.

Blue Blue can be both a soothing colour and one that suggests depression or sadness. Either way, it is associated with spiritual insight or wisdom. If a person is wearing blue in your dream it suggests that he or she has something intelligent, spiritual or truthful to communicate. You should listen carefully to these words, as they are likely to be valuable and to give you insight into your life.

Brown Murky colours like brown tend to be associated with confusion or anxiety. To dream in these colours can also signal depression. Brown is an earthy colour and depending on the dream can represent the stability and nourishment of the soil. The earth can either sustain in a positive way or be hostile and 'bog' you down in a muddy hole.

C

Gold Gold is typically associated with wealth and royalty (gold crowns) as well as the masculine element. In ancient cultures it represented the sun and a higher knowing. Dreaming of gold colours can mean that one is ambitious in accumulating wealth or that one has a 'golden opportunity' for knowledge and power.

Green This is the colour of nature and renewal. It can represent spring: the season of new beginnings. Harmony and nurturing are part of this season. This can translate to your own life, where new ideas that have been germinating are now suddenly sprouting and taking off.

Orange This is a spiritual colour in Eastern religions. This bright colour enhances one's feelings of inner peace and stimulates creativity.

Purple Royalty, priests and people of rank have worn this colour throughout history. It was considered a unique colour, rich in texture and shade. When dreaming of this colour, you may be aiming to succeed in your job or be in search of esteem and authority.

Red Red is the colour of fire and passion. It is also a symbol of masculinity. Depending on the rest of the dream, red can suggest aggression, danger, violence, blood, conflict or anger. Red screams out to be noticed and as such we need to heed the warning.

Silver Silver is the feminine equivalent of the masculine gold (the sun). It is associated with goddesses, queens and the moon. The colour silver represents magic, psychic ability and spirituality.

White Purity, birth, joy and enlightenment are all repre-sented by the colour white. In cultures where white is worn at a funeral, white is seen as a new beginning rather than the end. Blinding white or bareness, however, can represent a lack of colour or activity in your life. Like black, white is devoid of colour. You need to make sure that you have balance in your life.

C

Yellow This is the most cheerful colour of all. It is the colour of the sun and seen as a positive colour that is associated with fertility and life. Wearing yellow can suggest intellect and creativity.

Comb

A dream in which you are combing your hair denotes a desire for order and, possibly, for relaxation. However, if your hair comes out as you are combing it the dream denotes an anxiety about your inability to control certain aspects of your life.

Combat

We often feel as if life is a struggle, but the combat in your dream can show you how well you are dealing with con-trary forces. You should take note of how evenly balanced the fight is, whether the enemy is overwhelming you, whether the fight is fair or unfair, and how well you manage to acquit yourself.

Comet

Traditionally regarded as a sign of approaching disaster, a comet in your dream is more likely to signal the need for an important change to take place in your life.

Companion

The close companion in your dream is likely to represent your own attitude towards yourself, and the degree to which you are protecting and nourishing your own projects and emotional life. As the saying goes, 'be your own best friend'.

Compass

To dream of this instrument denotes an uncertainty about your direction in life. If you are having trouble reading the compass, it is a sign that you are confused and need guidance. If it is pointing to a specific location or direction take note as this can give you clues as to what you are looking for in life.

Computer

A dream with a computer in it is likely to represent productivity at work or in a creative enterprise. It can also symbolise your desire to be better organised. Dreaming of computers may also mean that you are overworked and are in need of human contact and fun.

Concert

Generally, to dream of a concert is a sign of your desire for harmony in your life. It suggests that you will be able to balance a number of contrasting forces or influences.

Confession

If your dream finds you laying your soul bare, it could be a sign that you need to face up to something in your waking life. Alternatively, it could be an indication that you feel overly scrutinised or judged by others.

Confetti

A symbol of celebration and, therefore, of happiness. However, confetti can also suggest short-lived pleasures and the fear or risk of being discarded.

C

Conflict *see* Combat

Contraception

A dream about contraception may simply reflect your anxieties about falling pregnant, or, if you are a man, about your partner conceiving. More symbolically, it may suggest that you fear the consequences of an activity or project, or are not yet ready to make a new beginning.

Contract

Dreaming of a contract or signing one suggests that you are having doubts or fears about a commitment in waking life. If you don't go through with the contract or agreement, it may be pointing out that you have a lot of hard work ahead of you. Are you concerned about taking a risk? It may also be that you don't trust people to keep their side of the bargain. Look to other symbols in the dream to interpret the meaning more fully.

Convent *see also* Abbey

This is traditionally a symbol of seclusion, of retirement from the world and from the conflicts of sexuality and the emotions. If this dream is a happy one, it is likely to symbolise your desire for rest and recuperation, for time out from emotional striving or conflict. But if the dream is anxious and unhappy, it is more likely to signal your fear that life and pleasure are passing you by, possibly because you are too focussed on your job or 'vocation'.

Cord

Generally, a cord represents ties that bind you to your family, friends or lifestyle. If you are trying to undo cords in your dreams, it is probably a sign that you feel tied down by the demands and responsibilities placed on you by others. If you are trying to hang onto a cord that someone else is pulling away, it may mean that you are worried about losing someone close to you.

Corkscrew

The presence in a dream of this common gadget may symbolise the birth of a new idea or project. If you have trouble using it, it is a sign to prepare for potential difficulties. If, on the other hand, the cork comes out with ease, the process should be relatively effortless.

Corn

Traditionally, ripe corn is associated with plenty and well-being. Dreaming that you are in a cornfield indicates that you will have financial and social successes ahead of you.

Corridor *see* Buildings

Cosmetics

A dream in which you are applying or purchasing cosmetics usually signals either anxieties about your age or appearance, preparation for a social event, or a desire to cover up something.

Countryside

Beautiful countryside in a dream is a symbol of happiness and emotional security. If you are in the middle of this beautiful landscape it indicates that you are close to achieving your goals. If you are viewing it from somewhere more distant, like a rocky cliff, the dream may be suggesting that you are currently involved in difficulties, but that there is a chance of happiness ahead.

Court

Not surprisingly, dreaming of being in court denotes your anxiety about being judged. This dream could imply a guilty conscience or fear of discovery. It may also reflect your feelings of being unfairly treated and your desire for justice. If on the other hand you are being 'courted', it is a sign that someone is interested in you either professionally or romantically.

Cousin *see also* Family

The cousin in your dream is most likely to be a displaced version of yourself—a close relative, but distant enough to enable you to maintain a detached perspective. This dream helps you to take a look at yourself or your circumstances in a more objective manner.

Cover

Placing a cover on something symbolises your desire to protect or secure it. Perhaps you are anxious about something getting away from you, or being spoiled. Paying attention to the nature of what you are covering will help you to interpret the meaning of the dream.

Cow *see* Animals

Crab

Because they wear their skeletons on the outside, these creatures suggest a defensive attitude to life. Their pincers also denote the need to exercise caution when attempting to explore the emotions or go to the heart of a matter. The crab is also a symbol of the zodiac sign Cancer, and so it is possible that the crab in your dream could represent a person born under this sign.

Crack

To dream that something has a crack in it suggests your subconscious awareness that some aspect of your life is flawed or incomplete. 'Cracks in a relationship' is a term used to describe faults that occur between two people in an intimate relationship. Cracks in walls or ceilings are often associated with disrepair and imperfection.

Cradle

An empty cradle symbolises your anxiety about losing someone or something precious to you through neglect or accident.

Crash *see* Collision

Crawl

If you are crawling in your dream, it is a sign that you feel cramped and that you need room to express yourself more fully. This dream activity also denotes a return to the helplessness or dependency of childhood.

Cream

This luxurious food is a symbol of prosperity and well-being. It can also symbolise something that has been obtained illegitimately, as in 'the cat that got the cream'. To dream of it suggests your desire for personal advantage, however it is gained.

Crickets *see* Insects

Crocodile *see* Animals

Crossroads

Decision and danger are symbolised by a dream of crossroads. Their presence in a dream warns you that care is required when making a decision or taking on new responsibilities.

Cross/Crucifix

Dreaming of a cross suggests that you feel burdened by other people's problems. It can also be a symbol of protection and hence a need to protect yourself from others.

Crossing

To dream of a road or level crossing suggests that you are approaching a point of transition in your life.

Crow *see* Birds

Crowd

Dreaming of a crowd highlights your feelings of being hemmed in and your need for space in which to express yourself.

Crown

Dreaming of a crown denotes success and desire to achieve. Think about what you'd like to be crowned for.

Crucifix *see* Cross

Crutch *see also* Lame

To walk with a crutch in a dream symbolises fear of

failure. It can also denote too much dependency on others. Think about whether you are a crutch for others to lean on or vice versa.

C

Crying

If someone else is crying, the dream may be telling you that you are neglecting another's needs. If you are the one crying, it suggests that your own needs are not being answered.

Crystal

Crystal in a dream signifies purity or something of great value. It may also signal a desire to protect something fragile from clumsiness or destruction—whether it's your own clumsiness, or that of those around you. Crystals are also credited with balancing and healing powers, so a dream in which crystals appear may provide a clue to something that is missing from your emotional or physical health.

Cup

This container is a symbol of our emotional life. It will help you to interpret the dream if you note whether the cup is full or empty and whether you are giving or receiving it. A cup also represents gifts of the spirit, such as joy, happiness, health and inspiration.

Cupboard see also House

Cupboards are associated both with our tendency to hold onto things, and with our need to be nurtured. Pay attention to the shape and condition of the cupboard. Is it well or poorly stocked? Can you find what you are looking for in it? These details may help you to assess the state of your own inner resources.

Curse

If someone curses you in a dream, it's a sign that you need to examine the sources of negativity that are affecting your life. Keep in mind that negative aspects in life will only have power if you let them.

Curtain

If the curtain is blowing open, dreams containing curtains are a positive indication of new possibilities or insights, especially in relation to your spiritual life. If you are closing curtains in your dream, it may be that you are avoiding a difficult or unpleasant issue.

Cushion

A symbol of the things we use to protect or 'cushion' ourselves in life. If someone is trying to take a cushion away from you, or you can't get comfortable, it could be a sign that you feel uncomfortable or vulnerable in your waking life.

Cutting

If you are cutting something in your dream, it is a sign that you will soon be required to make a difficult decision. It may have to do with 'cutting away', 'cutting out' or 'cutting up'.

Cycling *see* Bicycle

Cymbals

The crash of cymbals foretells some dramatic change or crisis in your life. It is a 'wake-up call' of some sort.

Cypress

These trees are traditionally associated with mourning and

graveyards, particularly if you are from the northern hemisphere. Dreaming of them suggests your anxiety about a loved one.

C

D

Dagger

If someone is using a dagger in your dream, it is a sign that you fear cutting comments or criticism. If you are using a dagger, it may mean that you need to behave aggressively in a particular task or business deal.

Dam

Dreaming of a dam is a sign of your tendency to repress or 'dam' your emotions or your energy. If you are building a dam in your dream, it suggests that you have been erecting defences around your feelings. If the dam is in danger of bursting, take heed: it is probably a warning that you may not be able to hold these emotions back much longer.

Dance

A dream that symbolises the achievement of, or desire for, harmony and well-being in your social and emotional life. Dancing can also represent the free expression or release of strong emotions.

Danger

The danger threatening you in your dream tends to represent, in an exaggerated or symbolic way, the problems you feel confronted by in your everyday life. In general, dreaming that you are in a dangerous situation suggests insecurity in some aspect of your waking life. Interpreting the danger symbolically rather than literally will help you to understand this dream. If the dreamer faces the danger, then problems in waking life will not be so confronting.

D

Darkness

Darkness in a dream may stand for something that you are unable or unwilling to properly see in your waking life. The darkness can also suggest depression, or symbolise your negative or pessimistic side. In this case, it is a sign that you need to take these emotions or doubts seriously, rather than trying to put them out of sight.

Darning

If you are darning in your dream, it may be a sign that you need to take the time and trouble to repair a relationship with a friend, family member or lover.

Date *see also* Calendar

If a dream is drawing attention to a particular date, it is probably because you are anxious about an upcoming event or can't wait for a particular day to arrive. However, this dream could also be reminding you of some traumatic event in your past that you have not yet come to terms with. It might also be the numbers that are significant to the dreamer. If so, why are these numbers important in your waking life?

Dawn

To dream of dawn is a symbol of new beginnings and hope. It can also be a sign of spiritual rebirth or of the dreamer's need to find new solutions or strategies to the problems in his or her life. The dream can also symbolise a successful transition out of a dark period in one's life. Generally, dreaming of dawn is a good omen.

Day/Daylight

If you are aware of daylight in your dream, it suggests that you will be able to find a solution to a situation or problem that has been troubling you.

Deafness

Dreaming of deafness can be your subconscious's way of telling you that there is something or somebody you are refusing to hear. This dream can also represent your fear of being cut off from your surroundings or other people. In general, this dream is a sign that you need to work on new ways to listen to your own needs or to communicate with others.

Death

This dream is less likely to be about an actual death than a symbolic representation of loss, change, or transition. Often it is a positive dream, signalling that some form of burden or anxiety is about to be lifted from you, enabling you to move forward in your life. In this sense, death is actually a dream of new birth, that is, releasing the old and embracing the new. Dreams of death often accompany or forecast important life transitions, and signal the dreamer's consciousness of his or her need to take on a different role or a new challenge.

Debt

Dreaming about debt may reflect financial worry at work or home. If you dream that you are in debt, it may suggest that you have been failing to return the love or attention of someone close to you. The symbolic meaning is that you owe somebody something and the time has come to pay. The debt is not necessarily associated just with emotions.

Decorate

If you are decorating in your dream it suggests either that you want more frivolity or celebration in your life, or that you are being overly superficial.

Deer *see* Animals

Defecate *see also* Excrement; Toilet

This dream suggests your desire to 'relieve' yourself of some burden or matter. It can stand for emotions that are blocking your ability to progress in your life. If you are having trouble finding somewhere to relieve yourself, it is a sign that your current circumstances are making it hard for you to unburden yourself.

Defend

If you are forced to defend yourself in a dream, it is a sign that you feel under attack in some aspect of your waking life, and that you need to stand up for yourself. If you manage to defend yourself successfully, the dream is a promising sign that you will overcome your obstacles.

Deformity

To dream of a deformity in one part of the body is often a sign that one part of your life has a problem or is out of balance with the rest. Use the interpretations of the different body parts to work out which part of your lifestyle or per-sonality the deformed limb may represent.

Deluge *see also* Flood

Because water is associated with our emotions, dreaming of a deluge or flood suggests that you fear being 'flooded' by powerful feelings. If you survive the deluge, however, this dream is a positive sign of your ability to cope with heightened levels of emotion.

D

Demolition

Generally speaking, this dream represents the way you feel about change. If you are in charge of the demolition, it is a positive sign that you are initiating the change and feel in control of it. But if something is being demolished around you, then the dream suggests that you feel powerless to control or direct the changes in your life. Demolition also represents the need to tear down current circumstances and build something more positive. The message is to look at what you have built in your own life that is not working. Tear it down and start again.

Dentist

A dream of going to the dentist suggests that something you have been putting off for a while needs your attention. If the dream is very anxious, or you are losing your teeth, it suggests your fears about helplessness, loss or impotence.

Departure *see also* Travel

To dream of making a departure, whether the setting is an airport or bus terminal, can signal your need to move on in life. It may also suggest your fear of losing people or things. The emotion that accompanies the departure in your dream will help you to interpret which meaning is indicated. It is common to dream of departure before a journey, in which case the dream is a sign that your subconscious is preparing you for this event.

Descend

To descend in a dream suggests the need to explore the subconscious, or to go more deeply into a particular matter or subject. If the dream is fearful, it is a sign that you worry that this descent is likely to be difficult by exposing you to painful thoughts or emotions. If on the other hand it is easy, it suggests that you are ready for the new knowledge you stand to acquire.

Desert

Generally, the desert is a symbol of barrenness or some kind of emotional or material lack. More positively, the desert can also represent a space in which material things and distractions are removed so that you can focus on achieving spiritual insight.

Desk

Dreaming of a desk can symbolise our anxieties about work or study. It can be a sign either of overwork, or of our belief that that we need to work more consistently if we are to achieve our goals. The desk may also represent a need for organising your thoughts in order to achieve those goals.

Despair

Experiencing despair in a dream can be a sign that the dreamer has moved on from a particular situation or emotion. In this case the dream represents the emotion you have left behind, rather than that which lies in the future. Despair in a dream is definitely a sign of healing and moving on.

Detective

If your dream involves a detective, it is a sign that you need to investigate a matter or emotion more closely. If the detective is following you, it is an indication that you feel watched or pursued. This dream can also signify your consciousness that you have behaved in a dishonest or underhand manner.

Devil

Dreaming of the devil represents the need for us to confront an issue in our life. If you see yourself in this role, it is a warning to think about your own actions and the way in which they impact on those close to you. The devil is also symbolic of an over-concern with earthly pleasures—either sexual or material. You are placing too much emphasis on these areas and the dream indicates that it's time that you get in touch with your emotions.

Devotion

To dream of caring for another suggests that you have become too emotionally detached from those around you. If someone in your dream is expressing devotion towards you, it is a sign either that you feel constricted by your close personal relationships, or that you are thinking too much about your own emotions and needs. Dreaming that you are being looked after by your mother suggests that you are experiencing emotional insecurity in your waking life.

Devour

Devouring something can be a symbol of the removal of some negative force or influence. This dream also carries the meaning of a return to basic, primitive emotions.

Diamonds

Diamonds are associated with permanence, hardness, clarity and great value. In a dream they may symbolise a long-term relationship or marriage or, if you are single, some other precious or enduring aspect of your life. If you lose diamonds in a dream, it is a warning that you need to take better care of your relationships or possessions.

D

Dice

Dice are symbols of risk or chance. Their appearance in a dream may be a sign that you are hazarding something on a single event or person. The numbers that turn up on the thrown dice may also have significance.

Dictionary

To dream that you are consulting a dictionary suggests that you are looking for some missing ingredient that will help to make your life more complete. The word you are searching for could be an important clue as to what this missing thing is. Such a dream indicates the need for meaning in our current situation, particularly if we have been feeling a bit perplexed in waking life.

Digging/Excavation

In general, a dream of digging implies your need to explore the more deeply hidden aspects of yourself. This is a dream in which the object of your search may also represent an experience or person that you may have tried to 'bury'.

Dinner

This dream suggests that you need to pay attention to your closest family or social relationships. Perhaps you need more sustenance than you are receiving, or are failing to provide others with nourishment.

Dinosaur

These exaggeratedly large animals tend to represent our most primitive fears. But because they are extinct, they may also stand for emotions or problems that belong in our past, or that we have outgrown. In this case, they can be our mind's way of telling us that we don't need to worry about these things any longer.

D

Diploma *see* Certificate

Dirt/Dirty

The impulses that we interpret as negative or wrong sometimes appear in our dreams as unclean. If you are covering someone in dirt, or they are aiming it at you, it may be a sign that you have been acting negatively towards another, or that they have been slandering you. Of course, this dream may simply be a reminder that it's time to clean your house!

Disappearing

A dream in which people disappear before your eyes highlights your insecurities, in particular your fears that people or situations are at risk of disappearing from your life. This dream suggests a lack of confidence or self-esteem on the dreamer's part.

Disaster

Generally, the disasters in our dreams are exaggerated representations of everyday worries. Often the dreamer will be solving or overcoming problems in the dream to keep safe, which tells the dreamer they do have the strength and knowledge to overcome just about anything. Interpreting the disaster symbolically rather than literally can help you to come to terms with these anxieties and reduce them to their proper size.

Disease *see* Deformity; Illness

Disfigurement

To dream that you are disfigured can suggest your guilt over an action you have recently undertaken. If another person in the dream is disfigured, the dream implies a doubt about the motives of someone close to you. Generally, any sort of disfigurement is associated with negative aspects of the dreamer coming to the surface. It represents not just guilt, but jealously, intolerance and other negative emotions that are usually hidden.

Disgrace

This is an insecurity dream that highlights your worries about being accepted or approved of by others. This dream does not necessarily foretell an actual disgrace. However, it may be a warning to you to act more considerately towards others.

Disguise

To be wearing a disguise in a dream suggests that you are refusing to look at a matter or situation head-on. If others in your dream are disguised, it may be an indication that you feel excluded, or are anxious that others are not dealing with you honestly.

Dish

A full dish tends to symbolise fulfilment in our emotional or family life, whereas an empty one suggests that something is missing or incomplete. A broken dish can suggest family arguments or conflict or even foretell the loss of a relationship.

Dishonesty

To act dishonestly in a dream can actually suggest the opposite, in other words, that you are overly concerned with making sure that your behaviour is above board. If others are behaving dishonestly towards you, it is a sign that you fear being cheated by those around you.

D

Disk

In a dream, a computer or floppy disk often stands for our desire for information or knowledge. This is often a work-oriented dream, and may be a sign that something is puzzling or eluding you in your work. A music or audio disk, on the other hand, tends to represent the desire for relaxation or time off.

Dislike

A dream in which you feel or express a strong dislike for something is often a positive sign, suggesting that you know your own mind and are not prepared to be overly influenced or pushed around by others.

Disputes

The dispute or argument in your dream may represent not only potential disagreements with friends or colleagues, but also a conflict between different aspects of yourself or your contrary desires. Paying attention to the nature of the dispute and the position you are taking in it will help you to interpret this dream.

Distress

Rather than forecasting unhappiness, a dream in which you experience distress is often a reference to an influence in the past that once caused you unhappiness, but which is passing out of your life. Psychologically this type of dream represents healing from past distress or hurt.

D

Ditch

Barriers such as these tend to symbolise the obstacles that prevent us from reaching our goals. A ditch may suggest your fear of getting bogged down if you try to move forward. Alternatively, if in the dream you are stuck in the ditch it may suggest that you feel exposed, and are anxious about being seen to be putting yourself forward. Dreaming of a ditch usually indicates that it's time to change in order to avoid routine in life.

Diving

Often this dream suggests the need to take some radical action or make a new departure. It can be a way for your subconscious to prepare you to 'take the plunge' into something new.

Divorce

This dream is not necessarily a dream about relationships, but about any division or split in your life. It may signal your need to escape from a particular situation or emotion that is no longer beneficial to you. If may also signify anxiety about money worries.

Dock see Quay

Doctor

Because doctors are authority figures who have responsibility for healing, to dream of one tends to signal a desire for some cure to take place. It can also be a sign that a cure has already taken place.

Dog *see* Animals

Doll

Dolls in dreams often represent children or the emotional aspects of childhood. If the doll is broken or abandoned, it may be a sign that you are anxious either about the welfare of an actual child for whom you are responsible, or that you feel that your own dependent or childlike qualities are at risk. If there is a negative association with the dream, it can mean the dreamer might feel as if they are treated like a child and not taken seriously.

Dolphin *see* Fish

Donkey *see* Animals

Door *see* Buildings, parts of

Dove *see* Birds

Dragon

A dragon is a very ancient symbol, which signifies different things in different cultures. In the Christian West, dragons tended to symbolise evil, as in the representation of Satan as a dragon. For the Chinese, on the other hand, the dragon is a symbol of wisdom and authority. Because dragons breathe fire, they can represent heightened emotions such as anger or passion. The emotions accompanying the dream will help you to determine the personal significance of this symbol.

A dragon also symbolises magic and prosperity. Psychologically it can represent qualities in a person around the dreamer. For instance, we often refer to dominating figures in life—particularly women—as 'dragon women'.

Draught

Being aware of a draught in your dream suggests your uneasiness or feelings of discomfort and/or insecurity. It is generally a sign that you feel unprotected in a relationship or work situation.

Draughts *see* Games

Dreaming

It's not uncommon to dream that you are dreaming. This is often a sign that the content of your dream is particularly difficult or disturbing, and reflects your subconscious desire to keep it at a safe distance from the 'real' or waking world. To dream that you are dreaming is also the first step towards lucid dreaming, that is, the ability to recognise the difference between the conscious world and the subconscious world.

Dress *see also* Clothing

If you are a woman and you dream of a beautiful new dress, the dream suggests that you want a more active social life or even romance. This dream can also suggest that you are anxious about the way in which you appear to others, or symbolise your desire to be thought attractive or fashionable by those around you.

Drink

To be drinking something in a dream may signify either your need for sustenance or your desire to 'imbibe' some emotional or spiritual truth. If you are worried about becoming drunk, however, it is a sign that you lack social confidence or are worried about embarrassing yourself in front of others.

Driving/Driver

Driving in your dream is a sign of your desire to take control over your direction. If you are having trouble making the vehicle go where you want it to, however, the dream suggests that you suffer from contradictory impulses or are unresolved about what direction to take. Other dream meanings associated with driving are as follows:

Acceleration If you are speeding up in your dream, it could be a sign of the need to take things more slowly, or to think through a matter more carefully. If the accelerator is jammed or out of control, the dream may be warning you of bad habits that are likely to get out of hand if you don't slow down.

Accident If you are driving and you have an accident, you should take it as a warning that your current lifestyle is out of control or about to lead you into trouble.

Backseat driver If your dream contains a pushy passenger who's trying to tell you where you should go, watch out! Chances are that someone is trying to manipulate you or that you feel pushed in a direction you don't want to go. This dream may be telling you that it's time to identify 'the backseat drivers' in your life, and take control of the wheel.

Brakes If you have to brake suddenly, it indicates that you should be prepared for obstacles ahead. This dream can also foretell a 'break' in your life, whether it is a lucky break, or simply a transition of some kind.

Expensive car If you are driving an expensive car like a Rolls-Royce or Mercedes, take it as a sign that you will shortly receive a worthwhile proposition, or that your material or emotional life is about to improve.

D

Hearse If the car you are driving is a hearse, it is a sign that emotions or matters from the past are weighing you down. However, this dream also suggests that you may be about to offload whatever it is that is troubling you.

Hitch-hiker If you stop to pick up a hitch-hiker, it is a sign that you can afford to be more considerate or generous towards others.

Tyre If you have to stop and change a tyre, it suggests that expenditure on your current lifestyle may be in danger of 'blowing-out' of proportion.

Drought

To dream of drought signals your fear of emotional or financial loss. However this dream also suggests that the problem is temporary, and that if you weather the situation better times will lie ahead.

Drowning *see also* Water

This frightening dream usually symbolises your anxiety about being out of control in some aspect of your life. For example, it can represent your fear of being overwhelmed by powerful emotions that you have not yet managed to integrate into your waking life, or suggest that you feel inadequate to cope with a stressful social situation.

Drugs *see also* Chemist

Obtaining or using drugs in a dream often suggests your desire to improve your health or well-being, perhaps through the use of a supplement or a better diet. However, if in your dream you are using or smuggling illegal drugs, it is more likely to be a sign that you are concerned about the legitimacy of some activity you are involved in or contemplating, or that you fear that others disapprove of your lifestyle.

D

Drums

Of all the musical instruments, the drums are those most associated with fundamental rhythms and energies. Thus, playing them in your dream tends to be a sign of your need to release primal energy or aggression, or to make contact with the more basic and raw emotions.

Drunk *see* Drink

Duel

Duelling is an activity that indicates conflict or competitiveness in a close personal or work relationship. But the duel is a very ritualised, formal kind of conflict, which may suggest that your aggression is under control, or that you are playing according to the rules.

Dumb

Being unable to speak in a dream suggests your frustration that people aren't listening to what you have to say. This dream implies that you need to work on ways to get their attention, perhaps by rephrasing your concerns or presenting them in a more positive way.

Dungeon *see also* Cell

A sign that you feel trapped or confined in an unrewarding situation, this dream may be telling you that you need to work on developing an escape plan if things are to improve. Jung believed that dreams about dungeons are associated with fears about getting in touch with the primal self.

Dust

To dream that something is covered in dust suggests that you have been neglectful in your social or emotional life. The dream may be warning you that it's time to make some changes, or to get out more and shake the dust out of your life.

Dwarf

These diminutive figures usually stand for a neglected or minor aspect of ourselves that needs our attention. This dream may be a warning to you not to overlook aspects of your personality that are in danger of shrinking or remaining stunted because you refuse to take them seriously.

Dye

If your clothes or bedding have become stained with a colour you can't remove, the dream symbolises your anxieties about being unable to control the process of change. It suggests that something is overwhelming you, or that you feel affected by someone else's actions, and that you are powerless to stop the process. If on the other hand you are the one who is dying something, it is a sign that you are preparing to take charge of the changes in your life.

Dynamite

Some situation or emotion is in danger of 'exploding'. This may not be a negative dream—on the contrary, it could be a sign that you need to change some aspect of your life, or that an emotion you have been holding back from expressing can finally be released.

Dynamo

A dynamo is a symbol of controlled energy. To dream of one either signifies your ability to take on a task that requires constant application, or that you have been working too hard at something, feel 'run-down' as a consequence, and need to recharge your batteries.

D

E

Eagle *see* Birds

Ears *see* Body

Earth

Earth is usually a symbol of nurturing (Mother Earth) and of the feminine. It reminds us of our 'roots': our family and our social background. The ground, like the earth, supports us (terra firma), and holds all our experiences. If you dream of being buried underneath the earth, your unconscious needs, habits or drives are no longer sustaining you and it's time for a change of attitude or more flexibility.

Earthquake

Just as the earth is firm and solid, an earthquake is a total disruption of this. You may be experiencing an upheaval in your life—as a result of which your emotions and sense of security are no longer stable. This may also be a positive dream; an eruption of emotion or feelings can indicate a major change occurring in your life, such as an important transition from which you can grow.

Easter/Easter egg

Easter is a Christian time of renewal and rebirth. Dreaming of this time could suggest symbolically a desire to return to our younger days. The Easter egg represents spring and new birth. Think about the part of your life that you wish to revive or the new ideas you'd like to give birth to.

Eating *see also* Food

To be eating in a dream suggests that you are satisfying your hunger, not necessarily for food, but also your other needs— whether emotional or sexual. To refuse food is to refuse the opportunity for growth and positive change. Sharing food at a table is a sharing of yourself with others. The dream may be interpreted in relation to the circumstances—how was the food consumed? What type of food was it?

Idioms such as 'What's eating you?' may apply to a life situation. Being eaten is a reminder that we are under attack or besieged by our own emotions or those of others. Do anger, fear, jealousy and other negative emotions consume us?

Consider the following idioms that relate to food and eating and try to interpret your dream in relation to their context: 'eat dirt'; 'eat one's words'; 'eat out of one's hand'; 'dog eat dog'; 'eat humble pie'; 'eaten out of house and home'.

Echo

Dreaming of an echo could be a message that you have to keep repeating yourself before someone takes you seriously. Perhaps you are lacking in confidence and need to convince yourself and others of your talents.

Eclipse

Dreaming of an eclipse of the sun indicates a loss of some type. It may be a loss of success or confidence in your own abilities. It may also be a loss of health due to excesses in

E

your life. An eclipse of the moon suggests not being able to attain your goals or that someone else overshadows you. We are told to 'reach for the moon' but 'the moon' is not attainable if it is eclipsed.

Education *see also* School

Education is closely linked with knowledge, so dreaming of being back at school may be telling you to apply the knowledge you learned then to a present situation. It could also be telling you to upgrade your knowledge and skills to improve your lifestyle. To dream of a college or university education may indicate that you wish to pursue new knowledge that will eventually lead to a more fulfilling life. If it is a dream where you feel frustrated and uncomfortable in a learning environment, it may reflect your anxieties about being unable to conform to what is expected of you. This could be at home, work or in a social group such as a tennis or golf club where there are rules and regulations.

Eel

When we say that someone is as 'slippery as an eel' it usually means that the person is not trustworthy. If you dream that you are trying to hold onto a slippery eel, it may be pointing to a situation in which you risk losing a grip on something (an issue or emotion) or suggesting that something is slipping away from you.

Egg

Generally, dreaming of eggs is regarded as a good omen among people of all cultures. An egg is a symbol of potential of the individual that is yet to be realised. If you dream of eggs in a nest, money and financial security is on its way (a nest egg). If the eggs are cracked or damaged then expect some kind of disappointment or loss.

Egypt

Egypt is regarded as a mysterious and exotic place linked with ancient knowledge and great wealth. Depending on the dreamer's association with Egypt, it may signal a need to get out of the rut and pursue interests that are more related to adventure and mysticism.

Electricity/Electrocution

Electricity is a powerful force that has the ability to energise, produce light and even cause death. It is also instant and quick. Consider the idiom 'blowing a fuse'. Are you burning up with anger? Perhaps you have been called a 'live wire' and you have excessive energy. The meaning of the dream depends on the circumstances, but generally an electric shock or electrocution may suggest that you are in for a surprise: a big shock, or a wake-up call about something. It may be a good idea to protect yourself from injury and become more aware of what is around you. A switch could indicate your need for control.

Elephant *see* Animals

Elevator *see* Buildings, parts of

Elopement

In ancient interpretations, dreaming of elopement was a bad omen because it indicated a clandestine union—one that was not approved of by family or society. Is there some kind of partnership—business or personal—that needs to be kept secret? Perhaps the dreamer wants to escape to a more romantic or exciting state that involves a union or partnership of some sort. Depending on the context of the dream, it could mean that you are running away from your predictable situation to one that is more exciting.

Embrace *see* Kissing

Embryo *see also* Baby

An embryo is the beginning of creation and as such it's very vulnerable. To dream of an embryo may suggest that your vulnerability is being exposed. It may be a new project, new beginnings of a relationship, a move or a job—whatever it may be, it needs nurturing and care so that it can develop to the next stage.

Emerald

Emeralds are associated with beauty. They were once thought to be powerful stones, which enhanced the memory and when placed under the tongue could help to predict the future. Their colour symbolised spring and fertility. Modern interpretation offers us the explanation that emeralds are precious stones and are used as adornments. As such they may represent something that is valuable, desirable and alluring to the dreamer.

Emperor/Empress *see* King; Queen

Employment *see also* Work

We tend to associate the type of job we do with our self-worth and how we compare with our peers. Status is the desired result of being 'gainfully employed'. Dreams relating to employment can suggest a need for change, concern over performance of tasks or getting along with colleagues and staff. An employer represents an authority figure, usually developed through our early relationships with our father. Depending on the context of the dream the employer indicates issues of independence, rebelliousness and proving yourself.

Empty

Depending on the emotion the dreamer felt during the dream, emptiness points to a lack of pleasure, enthusiasm or close ties. It reflects our feelings of unfulfilled ambitions, denial of opportunity and general isolation. Empty rooms or boxes may suggest that you have shed all that is not needed in your life, but that there is nothing to replace the old with: not yet, anyhow. This may be your opportunity to start with a clean slate and begin building on or refilling the emptiness.

E

Enchantress

An enchantress/fairy/witch image represents magic, illusion and seduction. The dream suggests that you should not be fooled by appearances but guided by your common sense instead. As the saying goes, 'all that glitters is not gold.'

Enclosure

Enclosures take the form of tunnels, cells, caves, or anything else that is restrictive. An enclosure represents defence mechanisms that we use to protect us from getting hurt by love, relationships and general wounds. What we usually regard as too frightening in ourselves to be let out can also be represented by enclosed spaces. If the dreamer sees restraints of some sort in his or her dream—such as walls, barriers or chains—it indicates that he or she feels constrained or trapped in waking life. It may be a warning for the dreamer to pull down what encloses them in order to rebuild and move forward.

End

Dreaming of an end or ending means it's time to move on; time for new beginnings. An ending can be either positive or negative depending on the individual dreamer. When change is inevitable, despite the dreamer's unwillingness, we need to decide what we need to take with us into our new phase and what we can leave behind. An end is usually felt in the dream as a loss, but like death or grief, can be a time of renewal. If you dream of reaching an end of a cave or tunnel, it could mean that you have found a way out of a difficult time in your life. But dreaming of being at the end of the queue can indicate that you feel 'last'—unimportant and forgotten.

Enemy

An enemy is an opposing force and in a dream the image of an enemy can come in many shapes and forms. But unlike an enemy in real life, the enemy in a dream could be anyone or anything—sometimes it could be the dreamer's opposing side (his or her own worst enemy). You need to reflect on what conflicting emotions or issues are present in your life and whether the best tactic is to fight or walk away.

Engagement

An engagement is a promise that you intend to honour—whether it is a business engagement or a relationship. Dreaming of an engagement—either broken or kept—suggests that you have doubts about fully committing and are looking for some signs of reassurance.

E

Engine *see also* Machine

The engine is a symbol of one's drive or energy. It includes the body as a machine, sexual energy and the drive to succeed. This dream needs to be interpreted in light of all other symbols in the dream. For instance, if you see a steam engine it could indicate 'full steam ahead' with a plan. A broken down engine may suggest the state of your physical health and that you need to listen to your body's needs.

E

Engineering

Dreaming of engineering works or of an engineer points to some aspect of your life that needs structuring or major adjustment. It is a positive dream because it gives the dreamer the feeling of being in control and using whatever assets are available to create the structure.

Entering/Entrance *see also* Door

An entrance suggests you are about to enter a new area of experience. For this to happen, you will need to make changes. If the entrance has two parts, as in the case of a porch, perhaps it may be telling you to balance two opposing aspects of yourself before you venture forth with the transition.

Entertainment

You may be in need of fun and leisure if you dream of being entertained and enjoying the experience. If you feel uncomfortable, however, you may be ignoring some vital warnings, such as 'all work and no play makes Jack/Jill a dull boy/girl'.

Entwined/Entangled

Depending on what is restraining you, dreaming of entwining is usually a sign of your need to extricate or untangle yourself from some emotional bind—whether that of a parent, spouse, partner or job. If you feel that the entwining chokes you, it is time for you to cut ties to whatever it is that you are allowing to restrain you. Perhaps you should be reclaiming your individuality.

Envelope

E

An envelope denotes either good or bad news. If the envelope is unopened in the dream the dreamer is fearful of the news. The dreamer is probably waiting on news in waking life and is fearful of the outcome.

Envy

Although envy is listed as one of the seven deadly sins, it is said that it's only when you envy someone that you finally come to terms with what you really want. Pay attention to envy in dreams—it is pointing you to where you want to be or what you want to possess. If someone is envying you, there is a good chance that you have achieved a significant goal in life.

Epaulet *see* Uniform

Eroticism *see* Sex

Escalator *see also* Elevator

Like a lift, going up an escalator suggests that you are reaching your full potential or goals; going down indicates the reverse. The positive aspect of the escalator is that if one is persistent there will be success at the end. Have you ever seen young people run up the escalator that is going down and still manage to get to the top? Unlike the open escalator, the lift is enclosed and therefore this is not possible to achieve. Unfortunately the lift is either taking you up, down or is stuck in between floors.

Escape

As the word suggests, escape reflects our need for freedom and release and, depending on the context of the dream, it may be telling you that you are avoiding facing difficult issues/decisions and therefore 'escapism' here may be a better term. If something is threatening you or burdening you with responsibility, this may also result in a dream of escaping.

E

Europe

Travel, culture, history, fashion, architectural and artistic beauty, the seat of Western civilisation—all these ideas are associated with Europe so that dreaming of living or travelling there suggests a personal longing for these elements or connections. If the dreamer has connections with Europe, it may also represent a desire to explore his or her roots or more traditional life.

Evaporation

Water transforms in its evaporative state and, just like water, we may transform ourselves or change state but remain basically the same. Investigate what it is about yourself or some situation that you wish would evaporate or go away, and deal with it. Evaporation can also mean a transformation in your ideas or emotions usually to a higher state. Evaporation is part of the water cycle and thus represents the cycle of life.

Evening

In dreams, evening represents wisdom and old age. It is also a time usually set aside for relaxation and quiet time. The dream may either be telling us that we should take more time to relax or to reflect or meditate. Peace and tranquillity is usually manifested as a starry evening sky, absolute darkness or a still night free of storms and clouds.

Evil *see also* Devil

If you sense evil or an evil presence in your dreams, accompanied by a feeling of foreboding and disgust, it usually indicates that something is going against your moral judgement. That something may well be your own urges—which, because they are uncontrollable, you judge as being unacceptable. When we fight against our own urges, it may feel like an evil force attacking.

Exams *see also* Tests

When you dream of being in an exam situation—usually unprepared, late or not being able to find the right room—you are having a typical anxiety dream. Self-worth, accomplishment worry and having to prove oneself are all issues cleverly disguised by the typical exam anxiety dream.

Excavation *see* Digging

Excrement *see also* Defecate; Toilet

This dream is about releasing waste, that is, what is no longer needed in the dreamer's life. It may be emotions, values, habits or relationships—all of which have been consumed, digested and now need to be let go of to make room for the new. Depending on the context of the dream, excrement can also represent self-disgust.

Execution

'So, shoot me!' as the saying goes, may well apply to the execution dream. If you dream of your own execution, you may be experiencing a period of depression or low self-esteem. The execution imagery may well be representing self-pity or even self-punishment. If you see someone else being executed, the dream may be of a more judgemental nature. You may well be thinking that someone ought to be 'shot' or 'strung up' for their offensive action.

Exercise

The purpose of exercise is to become fit, so if you are managing to do this easily in a dream, it suggests that you are keeping on top of things. However, if you are struggling and are too tired to complete your exercise routine, it may be time to slow down and reassess your priorities so that you can overcome obstacles.

Expedition *see also* Journey

An expedition has a more adventurous ring to it than just an ordinary journey or trip. It suggests setting out in uncharted or relatively new territory with the possibility of not returning. It is a dream that indicates that purpose, self-discipline and strong will are needed in order to achieve your goal. If you dream that you reach your destination, it indicates that your personal qualities will serve you well in life and that you can make unique achievements if you stick to your plans. If there is a disaster and you turn back, it is not a sign of incompetence but of caution. Perhaps you need to plan more carefully before setting out on a venture of any sort.

Explosion

When we say that we're about to explode, we really mean that we are overwhelmed by anger and that it needs to escape. An explosion in a dream is a release of energy or burst of emotion—usually reaching this stage because it has been bottled up and self-expression denied. It is also symbolic of pent-up sexual energy, resulting in orgasm.

Extravagance *see* Wealth

Eyes *see* Body

E

F

Fable

A dream that you are living a fable or fairytale may suggest wishful thinking on your part (living happily ever after). Perhaps you are trying to escape a situation that seems unbearable in your daily life. It could also be that you are pretending that everything is perfect and are not facing up to the truth. This happens to many of us who feel that 'keeping up appearances' is the best option in times of difficulty or unhappiness.

Face *see also* Body

When we first get up in the morning, we 'face' the day and we 'face' ourselves in the mirror. Therefore, the face can symbolise common fears about self-image and our concern with how others see us. The face can also hide inner feelings, as when we fake a smile, even though we feel miserable inside. This doesn't make us two-faced, as the way we present ourselves to the world may be the way we want to really feel. If the face or faces in your dream are grotesque, they may be representing your real feelings about some issue. Perhaps you feel inadequate or fear that others see you as such. Think of the idioms that best suit the emotion you felt during the dream: 'at face value', 'face the music', 'long face', 'face up to it', 'poker face'.

Factory *see also* Buildings

Dreaming of a factory indicates the state of activity and production in your life. It may be telling you that if you work at a steady pace, even though the activity is repetitive or stifling, you will ultimately reach your goal. However, it may also indicate that you need to get away from the daily grind and strive for a more challenging job or lifestyle. This dream may be interpreted either way, depending on the dreamer's state of mind. Alternatively, the dreamer may be experiencing a lack of control in his or her working life. If you feel alienated or even a little exploited, there is definitely a need to change your current working conditions.

Faeces *see* Defecate; Excrement; Toilet

Failure *see also* Exams

This is a universal dream, which usually expresses a fear or inadequacy that the dreamer is unable to admit or face in his or her waking life. Like the examination dream, dreams of failure are to do with competitiveness and comparison. You may be feeling that whatever you're striving for in your life seems to be unachievable or impossible. This, however, is only a reflection of your fears. A perfectionist, for example, always feels below standard. The dream may be indicating that if you tackle your problem differently, you will eventually succeed.

If the dream relates more to things 'failing', such as lights that won't work or a car that won't start, it may suggest that you need to take more control of situations and not allow external factors to overpower you. This may also be a warning that you are unprepared, and have not taken the

F

necessary steps to succeed in waking life. If you heed the warning you should be able to begin to rectify the situation.

Fainting

If you faint in a dream, it may suggest that you need to take better care of yourself, and not overdo strenuous physical activities, in order to avoid a 'collapse'. The dream could also be telling you that you are overworked and that your body needs a rest.

Fair/Fairground

The fair brings back our childhood memories of fun, excitement, rides and prizes. It suggests a letting go of social restraints as we indulge in a more imaginative state. The dreamer may need to get in touch with the childlike aspect of his or her personality. Your subconscious may be telling you to let go of the restrictions and boundaries you've set up in your life, to embrace creativity, and to see things through fresh eyes. The fair is also a symbol of social and public life, with an assortment of characters as well as the 'swings and roundabouts' of life in general.

Fairy *see also* Fable

Fairies usually represent wishful thinking and belief in the possibility of magic existing in the world, rather than reliance on the practical.

Falcon *see* Birds, Birds of prey

Falling *see also* p.17 (Typical dreams)

This is one of the most common dreams and one that we all have at some stage in our lives, usually at a time when we are feeling insecure and lacking in confidence. It is a typical anxiety dream that suggests our sense that we have no control. It has been interpreted as a dream of sexual surrender, where the fall and landing symbolise sexual intercourse. It also stands for the fear of failing—whether through 'falling into temptation', 'falling from grace' or 'letting ourselves and other people down'. Falling is also associated with isolation and the need to feel supported, especially if the dreamer is feeling misunderstood or not accepted for who he or she is.

F

Going to the edge and falling could be a warning that you are overworked or that you've set yourself such high standards that you are likely to fail. Dreaming of another person falling suggests your wish to be rid of them in your waking life. To see a house falling down suggests that you are struggling to let go of old attitudes and beliefs. If you witness something fall, you may be concerned about a potential danger.

Many people dream of falling and wake up before hitting the ground. Others fall and land—usually they are still alive in the dream and have felt no pain through their fall, despite their injuries. If you fall without hurting yourself, you will have minor struggles with your problem. If you are hurt, it will take you longer to build up the strength to face your fear and deal with it. On the more positive side, the dream may be giving you some good advice—to let go of old negative habits or dogmatic beliefs and enjoy life more.

Fame *see also* Success

Dreaming of being famous suggests your wish to be recognised for your talents. It may suggest that you need to give yourself credit for your own abilities rather than wait for others to acknowledge you. Once you realise your own potential, you can stand out above the rest. If you dream of others being famous, you may have an unfulfilled desire to be like them. On the other hand, you may be afraid of exposure and prefer to remain in the background.

Family

We spend our formative years with our family and that means that our attitudes, values and opinions are based on what we were taught. Whether or not we go against these values, our pattern of behaviour is moulded on what was displayed in our family unit. The absence of a mother or father is an important issue that often traumatises individuals. However, dreaming that your parents are dead or are absent in a family reunion could indicate that you have gained independence and are no longer reliant on their dominant role.

Children or siblings in dreams often represent aspects of ourselves. A helpless child or sibling in danger of drowning is really a symbol of the part of you that is in need of help. A father usually represents authority while a mother stands for relationships and the nurturing part of you. Grandparents are a symbol of wisdom and family traditions while relatives suggest your value systems.

It may well be that the family member you are dreaming of actually represents that person. However, if you dream of conflict in the family, it may be a reflection of conflict within different parts of yourself. Take note of the emotions that arise in the dream.

Fan

Ladies' fans symbolise sensuality and coyness. Dreaming of

using a fan may suggest that you wish to bring out these aspects of your personality to deal with a current situation.

Fare

Dreaming of paying a fare of any kind suggests that we have paid our dues in order to achieve our goal and are now ready to reap the reward.

Farm/Farmyard

A farm is a symbol of productivity and solid manual work. A well-kept farm is an indication of good health and prosperity ('farm fresh'). It also represents the down-to-earth side of the self. A run-down farm, however, is a sign of loss and emptiness. A farm is also symbolic of an idealistic or simple lifestyle, away from the fast pace of city life. The dreamer may be wishing for an existence that has these qualities.

Fashion *see also* Clothing

Fashion that is ever-changing and dictates what we wear plays a significant role in our lives. Dreaming that you are taking an interest in fashion, either in a glossy magazine or shop window, may suggest your desire for outward change. People pass judgement on what we wear—label, quality and style—and we use fashion to convey these qualities. Are you really what you wear, or are you putting on a show to convince others?

Fasting

Fasting is usually associated with cleansing. When we fast, our bodies are cleansed of toxins. A dream of fasting may be drawing your attention to a need for some type of cleansing in your life. Ask yourself what is toxic in your current life. It may also be telling you that you are 'going without' to punish yourself or to make a statement about a grievance of some sort. This dream may take the form of a hunger strike rather than fasting.

Fat

Symbolically, dreaming of a fat person or animal suggests prosperity. We speak of a 'fat wallet', 'living off the fat of the land', 'jolly fat man' and other such idioms which associate fat with ideas of good health and prosperity. This dream depends on how we think of our bodies in real life. If we see ourselves getting fat and are uncomfortable about this state, the dream may be communicating our sense of inadequacy. Many people hide behind their weight when covering up insecurities and fear. Alternatively, this dream may be a warning that the dreamer is overindulging—not necessary in food. If there is excess in your life the message here is of the need for balance.

F

Father *see also* Family

Fathers usually represent respected authority figures. Depending on the circumstances in the dream, seeing your father could suggest either that you are struggling with the authoritarian side of yourself, or that you feel inexperienced (inadequate) in some aspect of your life.

Fax/Fax machine

A fax machine is used for communication over distance. A dream of receiving or sending a fax stands for a message from a hidden part of ourselves that is coming into the a dream in a logical way—through modern communication equipment. This dream may also be a sign that we are trying to reach someone who is 'distanced' from us. Similarly, the fax machine may symbolise new ideas that the dreamer wishes to communicate to others.

Fear *see also specific fears such as* Flying; Drowning; Chased

This dream can be interpreted in many different ways, depending on the type of fear you suffer from and the form in which it is manifested in the dream. Fear is usually expressed as an obstacle dream. If you dream that you overcome the fear by some means—being rescued, running away, outwitting the enemy or saving yourself—it suggests that you will overcome whatever is hindering your progress. If you remain a victim in your dream, and feel helpless, you need to reassess the steps you are taking to address your fear.

Feather

There are many interpretations of feathers in a dream, just as there are many sayings in which feathers occur—'a feather in your cap'; 'birds of a feather flock together'; 'feather your nest'; 'as light as a feather'. Generally, when we think of feathers, we think of softness and lightness. As a result the dream may be suggesting that using a softer approach to a situation may be a better method for achieving your end.

Feathers also represent flight and the freedom often associated with birds. We may want to soar and fly like a bird, a desire that may be more a reflection of a spiritual than a physical need. The meanings associated with feathers have also changed over time, as feathers are no longer used as decorative items for the hats and boas of the past century. Dreaming of feathers was once considered a good omen that meant that one's social standing was about to improve.

Feet *see also* Body

We're familiar with the term 'getting cold feet', meaning that we are afraid of the action we are about to take. Reluctance to go through with something in a dream could relate to an issue in your life. Feet are also about movement—both negative and positive. 'Putting your foot in it' signifies that you have spoken out of turn whereas 'putting your best foot forward' is good advice on how to conduct yourself. Having 'itchy feet' indicates restlessness while 'getting back' or 'landing on your feet' signals victory over difficult times. The interpretation of this dream depends on what action takes place and what emotions are experienced. Feet are also the simplest form of transport and can suggest that the dreamer is, or will soon be, travelling over new ground. The feelings associated with the dream will indicate whether this is wise decision.

F

Fence

A fence is an artificial structure built to restrict and control movement, particularly of animals. A dream of a fence is a classic obstacle dream, often inviting an interpretation that reads it as a symbol of control over our inhibitions or our 'wild' self. As boundaries, fences can also represent our own boundaries within society, in relationships and at work. Often it's the conflict of work encroaching on our personal lives that is symbolised by a fence, and suggests our need to build a wall of resistance to keep them apart. We can also feel 'fenced in', confined, and 'stuck' in a place we may want to move out of. Fences also symbolise protection of property and of self, and the desire to keep out unwanted intruders. A fence between you and someone else is an expression of your desire to stay on your own turf and remain separate.

Ferry *see also* Travel

If you dream of being in a ferry, expect a major change to occur in your life. The ferry has ancient associations with being carried along the River Styx towards death. However, this journey is not a physical death but the ending of a phase in your life, whether to do with a relationship, a value system, or an activity. The ferry is symbolic of the vessel that carries you towards this transition.

F

Festival *see also* Party

A festival symbolises both celebration and tradition. Depending on the context of the dream and whether you are enjoying the feasting, it can be interpreted as giving you permission to enjoy life more, join in with a wider social group, or share good spirits and fun.

Fever *see* Health

Field

Dreaming of animals in a field suggest the dreamer's contact with his or her natural self. It may be telling you to get back to nature, or basics. Like a farm, a ploughed field indicates prosperity, while a barren one conveys the idea of stagnation. 'Playing the field' is an indication that we may desire freedom from social pressure or expectations. A field also represents the 'field' of activity, study or expertise that you are involved in. In this context it may be communicating a need for you to renew or consider your satisfaction in your chosen field.

Fighting

Depending on the dream, fighting tends to represent our need for independence and change. Dreaming of a physical fight is our subconscious way of dealing with anger, frustration and difficulty in expressing our feelings—whether the anger is aimed at ourselves or at others. Fighting also indicates defence—we fight for our values, our survival, our space, our health and our desire to win out against negative forces such as crime, pollution, injustice and people who attack us or our opinions. This is a dream of conflict that indicates the need for some sort of change. To dream of fighting may also suggest that you need to 'fight' more in your waking life for what is rightfully yours.

F

File

A metal file or a nail file could be an indication that you are being abrasive and that you need to take a softer approach with those around you. A dream in which you are filing something down to shape it to your specifications suggests that patience and perseverance is needed to achieve your goals.

Dreaming of office files, filing cabinets and the act of filing may be interpreted as symbols of the need for order in your life, to help you overcome chaos. Lining up in single file also suggests order and discipline. Consider how these images fit into your current life situation.

Film

If you dream of starring in a film, you may be trying to escape from reality by viewing your life from a different point of view. You may wish it were more like a movie with a happy-ever-after ending, but you need to question the story that you are creating on screen. Is it real or is it made up?

Finding

A dream of finding something can be telling you either that you have lost something in the first place or that you have 'discovered' or 'realised' something about yourself or your life that will change your perspective. It is a positive dream, because it helps you to become aware of some aspect of yourself that you hadn't acknowledged before and which can now be of use to you.

Fingers *see* Body

Fire

F

Fire is associated with life and passion and is one of the four elements of the twelve horoscope signs (air, water and earth being the other three). Fire is a good friend when it warms us, but if we get too close we get burnt. It's a symbol of regeneration, so dreaming of fire may indicate that you are entering a period of renewal and painful reflection. More negatively, fire can suggest anger, resentment and destruction. 'Burning with desire', and other such idioms refer to the effect of fire on our desires and sexuality. The dream may suggest that you need more vitality and passion in your life.

To dream of being burnt alive may express frustration at not being able to handle a new stage in life or new circumstances ('too hot to handle'). 'Baptism by fire' means coming to a new awareness of ourselves. If you dream of fighting a fire, you may want to cool or put out fiery passions. A fireplace symbolises contentment in the home but any fire that is out of control indicates extreme, uncontrollable passions that are potentially destructive and overwhelming. Seeing a fire engine or being a fireman in your dream is a sign that you are in control of explosive emotions.

Fireworks

Because fireworks are associated with festivities and celebrations, they suggest that the dreamer will soon be celebrating some good fortune. The explosive nature of the fireworks, as well as their dazzling display, indicates that whatever we are about to celebrate in our lives will be a little overwhelming and spectacular. The success may belong to someone you know, in which case you will share in it by being a spectator.

Fish/Fishing *see also individual fish entries*

The fish symbol was adopted by the early Christians to represent Christ and the Church. In a more general sense, when we dream of fish, we are getting in touch with our deeper selves and our search for a higher self or spirituality. For the Chinese, fish are a symbol of financial gain, while the image of two fish going in the opposite direction represents the astrological sign of Pisces. Consider why this dream appears at this stage in your life. Perhaps you are looking deeper—'fishing around'—for something? Catching a fish may indicate that you will achieve success—'a big catch'. Alternatively, you may be feeling as if you are living in a fish bowl, open to criticism for all to see. Perhaps you are 'a big fish in a small pond' and you need to expand your horizons.

A cold fish is unfeeling and something that smells fishy suggests that not everything is as it seems. Pay attention to the fish in your dream and monitor your reactions to this symbol.

Flag

A flag represents beliefs and principles that you hold in common with other like-minded people. It is a symbol of common good, patriotism, loyalty, and comradeship and provides an object for people with common beliefs to gather around or follow. Dreaming of a flag could be a sign that you need to reflect on your principles and where you stand on issues that affect you and others around you.

Flattery

Flattery is insincere, so if you dream of being flattered by someone it indicates that you are not being truthful to yourself about an issue. It also suggests that you have a need for attention or recognition. Receiving or giving a compliment, on the other hand, is genuine and reflects self-acceptance and confidence.

F

Fleas *see* Insects

Fleas are annoying and cause irritation. In a dream they are signs that we need to get rid of situations or people that are causing us to feel irritated.

Fleece

When we think of fleece we think of woolly sheep, security, comfort and warmth. These are creature comforts we crave for and hold in high regard. Are these comforts being met in your waking life? On the negative side, this dream may be a sign that you are feeling 'fleeced' or cheated.

Fleet

To dream of a fleet of ships reflects our hopes and aspirations. If the fleet is coming in it means that the dreamer may very well gain what they are hoping for.

Flies *see* Insects

Floating

Floating involves being in a state of complete relaxation and 'going with the flow'. That means that we are allowing events to unfold at their own pace and to carry us along. A dream in which you are floating may be an indication that you need to let go and trust in the natural order of things. If you feel uncomfortable or distressed in your floating dream, perhaps you should consider taking charge of your life more and not being too passive.

Flocks of Birds *see* Birds

Flogging

F

Any dream about punishment has to do with the dreamer's feelings of guilt. Do you think you deserve to be punished for some inadequacy or some action that you haven't been proud of? Perhaps you have a cruel taskmaster and you are being driven beyond your limits? The taskmaster could represent you or someone in authority.

Flood *see also* Deluge

Like fire, flood is an uncontrollable force of nature that can be frightening and overwhelming. Feeling inundated brings about anxiety and an inability to cope and sometimes this can suggest depression for the dreamer. We talk about a 'flood of tears' or a 'flood of memories' both of which indicate a release of bottled-up feelings as well as relief.

Floor *see also* Buildings, parts of

The floor represents support. It is the base structure on which you build your life (house). If the floor is weak, your support structure will also be weak and unable to see you through life's difficulties. If you are cleaning, polishing or repairing the floor, it suggests that you are willing to put effort into improving your standard of living. A slanted floor indicates that you are off-balance and deviating from your original plans. This may result in you not being able to achieve your goals.

Flour

Flour is an ingredient used to make foods such as bread, cakes, biscuits and other foods that are generally known as 'fillers'—meaning that they provide us with a hearty meal. Dreaming of flour suggests you may need to take on a more basic or practical approach so that your life may be more 'fulfilling'.

F

Flowers

Flowers represent beauty and pleasure. To be given a bouquet is to feel rewarded and appreciated. It is also a token of love and tenderness, as well having sexual significance—the genitals resembling the shape of specific flowers. In Christian symbolism, living flowers are a representation of immortality, whereas cut flowers are associated with death. Traditionally, each individual flower had a special significance in dreams. Some of these meanings are still associated with specific flowers, depending on the dreamer's cultural, spiritual and geographical background.

Bluebell These flowers suggest arguments erupting in your household.

Buttercup Buttercups are about taking stock of your financial affairs. They are rich, golden flowers that are often associated with childhood and plenty.

Carnation Carnations are flowers of passion and were once traditional buttonhole flowers for men.

Chrysanthemum White chrysanthemums are associated with loss. This could be because, in the northern hemisphere, these autumn flowers come out around All Souls' Day in November, a time when people visit their departed loved ones in cemeteries.

Clover This is a fortunate omen if it has four leaves, but if there are three it means that someone will ask you for money.

F

Daffodil Daffodils are flowers you give someone to mend a friendship. These flowers suggest plenty, optimism and emotional well-being. Because of their associations with spring, they can also be a symbol of new beginnings or a fresh start in life.

Daisy Dreaming of daisies signals emotional openness or simplicity. This dream can also be associated with a young or naïve person—'as fresh as a daisy'.

Forget-me-not This flower is just the opposite of its name. It means that your partner cannot fulfil your emotional needs.

Iris Irises are an indication that good news is to come.

Lily Lilies are a symbol of chastity and innocence. Water lilies grow from mud, through water and then reach for the light. They are a symbol of our regeneration and purification.

Lotus Lotus flowers represent new life and immortality. The ancient Egyptians copied this flower profusely in paintings and held it in high regard for its healing properties.

Marigold These are happy flowers once thought to break the power of enchantment.

Mistletoe This is a romantic plant and reminds you to be attentive to your lover.

Myrtle Myrtle is a flower of happiness and tranquillity.

Peony Peonies are about the dangers of self-restraint. Let yourself go.

Poppy This is the flower that symbolises memories of war; its bright red colour reminding us of the futility of bloodshed.

Primrose Primroses are a symbol of new friendship.

Rose Roses represent love and femininity.

Flute *see also* Musical instruments
A wind instrument, the flute represents deep emotion and enticement. It evokes feelings of harmony, joy and 'lightness'. Therefore, dreaming of a flute symbolises your need or desire to express these feelings.

Flying *see* p.17 (Typical dreams)

Flying birds *see* Birds

Flying saucer *see* Alien

Fog
When we speak of being 'in a fog', the saying indicates that we are confused and unable to see the real issues that

are affecting us. If you dream of walking in a fog, it is best not to take action at this time, but to wait until you are feeling more confident. At times your ideas can be clouded by others' judgement. Wait until the feeling of 'not having the foggiest idea' has lifted before making a decision on any issue.

Following

If you dream of following someone it means that a habit or an attitude is leading you. Perhaps you are pursuing something that will give you a stronger sense of identity. This might be a worthy cause, an ideal or an organisation. This dream may also be questioning whether you prefer to be a 'follower' or to take a more of a leadership role, particularly at work. Following an animal suggests that your basic drives or instincts are leading you. If you dream of being followed, you need to work out whether the dream is positive or negative. If it is a positive experience, the dream is assuring you that you have initiative and only need to put it into practice. If the experience is negative and you feel 'stalked' rather than just followed, then you need to deal with past fears, memories or guilt that are pursuing you. Put them 'behind you'.

Food

Food is a symbol of nourishment for the body, the mind and the soul. If you dream of eating food, it means that you are satisfying some craving or desire for nourishment. Different foods represent various needs that we crave at different times.

Bread is a staple food and represents our basic needs.

Cake is a symbol of decadence and sensuality, particularly if it is filled with cream and other tempting dressings such as chocolate.

Ham/Cured meats These represent our need for preservation. (*See also* Ham.)

Meals Meals around a table with others indicate sociability and a feeling of belonging.

F

Meat Meat is associated with flesh and as such is a symbol of physical gratification.

Milk A human's first food, milk represents infant needs or the nurturing of oneself.

Onion Onions are multi-layered and can often represent parts of ourselves.

Sweets Like cakes, sweets represent indulgence and a craving for what is normally regarded as temptation.

Vegetables These are basic foods—necessary for good health, but not always craved. Like bread, vegetables form part of a staple diet and, despite some blandness, they are important to maintaining our health.

Football *see also* Games; Ball

Football is a competitive game of skill and teamwork, which represents how we identify with a group of people or connect with this group. If you dream of being in a football team, take note of your relationship with other players. Are you part of the team or are you a star? Perhaps you are sitting on the bench waiting to be called, or you are being 'kicked around'. Identifying your role will shed light on how you relate to people around you.

Footprints

Seeing footprints in a dream reveals your need to follow someone—either their expertise or their approach to life. If the footprints are in front of you, there is help ahead, but if you see footprints behind you then you need to examine the way you've done things in the past, with a view to making some changes.

F

Foreign country *see also* Overseas

Dreaming of being in a foreign country highlights the need for a different mental or emotional attitude to be applied to a situation. It also indicates that new experiences are ahead of you.

Forest

In fairytales, there is always a fear of the hero or heroine being lost in the forest. As a result, the image of the forest as a place of hiding, of loss and of dangerous encounters is probably imprinted on our memories from childhood. In the forest also live witches, ogres, trolls, fairies, elves, and wood people: in other words, the positive and negative forces in our lives.

In psychological terms, a forest is a symbol of testing and of coming to terms with our own true natures. The trees may obscure our way ('can't see the forest for the trees'); that is, represent narrow-mindedness or old patterns of thought. On the other hand, the trees are part of the nature that makes up the forest and each of us must come to terms with his or her nature. If the forest is covered in dead leaves, it may mean that a situation or a relationship has come to an end.

Forget-me-nots *see* Flowers

Forgetting

If you dream that you keep forgetting something, take the dream literally. It may be telling you that you need to pay attention to appointment details or deadlines that you may miss.

F

Fork (in the road)

Dreaming of a fork in the road means that you will have to make a decision on an important matter. Symbolically, the fork in the road represents a junction on our spiritual path where guidance will be needed to make a decision as to which direction to take.

Fork (utensil)

A dream of stabbing someone or being stabbed with a fork represents the force that drives us, often in a negative manner. The three-pronged fork is traditionally associated with the devil and is therefore a warning of trickery. However, in general terms, the fork is a symbol of indecision as indicated by the idiom, 'taking a stab in the dark'.

Fort *see* Buildings

Fortune-teller

Fortune-telling is associated with looking into the future for guidance and trusting in the opinion of those equipped with seemingly more knowledge. If you dream that you consult a fortune-teller, consider whether you are impatient to gain knowledge of some future event. Keep in mind that you are trusting someone who appears to have the knowledge, but that in fact only your actions can affect the future. This can also be a warning dream that tells you to beware of false prophecy, and to find out something for yourself rather than believing what someone else tells you.

Fountain

A dream of a flowing fountain is a sign of life, health and our ability to express our emotions fluently. A dried up or clogged fountain indicates problems in our emotional lives and the need to release negative or unproductive feelings.

F

Four *see* Numbers

Fox *see* Animals

Fraud

To dream that someone has cheated you indicates that you are too trusting of people and that you need to protect yourself better. If you are the one committing fraud, you should explore your reasons for feeling that you do not deserve to have things, so that you need to cheat to obtain them.

French

French is associated with a cultured and sophisticated society, so dreaming that we speak the language, or are part of the culture, represents a desire to embrace these qualities.

Friends

Friends appearing in your dreams indicate the need for you to explore the qualities that friends bring into your life, such as love, support, loyalty, comradeship and fun. If they tend to be negative qualities—such as competition, jealousy, and possessiveness—it is time to reassess the friendship.

Friends can also represent aspects of your own personality that you need to acknowledge more. Perhaps you need to be a better friend either to yourself or to someone else. What is the relationship you have with the friend in your dream? Does the friendship need repair or do you want to cut off from that person?

Frog *see* Animals

Frost *see also* Ice

'Icy frost' and 'frozen in time' are phrases that suggest a lack of movement and life. Discover what your dream means by examining your present state. Are you unable to move forward? Are your feelings frozen? Is there a decision that you need to make but are unable to do so? This dream may also be indicative of how you are treating others in waking life—in other words it could be time to 'defrost' and show some warmth.

Fruit

Fruits are associated with reproduction and ripeness (coming to maturity). We talk about the 'fruits of our labour' to indicate the prosperity that follows a time of hard work. Each individual fruit is thought to represent some aspect of sexuality, fertility or the life force.

Apple Apples are the 'forbidden fruit' described in the Bible, and in religious symbolism represent the fall of mankind or the origin of sin in the act of taking a bite of what is forbidden. Over the centuries the apple has also become a symbol of sexual or maternal love, as in the expression 'the apple of my eye'.

Banana Bananas are unique in their elongated shape, and represent male sexuality. To dream of a big, yellow banana signals that you need to slow down and take better care of your health, especially your diet. It could be your body's way of telling you that you're missing out on some essential vitamins and minerals.

F

Berries These natural fruits grow wild, and as such have significant meanings. In olden times, raspberries were thought to represent tiny hearts and therefore dreaming of them denoted romantic emotions. Gooseberries, on the other hand, were an ancient symbol of fertility. Strawberries are thought to represent a happy marriage. Today we enjoy eating strawberries with cream or in champagne. They are also great to decorate sweets such as cakes and slices. Strawberry jam is also a popular spread. Because of their versatility, strawberries are associated with foods that blend well together—hence a marriage of two tastes.

If you dream of blackberries, beware! The path towards your goal is likely to take you through a thicket of obstacles. You'll get there in the end, but you'll have to be prepared for a few scratches along the way. If you're eating blackberries, it's a sign that you may soon be enjoying the fruit of your labours.

Cherries Cherries symbolise good health, fertility and sexuality.

Figs, peaches and plums These soft, luscious fruits represent the female genitals. Figs represented life and prosperity to the Romans and they regarded the fruit as sacred and erotic. The fig is an ancient symbol of sexuality and fertility. It also represents prosperity, so a dream in which you are eating this fruit may suggest that good times are coming.

Olives Olives are emblems of peace and kindness, as the oil pressed from the olive can be used for many purposes.

F

Orange As oranges are associated with vitamin C, dreaming of this fruit suggests that you may have been thinking of boosting your vitamin intake. Oranges are also citrus and zesty—perhaps this form of energy is lacking in your life. If the oranges are being squeezed you may take it to mean that you are feeling drained by someone or something.

Pomegranate These were once the Christian symbol of resurrection due to their many seeds. The pomegranate was also considered a symbol of fertility and new life.

Funeral

Because a funeral is an acknowledgement of death, dreaming of attending one is a sign of our need to accept death or an ending of some kind. It may be a loss of part of your life, your beliefs, or your relationship that you need to come to terms with in order to move on. A funeral allows mourning to take place, and this is a healthy response to a painful loss. If you dream of the funeral of a parent, it may suggest that you are cutting the umbilical cord and becoming independent. Dreaming of your own funeral is a common dream that symbolises a feeling of 'deadness' in your life and a wish to make the most of life while you still have it. It also indicates leaving the old self behind. Dreaming of someone else's funeral may be a sign that you wish that they were dead—a reflection of a fantasy that you engage with during your waking hours.

Fur

Animals have fur to protect them against the elements. If your dream has fur in it, consider what you are trying to protect yourself from. If you dream of wearing a luxurious fur coat worthy of a movie star, pay attention to the emotion in the dream. Is the fur coat a symbol of fame and stardom and is it wishful thinking on your part?

F

Furniture

In dreams, furniture represents the attitudes and values or notions of identity that we have inherited from our families. It can also symbolise our 'emotional baggage', that is, needs that were not met in the past that we now feel in-secure about.

Different pieces of furniture represent various parts of our attitudes or ourselves.

Bed/Mattress These contain many meanings. For some they represent a place of rest or refuge. For others, they highlight their relationships, particularly with sexual partners, and their issues with intimacy. Lying in bed is also a passive activity, whether one is recovering from an illness or just daydreaming. As a result this dream could indicate some form of depression.

Carpet Carpets can be threadbare or plush. These opposite conditions reflect the dreamer's financial state or level of satisfaction with life's comforts. 'Sweeping something under the carpet' indicates hiding some emotion or secret, while 'rolling out the red carpet' suggests receiving recognition for one's efforts.

Chair/Sofa These are for resting and relaxation, so they usually express the dreamer's passive attitude or openness. This dream may be suggesting that you need to take more rest and be open to new methods of relaxation that will reduce anxiety.

Cupboard/Wardrobe These are where things are kept hidden, locked away and out of sight. Hidden memories, our ability to be open to people and a sense of isolation are all possible meanings of these pieces of furniture. The cupboard has a sexual significance, through its ability to represent the womb. If we have 'a skeleton in the closet' we have secrets and desires hidden from those around us. The term 'coming out of the closet' is used to describe homosexuals acknowledging and informing the 'outside world' of their sexuality.

Table Tables are pieces of furniture that are used for sharing things with others, whether a meal or a conversation. A bare table could indicate that you do not give of yourself. Your place at the table reflects your desired social status. Are you at the end or at the head? If you see yourself laying out the table, you are concerned about social image.

Future

Dreaming of the future, or dreaming of actual events unknown to the dreamer, have both been considered prophetic dreams. This phenomenon has puzzled experts and as yet there is no agreement as to how one can accurately foretell the future. If you dream of a future event take note of whether the dream recurs and analyse the symbols before you take the dream too literally. The symbols in the dream may just represent the needs you want to have fulfilled, or your fears of what the future holds for you.

G

Gale *see also* Wind

A gale is an uncontrollable force of nature, indicating that we feel we have no control over certain situations in our lives. If you struggle but do not perish in the gale, it suggests that you will overcome difficult circumstances.

Gall

Gall is a symbol of bitterness and irritability. Do you recognise this feeling? See what you can do to express it in a positive way.

Gambling *see also* Games

Dreaming of gambling symbolises a reckless code of behaviour and refusal to take life seriously. If you dream of winning, it usually means the opposite. The dream could be cautioning you to change your ways before you risk losing. Alternatively, the dreamer could be feeling as if he or she is taking a risk in their waking life. In this case the dream may be a warning from the subconscious to proceed with caution.

Games

Dreams of playing games represent the way we cope with life. If we play well, it stands to reason that our lives are on target and we are managing well. If we play badly, we need to consider upgrading our skills in order to improve the score. Ball games are often team sports and, therefore, they indicate the way in which we relate to people in a social context. They are also strongly competitive games. Consider how competitive you are in the game of life and whom it is you struggle against to reach your goals.

Thinking games, such as chess, are more to do with ideas and with how well you make your moves and reflect your successes in life. Card games and gambling are symbols of balancing calculated risks and recklessness.

G

Gangrene

To dream of having gangrene or that someone else has this infection indicates decay and loss of some aspect of your life. It can also suggest that you are holding onto some aspect of your life that is physically or emotionally toxic.

Garage

Regardless of how you see the garage—whether it is a tool shed, workshop or car park—it generally represents how you maintain your motivation, your passions and the resources available to you. It is a symbol both of your energy reserves, and the things that you don't need but you can't let go of, 'just in case'. If you dream of a car repair garage, you need to take care of your ambition or drive.

Garbage

The act of throwing out garbage represents what you no longer need or what you consider to be useless. Depending on the type of garbage you see—in other words, whether it is furniture (values), food (nourishment) or flowers (beauty)—you may be discarding valuable parts of yourself.

On the other hand, you may feel it's time to let go of some parts of yourself that you have outgrown or which are no longer useful to you. In general, this type of dream indicates that the dreamer is discarding what is no longer productive in his or her waking life.

Garden

A garden is a symbol of the dreamer's inner self. Ideas and values are cultivated or 'grow' and expand throughout a lifetime. It's important to note the condition of the garden. If it is a tidy garden, it indicates that you have an organised and conservative mind. An untidy or overgrown garden, on the other hand, reflects your lack of order and direction. It could also be pointing to past disappointments and a fear of new setbacks. A beautiful garden is a sign of happiness and prosperity, while an overgrown one is a warning to be more focused on your goals. It may be time to 'weed out' the unpleasant aspects of your nature.

G

Gardener

The gardener is the nature loving, wise aspect of ourselves that takes a 'down to earth' approach to life and is the keeper of the natural order of things.

Garland

Garlands have traditionally been associated with honour and recognition. They have been awarded to champions and heroes for performing extraordinary deeds. Dreaming of receiving a garland may be an indication that you feel a need to be recognised by others for your talent and effort.

Garlic

Garlic was once regarded as so potent that it kept vampires

away. The smell was so pungent that evil spirits did not approach the wearer. In many countries, garlic garlands were hung over doorways for protection. Today, the meaning of garlic has changed in a practical direction. Garlic has been recognised as a natural herb with strong detoxifying qualities that guarantee better health. Depending on the nature of the dream, seeing or eating garlic indicates your desire to ward off something, whether illness or other people.

Gas

Gas is a natural resource that provides us with energy. However, if it is misused it can cause injury and death. Dreaming of wearing a gas mask could indicate that you are prepared for possible dangers ahead of you. A gas leak represents a fault that, if it is not repaired, will be dangerous. This may have something to do with the dreamer's relationships. If you are unable to light a gas appliance, it suggests that there is energy lacking in some area of your life. You should also consider taking this dream literally, as your subconscious can sometimes take note of things that your conscious mind overlooks. Have your appliances and connections checked. Other idioms to note are 'full of gas' (empty words) and 'step on the gas' (accelerate).

Gate

A gate is a symbol of transition or change from one stage to another. When we walk through the gate we are entering another state. In dreams this may mean a transition from one period of life to another, such as from adolescence to adulthood, from the single state to being married, from school to employment or even from life to death. The pearly gates of heaven are a symbol of the passage across the threshold of life into the realm of death. If you dream that the gate is locked and you are trapped either inside or out, you may need to look at other symbols in your dream. Ask yourself whether the gate is a barrier or an opportunity for new things.

Gems *see* Jewellery/Jewels

Genitals

Traditionally associated with reproduction, genitals represent the sexual identity of the dreamer. It is not uncommon to dream of having genitals of the opposite gender. It usually refers to the feminine or masculine side of ourselves that we wish to connect with. If you dream that you are mutilated or injured in the genital area, consider what it is that is hurting your sense of sexual identity. It may have to do with past sexual or emotional abuse or a lack of confidence in your sexuality.

G

Ghost

When we dream of being haunted by a ghost, we are not actually being haunted by a spirit, but by our own feelings of guilt, memories and unfulfilled ambitions. The 'could have beens' and 'should haves' are the ghosts that haunt most of us. Such a dream can be indicative of unresolved issues associated with the person who is haunting us. In this case the answers that the subconscious mind is trying to find to these issues may be present in other symbols within the dream. If the dream is recurring, it is a sign that the issue remains unresolved.

Giant

As children we saw adults as giants. Our parents seemed frightening in comparison to our small stature. This dream may be indicating that you feel powerless, or that whatever issue you are facing seems too big for you to handle. Perhaps that is why you are reverting back to your childhood fear of adults. Recognise your own power and outwit the problem—just as David did with Goliath.

Gift

To give a gift is to give of one's self. If you dream of accepting a gift, you may actually be acknowledging your own talents and skills ('gifts').

Gig

A gig is an occasion to let loose and enjoy yourself without the usual inhibitions. It is more informal than a concert or a dance, so the dream may be communicating a need for some free time in which you can be socially at ease.

Girl

If you are female, and you either dream of yourself as a girl or see a girl, the dream generally relates to the more emotional, young and vulnerable aspect of yourself. It may also reflect how you feel about a sister or daughter. For a male this dream is a reflection of his undeveloped emotions. Regardless of whether the dreamer is male or female, this dream suggests a need to be in touch with the more feminine aspects of self.

Girlfriend *see also* Boyfriend

If you are a man and dream of a girlfriend or ex-girlfriend, the dream is usually more about the balance of the masculine and the feminine in the dreamer than the actual relationship itself. If a girlfriend appears in a woman's dream, it is a reflection of the type of friend the dreamer would like to be.

Giving

'Give and take' is a phrase used to describe a healthy relationship, so if you dream of giving something to someone it usually suggests that you are giving something of yourself. Examine your feelings about giving in the dream. If you grudge giving something away, then you may need to be more sharing, whereas if you're too eager to give or 'dump' on others, you may need to reassess your reasons for this dependency. If the receiver does not appreciate your giving, it indicates that you are not in tune with what the other person needs.

G

Glass

Glass is a transparent barrier that allows us to see what's on the other side. For this reason it represents the invisible barriers that we put up ourselves or that others impose on us. These barriers might be emotional distance, social barriers, fears or a lack of self-confidence. When professional women refer to the 'glass ceiling' and their difficulty in breaking it, they mean that they can see what they could possibly achieve but that the glass (tradition / male dominance) is a barrier that needs to be broken or opened up. If you dream of breaking glass it may indicate a broken promise, relationship or a shattered dream. This distressing dream may be turned into a positive one if you take it as a sign to free yourself of emotional restrictions and be ready for a new direction.

Glasses

Glasses relate to the way we see the world around us. Wearing glasses, particularly sunglasses, is a way of hiding oneself. Being 'long-sighted' suggests that you have a long-term vision of your future, whereas if you see yourself as 'short-sighted' you are only concerned about tomorrow. Apply these terms to whatever is going on in your life and pay attention to the dream. It may be telling you to change your viewpoint or shift your focus on things.

Gloves *see also* Clothing

Gloves are a symbol of protection—keeping your hands clean. This can be a literal meaning, or it can also indicate that you want to avoid getting involved in any 'dirty business'. Expressions such as 'iron fist in a velvet glove' and treating someone with 'kid gloves' all have variations of meaning. Generally, however, it is about protection and covering up.

G

Glue

Depending on the dream, glue is associated with permanence and fixture. Terms such as 'stick to me like glue', 'stick to it' or 'sticky situation' will help you work out the meaning of the glue in your dream.

Goal

Scoring a goal suggests success, but missing a goal means we need to work harder on our skills in order to score.

Goat *see* Animals

God *see also* Religion

Dreaming of God or a god-like figure is a symbol that we acknowledge the divine—that there is a power greater than ours. God may also represent an authority figure—a mighty father figure who is able to take charge and protect us, which can be a comforting image. Think about what is burdening you and try to come to terms with the idea that although the 'buck stops with you' in some situations, there is always a higher force that takes care of you. Alternatively, this dream may be suggesting that you have to learn to be responsible for your actions.

Gold *see also* Colours

The emphasis of this dream is on value—gold represents something precious and valuable to the dreamer. It may be the valuable part of ourselves so that finding gold means finding new aspects of others or ourselves. Gold does not tarnish and therefore stands the test of time. Think of the values you hold to as the most important in your life. Do you have a heart of gold or are you a gold digger?

G

Golf *see* Games

Gong

A gong is loud and demands attention. If you hear a gong in your dream, it suggests that you are being called for something, or that you need to pay attention to some issue in your life.

Grain

Grain is associated with success and harvest. A grain of wheat indicates the germ of an idea that is then harvested with success. It may mean that you have created opportunities for yourself over time and that it is now time to reap your reward. A wheat field also suggests personal growth from a humble seed to a field (from immaturity to experience). How successful the harvest will be depends on your feelings in the dream. If they are negative, you may need to change the type of grain you are sowing in order to bring about ultimate success.

Grandparents *see also* Family

Grandparents in a dream are symbols of love, protection, security and tradition. If you dream of searching for a grandparent, you are likely to be searching for the qualities they stand for.

Grass

If in your dream the grass is greener on the other side of the fence, consider how this term reflects your emotions. Do you feel that others are better off than you are? Perhaps you ought to reflect that the grass is not always greener there. Green grass is a symbol of success and growth, while dry or burned grass generally means failure and misery. Dreaming of the latter may mean that it is time to move on to greener pastures. Planting a lawn and helping it grow suggests that you will overcome financial difficulties through your own efforts and hard work.

Grave *see also* Death

Dreaming of a grave reflects your own feelings towards death or about someone who has died. It is also recognition of some aspect of your life that has 'died' or come to an end. Because it usually signals transition, rejuvenation or new beginnings, this is not a negative dream.

Gravel

Gravel is dangerous to skid on, whether you're driving on it or scraped your knees falling on it as a child. The message of the dream may be to not take risks at the moment, but to wait until you are on solid ground (bitumen).

Grease

When we eat something greasy, we feel guilty that it's bad for

G

our health. If we spill grease on our clothes, we are concerned about getting the stain out. Greasy dishes in the sink make us look like sloppy housekeepers. Generally, grease means that we aren't careful enough and that we aren't taking care of ourselves. A greasy or slimy character suggests someone who is not to be trusted. How does grease fit into your life?

Green *see* Colours

Groom *see* Bridegroom

G

Guard *see also* Jail

A guard is a symbol of both protection and imprisonment. Depending on the dream, the guard is a warning to you of some kind. Either you need to be on your guard in relation to some action, or you feel that you are being kept away from your heart's desire.

Guillotine

Do you feel that you are losing your mind? Or are you losing your head over someone? Despite the guillotine being a weapon used to execute people, we associate it more with the killing of our common sense. You may be cutting off a part of your personality. Do you feel irrational or impulsive? Perhaps you have a desire to 'cut off' your head (rational thoughts) and make decisions based on the heart. The guillotine is also associated with revolution and passion. The dreamer may be acting out of haste in order to bring about drastic change in life. The warning here is to use your head and not your heart to make decisions.

Guilt

To analyse this emotion, you need to look at the other

symbols in the dream. Maybe you are feeling guilty because of something that is going on in your life. Alternatively, the dream may be telling you that you should feel guilt for some deed.

Guitar *see also* Musical instruments

As with all musical instruments, the guitar expresses our deepest feelings through its sound. Romantic, exciting and up beat, the guitar represents these parts of our creative selves.

Gun *see also* Rifle; Weapon

A gun is a symbol of aggression. Shooting someone means that you feel aggression towards some person or the part of yourself that this person represents. The gun also represents the male sexual organ and drive. If the weapon doesn't fire, the dreamer has feelings of sexual inadequacy. Depending on the circumstances in the dream, the gun can be interpreted in many ways. You may be using the gun to protect something that is of value to you. Killing someone may be a message that you have violent feelings towards this person and wish to eliminate him/her from your life.

Gypsy

Gypsies are often thought of as a nomadic, mystical race who lead a carefree, unconventional lifestyle. Do you want more freedom in your life? Do you feel stifled and wish to express yourself in a more creative and less conservative manner? A dream of gypsies is often related to the dreamer's own feelings of restlessness and need to be released from the mundane burdens of life. The message here is the need for 'time out'.

H

Haemorrhage *see also* Blood

Do you feel drained or emptied in some way? Blood is a significant dream symbol of our energies and life force. Similarly, its rich red colour suggests strong emotions or passions. Therefore, a dream in which you are unable to control a sudden flow of blood tends to suggest loss of strength or potency, whether in your emotional, spiritual or physical life. Alternatively, it may suggest the sudden release of pent-up emotion. Think of what is 'bleeding you dry'.

Hail

Because of its associations with frozenness, and also water, hail is most likely to stand for a temporary blockage or numbing of your emotions. Perhaps your inability to express your emotions has led to them becoming 'frozen' so that you are unable to express them freely. It could be that you are in a situation where you feel that you have to remain strong and self-contained when you might otherwise prefer to express grief or anger more openly. Either way, hail is a reminder that when emotions are blocked they may become more painful rather than less, when they eventually 'fall' both on others and on yourself.

Hair *see* Body

Hairdresser

Dreaming of a hairdresser can have several meanings, depending on the context and the emotions that accompany the dream. On the one hand, it can mean that you are looking for physical intimacy, on the other hand, that you wish to be taken care of by others. Being at the hairdresser can also suggest your anxiety about the way that you appear to others. Do you feel unprepared for some social event or situation that is coming up?

Hall *see also* Buildings

H

To dream of a large, hall-like building or space tends to suggest some emptiness or vacancy in your life. Perhaps you lack friends or a social life, or don't have enough activities to fill your time. Alternatively, if the dream is a pleasant one, it may signal your desire to have more space, or feel less pressured by those around you. If the hall is filled with people, it is likely that the dream represents the public aspects of your life.

Halo

Dreaming of someone with a halo suggests feelings of serenity, protection and purity. If on the other hand you are wearing a halo in your dream, it could indicate that you feel pressured into a role that isn't allowing you self-expression.

Ham *see also* Food

Eating this meat in a dream could signal your sense that you are living 'on the pig's back'. But because ham is prepared by a process of 'curing' the dream may also suggest concerns about health.

Hammer

Dreaming of a hammer can be a sign that a problem in your

life requires a forceful or aggressive solution. Hammering in a dream can also be an indication that you are determined to 'nail' an issue or problem that has been bothering you.

Hand *see* Body

Handcuffs

These are powerful symbols of restraint, whether by our own self-doubt or negative qualities, or by a particular person or situation in your life. If you are trying to handcuff someone else in your dream, the dream suggests you have a possessive attitude towards somebody close to you. It may be a warning that your desire for intimacy has aggressive undertones and that you need to take a more relaxed approach.

H

Handwriting

Because everybody's handwriting is unique, handwriting in a dream tends to symbolise individuality. If you are writing in your dream, it probably indicates your desire to express yourself creatively in some way. But if you are having trouble reading the handwriting, it could be a sign that you feel baffled by or unable to 'decipher' the personality of someone close to you.

Hanging

If you are hanging from something in a dream, it may be a sign that some issue in your life is suspended or lacking a conclusion. If in your dream you are trying to hang something up, however, you may be reflecting your wish to put order into your life by trying to keep things in their place. If you are hanging the object high up, it could be sign of your insecurity about keeping something you possess that you believe others want. If you are hanging something upside down you may be longing for a complete change in your life.

Harbour

Generally, a harbour is a symbol of security and of the desire to be protected. Harbours are places of safety and calm where you can take refuge from the storms and heavy seas you are likely to encounter in your life journey. Because of these associations, dreaming of a harbour may also symbolise a reassuring relationship, whether with a partner, parent or friend.

Hare *see* Animals

Harem

In Western European culture the harem has traditionally been a symbol of sensuousness and exotic pleasures. To dream of a harem is likely to signal your desire to explore your sensual nature, although for a woman this dream may also suggest the need to belong to a community of women or 'sisterhood'. For a man it could be a compensatory dream, an escape from a situation in which he feels put under pressure by a female partner or partners, into a fantasy of hedonistic sexual pleasure.

Harp

This instrument can be a sign of your achievement of or desire for positive or harmonious 'vibrations' in your emotional or spiritual life. Alternatively, it may signal your desire to be more 'in tune' or harmony with others close to you.

Harvest

To dream of a harvest tends to symbolise your desire either for prosperity or for the completion of a project. If you're worried about whether the harvest can be brought in in time, it may be an indication that you feel rushed in a project. But if the harvest is going to plan, it is a positive sign that things are on schedule. To dream of a perfect harvest is associated with prosperity in a material as well as a spiritual sense. It represents happy conclusions of all things, as well as good health, joy and happiness.

Hash

When we describe a person as 'making a hash of something', it implies that he or she is making a mess of the job. Therefore this dream is likely to suggest a concern that you or someone you are working with isn't up to a particular job or situation. This kind of dream can often be a positive experience which, by allowing you to express your doubts, frees you up to performmore successfully.

H

Hat

Putting on a hat in a dream can signal the awakening of your creative impulses or your desire to find a solution to a problem. It can also symbolise completion, as in the expression 'to cap it all off'. Hats can also represent positions or roles in life. Changing hats in a dream means that there is a desire to change your position in life.

Hate

To dream of experiencing such a strong emotion is an indication of the presence of powerful negative feelings in your life that should not be ignored. This dream is positive if it prompts you to consider what aspects of your relationships with others are causing you unhappiness.

Hawk *see* Birds, Birds of prey

Hay/Haymaking

Hay and hayfields suggest warmth, prosperity and friend-ship. They can be a symbol of good times or of an increase in productivity in your work or social life. For some people they also carry childhood or family associations. The proverb 'making hay while the sun shines' signals the need to make the most of favourable circumstances while they last.

Head *see* Body

Headlights

If you dream of approaching headlights, it is likely that you feel as if your actions or feelings are under scrutiny or are being unfairly judged.

Health

To dream of your health denotes the need to slow down and take a more considered approach to a hectic lifestyle. More symbolically, this dream can be a sign that something is out of balance in your emotional life.

Hearse *see* Driving

Heart *see* Body

Heart surgery

If you dream of having heart surgery it is a sign that you need to pay more attention to your emotions. This dream tends to refer either to the desire to get rid of an emotional blockage, or to free yourself from a negative emotion alto-gether. The dreamer might feel that someone is manipulat-ing or playing with their emotions in waking life.

Hearth

A hearth or fireplace symbolises the need for security, whether the context is our family life or our relationship with ourselves. This image is a symbol of emotions or passions that are contained and directed so as to provide warmth for us and those close to us. But if the fire is getting out of hand, it could be sign of your fear that some powerful emotion is in danger of threatening your cosy or familiar existence. If, on the other hand, the fire is in danger of going out, it suggests that there is an emotional problem or 'cooling' of feelings between you and someone you are close to.

Heat

H

Dreams of being too hot often have a simple physical cause. You may just be feeling warm and need to throw off the blankets. More symbolically, hot climates or high temperatures in a dream can stand for the 'heat' of strong emotions or passions such as sexual or romantic love, anger or jealousy.

Heaven *see also* Religion

A dream of heaven is often compensatory in nature; in other words, it serves to console us at a time when our actual lives may be filled with difficulties. It can be particularly reassuring when the health or well-being of ourselves or of someone close to us is in question. In this situation, the dream suggests the need to accept our absence of control over the processes of life and death. Less positively, this dream can also be regarded as a temporary wish to retreat from the realities of life. In other words, it can be a wish dream, a desire for a little heaven on earth.

Hedgehog *see also* Animals

The hedgehog is a symbol of prickly defensiveness. If you

dream of this animal, it could be a warning that you need to consider how effective your current strategy for dealing with threatening people or situations is. Instead of 'rolling into a ball' it may be necessary to engage more actively with a problem or issue. A hedgehog may represent the dreamer's need to be more protective of his or herself in waking life.

Hedges

A green and flourishing hedge suggests contentment, prosperity and protection, while a hedge full of thorns can symbolise the obstacles that lie between you and your goal. If you get lost or scratched while trying to get through a hedge, it is a sign of frustration in your work or emotional life.

H

Heel *see* Body

Hell *see also* Religion

This dream probably suggests your feeling that things in your life can't get much worse. Chances are that if you experience this dream, however, you have already hit rock bottom and your life could be about to take a change for the better. It is worth noting that we can make our own hell, and this may be a warning for us to take a more positive attitude in life.

Hen *see* Birds, Chicken

Herbs

Determining whether this dream is positive or negative depends on the kind of herb you dream about. If it is fragrant and wholesome, it is likely to signal good health and a positive mental attitude. Poisonous herbs such as rue or hemlock, however, suggest a negative influence in your life that requires an antidote.

Hermit

It's likely that the hermit in your dream symbolises either your own need for solitude, or your fears about loneliness. As in the tarot, the hermit can suggest the wisdom and spiritual awareness that can come from reflection or withdrawal from material pursuits. It can also suggest a fear that some activity or quest is unbalancing your life and forcing you to become too socially withdrawn. You should use the feelings that accompany this dream to help you to interpret its meaning. If there are negative feelings associated with the dream, the dreamer is taking a mature or wise outlook in their current situation.

H

Hero/Heroine *see also* p.14 (Archetypes)

The hero or heroine in our dreams often reflects our own initiative or potential for growth and change. If the hero or heroine in your dream is someone completely unlike you, the dream may be offering you the opportunity to get an objective view of your own goals, potential and actions. Alternatively, this figure could represent those qualities you most admire in others and wish you could achieve yourself.

Hiding

It is common to dream either that you are hiding yourself or something else. If it is you, or the person that corresponds to you in the dream, who is trying to hide, the dream may be suggesting your desire to protect yourself from something or somebody. This could be a threatening situation or negative person, or even some aspect of your own personality you don't want to face up to. If in the dream you are hiding an object, the nature of this object will help you to interpret what it is you would rather not face up to, or what it is you wish to protect from others.

High school *see also* Education; School

This dream tends to refer to our relationships with large groups of people, perhaps at work, or in a social context. Because it draws on memories of a time when we were younger and less independent, it can also suggest emotional immaturity, lack of confidence or a desire to impress others with our talents and achievements. This was also a time when we needed to fit into a group and peer group pressure was at its highest. Perhaps you are experiencing these feelings in a real-life situation.

Hills

H

Climbing a hill suggests our desire to surmount difficulties, or to gain a clear perspective on our situation. Being on the top of a hill looking down signals our achievement of a spiritual insight or awareness. Not being able to reach the top of the hill, on the other hand, suggests the sense that some hard slog still lies ahead of us. Going downhill can either be a symbol of relief, or a sign that circumstances are preventing us from achieving our goals.

History

It's not uncommon for dreams to have historical settings—especially given our familiarity with these settings from television, film or books. Generally speaking, these settings will stand for some aspect of the dreamer's self or his or her life. For example, a Western or frontier setting might represent the dreamer's sense of adventure or pioneering spirit, while a medieval one is more likely to be concerned with issues of romance or power. Interpreting such a dream requires you to think about the personal associations that these different historical periods carry for you.

Hitch-hiker *see* Driving/Driver

Hives

Because of the bee's reputation as a tireless worker, a dream with hives in it suggests issues of industry or productivity. Perhaps you feel overworked in your current job or under too much pressure to conform to the requirements of your fellow-workers. However, this dream could also suggest a desire to work together with others to achieve increased productivity or a worthwhile goal. Because the activity of a hive centres on a queen bee, this dream may also contain a reference to a powerful female figure, whether in a domestic situation or at work.

H

Hoe

This common garden implement suggests the desire to improve one's physical or emotional environment by getting rid of issues or emotions that are no longer relevant, or that interfere with our growth. In general this dream is a positive one that signals our willingness to cultivate either ourselves, or the things that nurture or support us in our lives.

Holding

If you are conscious in your dream of holding something, the object probably represents something that you're trying to protect or are afraid of losing. In general, holding suggests a desire for control, ownership, intimacy or, more indirectly, for knowledge or awareness (as when, for example, we feel we have finally 'grasped' a concept or idea). If what you are holding is struggling to get away from you, however, the dream may be telling you to reconsider a possessive attitude, or to let something go which is no longer serving a valid purpose. Holding yourself in a dream symbolises an overwhelming desire for intimacy and protection.

Hole

Generally speaking, a hole can stand either for a trap or bad situation in life we fear falling into, or for a place of refuge that appeals to our impulse to hide or feel protected. Holes in clothing, on the other hand, tend to represent our sense of our own failings, the things that are incomplete or missing from our personalities or lives. A pothole in a road may represent the need to stay alert and watch for dangers that lie ahead.

Holiday

Dreaming of a holiday suggests our desire to slow down, relax, or take time out for ourselves. If the dreamer is feeling overworked or harassed, this is likely to be a compensatory dream that offers in imaginary form the relief that is not available in his or her waking life. Alternatively, the dream could simply be telling you that you are too focused on a single issue or problem, and need to give yourself a break or cultivate more variety in your life.

Holy Communion *see also* Religion

To dream of this solemn ritual suggests a desire for transformation to occur in some area of your life. It can also symbolise your sadness at the absence of a friend or a relationship.

Holy people

The holy person in your dream may represent someone you have a deep respect for. There will usually be some aspect of the dream figure that will help you to identify them with a person or persons in your waking life. Interpreting this dream requires you to pay attention to the way you feel about the person in your dream. Alternatively, this dream may represent your own aspirations to a more spiritual or 'perfect' life.

Home *see* Building, parts of

Homosexuality

If you are gay or lesbian you probably won't be surprised to have dreams that involve sex with someone of the same gender. Dreamers who identify as heterosexual in their waking lives may be more surprised by such a dream, however. This dream suggests that our unconscious is a place where identity is less cut and dried than we may consciously experience it to be. But such a dream can have a wide variety of meanings. Generally, instead of worrying that such a dream signals a crisis in your identity (your waking life will indicate whether this is the case) it may be more useful to regard it instead as an aid to exploring your feelings about your relationships with friends or family members. After all, sex in a dream often stands for any kind of intimacy or communication, in both its pleasurable and dangerous aspects. This dream could also be compensatory—a sign that you feel overly pressured into a particular role and identity and need to express yourself differently.

Honey

This substance represents an intense experience of sweetness or pleasure. By extension, it can also contain a reference to someone we love or who gives us pleasure.

Honeymoon

Because we often use the term 'honeymoon' or 'honeymoon

stage' to refer to an initial period of infatuation or a stage at which things are going well, this dream tends to symbolise new beginnings, optimism or the desire to undertake a new and exciting project. It may also foretell the arrival of a pleasurable or unexpected event.

Hood

A hood is most commonly used for concealment or protection and as such is associated with our desire for these things. If someone else in the dream is wearing a hood, the dream could be expressing your frustration with someone near you who you feel is hiding their feelings from you or refusing to deal with you openly. Because a hood can have a menacing aspect, dreaming of someone who is wearing one may also point to an aspect of yourself that you fear to explore. Are you afraid of revealing your ideas or parts of yourself?

Hook

A dream involving a hook may indicate the desire to bring something closer to yourself. We talk about 'getting hooked with/on something'. It indicates our need to connect totally with someone or something, but in doing so shows our feelings of dependency and immaturity.

Hoop

This perfectly round toy signals our need to find balance, completion and harmony in our lives. It may also suggest nostalgia for childhood. Less positively, it may represent the sense that we are going round and round in circles when we should be making progress in life.

H

Horn

The horns of animals such as deer are a traditional symbol of masculinity and potency. For this reason they may stand for the part of you that is most 'animal' or aggressive. Musical horns, on the other hand, suggest a summons or call of some kind—whether spiritual, or from another person.

Horoscope *see also* Zodiac

In general, dreaming of a horoscope symbolises either your desire to know the future, or to explore your own identity. If you dream of a particular sign of the zodiac it may be a clue that the dream is about a person close to you with that particular birth sign.

Horses *see* Animals

Horseshoe

A traditional symbol of good luck, the image of the horseshoe is also strongly associated with weddings. This association may determine its significance in your dream.

Hospital

Dreaming of a hospital usually indicates either the desire for healing, or anxieties about your own health or well-being or those of someone close to you. The events taking place in the dream, and the behaviour of the doctors and nurses, will help you to decide which meaning is indicated.

Hotel

Dreaming of a hotel indicates a short-term situation, such as a relationship that we realise subconsciously is unlikely to last, or a brief holiday or escape. For businesspeople or trav-

H

ellers on the other hand, this dream is more likely to express attitudes towards their work.

Hourglass

The appearance in a dream of an hourglass is an indication of time concerns—perhaps eagerness for a particular date to arrive, or anxiety about an appointment that can't be put off. The dream may even be reminding you to hurry up and finish some project or activity. More symbolically, the hourglass can express our feelings about the passing of time or our own ageing process. In medieval art for example, death was often depicted holding an hourglass, which was widely recognised as a symbol of mortality.

House *see* Building

Hunchback

Dreaming of a hunchback suggests that you or someone around you is carrying too great a burden and that their life is at risk of becoming pushed out of shape or 'deformed' as a result. It may be associated with a feeling of being shunned or shut out in waking life.

Hunger

A dream in which we are hungry can be simply a projection of our physical state. More symbolically, the physical experience of hunger can stand for something we lack in some other sphere of our lives—whether it is a hunger for love or intimacy, for fame, for money or for celebrity. Your own life situation and aspirations will help you to interpret this dream.

Hunting/Hunter

The figure of the hunter stands for our aggressive, go-getting tendencies, whether in romance (where it is likely to suggest that we are taking an active, pursuing role) or in our working life. This dream could be telling you that you need to take a more aggressive approach to getting what you want.

Hurricane *see also* Disaster

Like tidal waves or earthquakes, hurricanes are symbols of some force or element within our lives that is out of control. For example, the hurricane in your dream may represent your unconscious belief that some emotion or passion you are experiencing is so powerful that it is likely to 'blow you away', cause destruction to your current lifestyle, or even damage those around you. Alternatively, the hurricane could represent an external factor that threatens to bring havoc into your life or significantly alter it in some way.

Hurt

The physical hurt we imagine in a dream usually stands for an emotional pain. The nature of the hurt, and where it is located, will help you to locate the source of this pain so that you can begin to find ways of healing it.

Hut

Like hotels, huts suggest a temporary residence or insecurity. This building may also convey the dreamer's sense of having a reduced lifestyle or income. More positively, dreaming of a hut may suggest your desire for a holiday or for a simpler, less cluttered lifestyle.

Husband *see also* Family

This figure does not necessarily represent your actual husband (especially if you are unmarried!) but may stand for someone in your life who occupies a protective or supportive role towards you, particularly if they are male.

Hyena *see* Animals

Hymn

To hear or sing hymns in a dream may suggest a desire for spiritual growth. It can also be a sign of our own desire to be praised or appreciated.

Hysteria

A dream in which you or someone around you is hysterical suggests your anxiety about emotions that are out of control. It may also be a representation of your fears that a situation or relationship is no longer working, or is about to take a turn for the worse.

H

I

Ibis *see* Birds, Waterbirds

Ice cream

Eating ice cream in a dream usually symbolises a desire for pleasurable or sensual sensations. However, if the ice cream is too cold or you find yourself concerned that it's going to melt, this dream could stand for some of the worries that prevent you from fully enjoying your sensuality.

Ice/Icebergs

Dreams involving water often relate to our emotions, so dreaming of ice is likely to suggest a hardening of your feelings about somebody. If ice is a sign of emotional coolness, or even a loss of libido, a dream of thawing ice symbolises the thawing of a hostile relationship or the end of a period in which you have been forced to keep your feelings 'on ice'. If you are skating on thin ice the dream suggests your sense of insecurity at home or at work. Icebergs symbolise a distant emotional threat.

Icicles

Icicles can be a symbol either of male impotence, or the inability on the part of a man to make emotional connections. If the icicles are melting, the dream suggests that this coldness may also be about to disappear.

Idiot

To dream of an idiot can suggest a sense of frustration at being unable to communicate. This type of dream can also indicate that you are using your intellect rather than your heart in real life. You may want to go with what you feel.

Idol *see* Statue

Igloo

This dream image is probably a symbol of the way you feel about either your domestic situation or your inner self. Made of blocks of ice, the igloo can suggest coldness, frigidity and the barrier you put up. More positively, it can also be a symbol of refuge in a hostile landscape. The inside of the igloo in your dream will help you decide which meaning is intended.

Illness *see also* Sickness

To dream of a particular illness may be an early indication that some aspect of your physical health needs attention. More symbolically, illness in a dream can also stand for an emotional problem, in which case the nature of the illness may help you to 'diagnose' the feeling that is concerning you. If you dream that someone else is ill, the dream may be a reflection of your concerns about either that person, or your feeling that all is not well in your relationship with them.

Illumination *see also* Light

Like all dreams involving sudden light, a dream in which something is lit up or illuminated may stand for an insight into something that was previously hidden from you. To dream of an illuminated manuscript suggests a knowledge or possession of great value. It may even be a symbol of your sense of your own uniqueness or the value of one close to you.

Imitation

A dream in which you are mimicking someone else suggests insecurity about the value of your own skills or contribution. This can be a particularly difficult dream for those who work in creative fields and feel the pressure to be 'original'. However, imitation is a part of all creative work, and this dream can be a reminder of the debt one owes to others. Take note of what is being mimicked as this might be highly valued by the dreamer and perhaps there is need to explore this in real life.

I

Immersion

Like most dreams involving water, dreaming of immersion has significance in terms of our emotional lives. This dream may suggest that you feel as if you are 'drowning' in your emotions, to the extent of finding it hard to breathe. It also indicates that the dreamer is out of their depth emotionally in real life. Take note of this dream, as it may be a subconscious message to find a comfortable level of emotional expression.

Immobility

Its not uncommon to find yourself immobilised in a dream. This is a classic symptom of anxiety, which dramatises and exaggerates our sense of helplessness. Less dramatically, if you find yourself unable to move in a dream, it may suggest loss of energy or of entrapment in a situation such as a job or relationship which, like yourself in your dream, feels as if it is 'going nowhere'.

Imp

The imp in your dream might represent your own mischievous side. In this case it may stand for your own sense that you have been misbehaving or acting against the interests of others. However this figure might also symbolise a person or force that is trying to stop you from achieving success.

Imprisoned *see* Captivity

Incense

This fragrant smoke may suggest your desire to make contact with your more spiritual side. However incense may also stand for some awareness or pleasure that is short-lived, or in other words is likely to 'go up in smoke'.

Incest *see also* Sex

This dream is unlikely to reflect a current sexual desire or interest. On the contrary, dreams about incest often draw upon the desires we had as very young children for the undivided attention of parents or other family members. In this respect, they can be a reminder of the way we were as infants, when the borders between ourselves and those closest to us were less secure or defined. As a result, dreams of incest can be a reminder of our need for security, love, and intimacy. Alternatively, this dream may be prompting you to recognise aspects of your family members in a current sexual partner.

Income

Dreams about our income in whatever form (e.g. wages, tax) tend to symbolise the things that sustain our day-to-day life. For example if you dream of a pay rise, it could be a sign that your self-confidence has increased and that you want others to appreciate your value. Similarly, to dream of a drop in income may suggest emotional neediness or insecurity. To dream of paying or calculating tax can suggest not only money worries, but also our sense that we are obligated to others.

India

For a Western person, India has a range of associations. It can be associated with the exotic and colour, with the desire for spiritual awareness, with respect for the sacred, and with the desire to unite the disciplines of mind and body. India is also associated with the extravagance of the Raj, with the non-violence and spiritual example of Gandhi and with social problems such overpopulation, poverty and sickness. Thinking about the personal associations that this large and varied country holds for you will help you to interpret its significance in your dream. For example, dreaming of India may express your desire to travel, but it could also suggest your quest for higher awareness.

I

Indigestion

Often a dream of indigestion will have a physical cause. However, if there is no direct physical reason for this dream, a symbolic meaning is more likely. Generally this dream suggests either that you have 'bitten off more than you can chew' (or digest) and need more time to think it over, or that there is something in your life that isn't agreeing with you. Ask yourself what's making your stomach churn. This dream could be a sign that you need to do something differently, or tackle problems in more bite-sized pieces.

Infant *see* Baby

Infection

Like dreams of sickness, dreams of infections usually have an emotional meaning. For example, the infection in your dream may symbolise negative attitudes you have internalised from those around you: attitudes or emotions that are 'festering' within your mind, or threatening to invade your waking thoughts. This dream may be warning you to re-examine the negative influences on your life, and consider the ways in which they might be overcome.

Injection

A dream in which you are having an injection suggests feelings of vulnerability or invasion. The dreamer's inner space has been 'punctured' or penetrated, perhaps with painful or fearful consequences. But such a dream is not always negative. After all, injections are also associated with healing or inoculation. Therefore, to dream of an injection may signal your desire to recover from an injury, or to develop the strength and skills needed to ward off future emotional harm.

Injury

Injuries in dreams represent the harm that we feel others have done to us. If this is a persistent or very troubling dream, it may be a sign that the dreamer is in need of inner healing, perhaps to recover from the emotional damage inflicted in childhood, or at some other vulnerable period of life. However, we all feel 'wounded' by others from time to time, and this dream may be no more than a dramatic way of expressing this sense of hurt.

Inquest

An inquest in a dream suggests the urge to investigate a past matter or emotion. Because inquests are associated with suspicious or mysterious events, this matter may be one that is associated with the dreamer's feelings of guilt or ambivalence. Either way, it suggests the desire to settle a matter once and for all, perhaps as the condition for putting it behind you and moving on.

Insane

To dream that you or another is insane suggests your fear of emotions that are out of control. This dream could be warning you to avoid a particular person or situation in case you get caught in negative emotional currents. Alternatively, it could be a sign that you haven't been expressing or exploring your emotions enough, and that they have built up to the point where they demand release, or are threatening your stability. Whatever it is, get if off your chest.

I

Insects

Generally speaking, the insects in our dreams stand for the things that 'bug' us in our waking lives. Like insects themselves, these things may be small, but they can also be annoying and when there are large numbers of them, threatening or scary. You probably have your own personal list of the insects you avoid. However, over the centuries most common insects have also accumulated broad cultural associations and these may be reflected in your dreams.

Ants Traditionally, ants symbolise industry, hard work and discipline. However, they also have more sinister associations including lack of individuality, lack of imagination and militarism. Dreaming of ants may suggest pride in your work, but also your sense that you are overly regulated in your job or home life, or don't have enough opportunities for pleasure or self-expression.

Bees *see* Bee

Beetle Like ants, beetles have several different popular associations. For example, they are associated with dirt (in which case they may suggest your disgust at your surroundings, whether at work or home) but also—because of their hard shells—with a desire to be protected. Another traditional association with the beetle is blindness. A dream with beetles in it could be suggesting that you are scurrying around in the dark, unable to see what's going on around you.

Butterfly *see* Butterfly

Caterpillar Caterpillars are symbols of change or metamorphosis into another state. The caterpillar that is destined to turn into a butterfly could be a symbol of those parts of yourself that also have potential and are waiting for the right moment to emerge from their cocoon or to discover their wings. As a result this dream may signal your desire for a change of activity or environment.

Cricket The phrase 'merry as a cricket' conveys this insect's traditional associations with good times and a cheerful attitude to life. This dream could be a sign that you or someone close to you is feeling particularly 'chirpy' or happy. It could also be a compensatory dream when you are feeling blue.

Fleas These tiny, biting creatures tend to stand for the things that annoy us or make us uncomfortable. Because they are hard to see with the naked eye, they can also suggest those emotions or impulses that lurk at the edge of our consciousness and which, as a result, we find hard to identify so we can deal with them.

Flies In Western culture these tend either to be a symbol of uncleanness, in which case they may stand for troubling emotions or thoughts we would rather brush off, or of annoyance.

Grasshopper Traditionally the grasshopper was compared with the ant and regarded as a symbol of laziness. Dreaming of grasshoppers may suggest your guilt that you're whiling away your time while failing to be productive, or your sense that you should be saving more.

Lice/Parasites These creatures probably represent those things or people that you feel fasten onto you, drain your energy and prevent you from making the progress you desire. If the lice are in your hair, they could be a symbol of some force—such as a rival or a dependant—which you fear is making you less sexually attractive or desirable.

Locusts As the expression 'a plague of locusts' suggests, these insects are symbols of misfortune. Their appearance in a dream could be a sign that you feel your problems are reaching 'biblical' proportions.

Maggots Because of their associations with death and waste, a dream of maggots may suggest your anxieties that you aren't living fully enough, or that there is something badly wrong with your home life. Alternatively, you may feel that others are using you or behaving in an inconsiderate way.

Mosquitoes Their habit of attacking at night makes mosquitoes a symbol of persecution, perhaps by unseen enemies. Of course the mosquitoes in your dream could also represent your own tendency to attack others, or to undermine your own best interests.

Moth In traditional European mythology, moths symbolise the soul or psyche. As a result, this dream may have spiritual connotations, or be associated with a person who is no longer alive, but with whom you still feel emotionally connected.

Spider A dream of spiders can signal a desire to be productive and creative. Alternatively, it may suggest that you are feeling caught up in or smothered by the emotions and conflicts of those around you, especially in your home or family life. Traditionally, spiders were thought to symbolise powerful maternal or female figures. They are considered lucky in a number of Eastern cultures. The size of the spider in a dream will indicate the degree of luck.

Wasps In traditional dream lore, these stinging insects were believed to be a sign that the dreamer had jealous enemies. In modern times, dreaming of wasps is an indication of your fear of being stung by another's 'waspish' tongue, or even your concern about the damage you may do with your own.

Insomnia

A dream in which you are unable to sleep may appear very contradictory indeed! In general, this dream probably signals anxiety, not necessarily about sleeplessness, but about the problems or issues in your life that are most likely to keep you awake. This type of dream is one step away from lucid dreaming (see p.viii (Introduction)). If the dreamer can recognise they are asleep during the dream they can take control of the dreamscape.

Interview

Like dreams of examinations, dreams of interviews tend to represent anxieties about being tested or made to perform. It is also common to dream of an interview before a real one is actually scheduled to take place. In this case the dream is ensuring that you are prepared for this event. This is true even when the dream is negative—in which case the dream is allowing you to express your worst fears, so you can go into the real situation with confidence and make the best of it.

Intestines *see* Body

Intoxication *see also* Alcohol

This dream reflects anxieties about your consumption (not necessarily of alcohol) or about habits that threaten you with loss of control, whether in relation to money or your emotions. More positively, being intoxicated in a dream could be a sign that you are preparing to relax, enjoy yourself more, or behave less responsibly for a change. This dream can also symbolise a desire for a change in attitude and perspective.

Inventor

If you dream of this figure, there is a good chance that there is a problem or project in your waking life to which you are trying to find a solution. Is the project brimming with ingenuity or does nothing appear to be working? The progress experienced by your dream inventor will help you to evaluate the obstacles you are likely to face.

Invisible

Something in your dream that is invisible, but is affecting you, is likely to be a sign of some force in your life, such as a parent or other authority figure, who is continuing to play a role in your life. If you yourself are invisible, the dream suggests either that you feel unable to make the impact on others that you would like, or that there is something in your past that you would rather forget. Generally, if the dreamer feels as if they are constantly put on public display in real life then such a dream is playing out an internal waking desire.

Invitation

An invitation in a dream may symbolise a new opportunity in your waking life. How you respond to the dream invitation may help you to interpret your feelings about taking up an offer, or beginning a new project. Alternatively, dreaming of an invitation may signal your desire for a social or work opportunity to become available to you.

I

Iris *see* Flowers

Iron/Ironing

Iron is a traditional symbol of strength and stamina. However, it can also represent inflexibility or a lack of emotion. If the iron is rusted, it suggests a fear of losing something precious as a result of the effects of time or neglect. A dream in which you are ironing may symbolise your desire to look your best for a particular occasion. It may also suggest your intention to 'iron' out a problem, or solve an issue.

Island

Islands are symbols of both escape and isolation. They can also represent the self in its most solitary or independent state. For this reason interpreting the meaning of this dream requires you to decide whether your dream island symbolises freedom and self-expansion, or rejection and low self-esteem. For example, if you dream of being cast up on a desert island, the dream is probably representing your fears of loneliness. If you feel relaxed and fulfilled on your dream island, or it resembles a paradise rather than a desert, the dream is highlighting your wish to escape from a crowded schedule and spend more time by yourself.

Itch

An itch prompts you to scratch, and itchiness in a dream may be telling you that you need to seek relief from something that is bothering you. This dream may also signal your sense that someone around you is causing you irritation. Expressions like 'the seven year itch' suggest an additional, more sexual meaning for this dream.

I

Ivory

In traditional gypsy lore, a dream of ivory was said to foretell prosperity and success. Today ivory is more likely to symbolise something of great value that we feel needs protection or conservation. For example, the ivory in your dream could stand for a person whom you admire for their beauty or pure soul. It could also represent your own internal qualities or attributes. An ivory tower continues this theme of soul searching, but suggests isolation and an absence of close communication.

Ivy

Ivy is associated with vigorous growth and tenacity, but these positive qualities can also turn into dependency and a tendency to cling or smother. In Christian tradition, ivy is a symbol of immortality or eternal life and this religious meaning, which is most commonly associated with Christmas, may also be reflected in your dream.

J

Jack

In contrast to the king in a pack of cards, the jack stands for a more youthful or irresponsible male. This dream could represent either yourself or someone close to you. The figure of the jack suggests a person who is too impulsive or emotional, who is not yet ready to settle down, or is too dedicated to having a good time to take on responsibility. A 'jack of all trades' suggests someone who can't decide on the right profession to pursue and who runs the risk of superficiality as a result. Either symbol associated with a jack suggests the dreamer may be acting in haste. So take caution and look at the finer details.

Jackal *see* Animals

Jackdaw *see* Birds, Crow

Jail *see also* Prison; Cell

Like all images of confinement, being in jail symbolises the obstacles to our freedom. It may be the freedom to express yourself creatively, to move away from home, or to escape an emotional situation that has become imprisoning. This powerful dream could be a prompt to consider your feelings about your environment, and to think about how you might expand your horizons.

Jailer

If jails represent the obstacles to our freedom, the jailer is the figure who is at the source of these restrictions. He or she may stand not only for another person in your life, such as a parent or authority figure, but for your own inhibitions or negative attitudes. If the dreamer is the jailer then they create their own obstacles in waking life.

Jar

Trying to open a jar in a dream suggests a desire to enjoy the fruits of your labours. If the jar opens easily, the dream suggests confidence about your ability to overcome your obstacles. An empty jar symbolises disappointment and impoverishment, whether it represents yourself (in which case it may be a sign that you are depressed or lacking in energy) or a lack of nurturing in your life.

J

Jaundice

If you dream of suffering from jaundice, it is most likely a sign that you lack energy or are overworked. If may also suggest that you have anxieties about diet and nutrition.

Jazz *see* Music

Jelly

This wobbly substance suggests an issue that is hard to get your teeth into. Perhaps somebody is avoiding a confrontation, or you yourself can't seem to define an issue or problem that is bothering you. To dream of jelly may also suggest a sense that you are failing to be firm on a particular issue or problem. At worst, it denotes a sense of unreliability or 'spinelessness'.

Jellyfish

Jellyfish on a beach indicate that you are feeling surrounded by dangers that are hard to see and therefore to avoid. These may come from people or situations that don't seem openly confrontational, but are nonetheless a source of danger.

Jesus *see* Christ

Jewellery/Jewels

In a dream, jewellery and precious stones are likely to symbolise the things you value most in life. These could include your own talents or creative abilities, those whom you love, or even abstract qualities such as courage, determination or fair-mindedness. Dreaming of finding jewels or treasure suggests your desire to achieve or produce something worthwhile. In this case the dream could be compensating for your sense of frustration or lack of productivity in a current job or hobby.

J

Jilting *see also* Wedding

Dreaming of being jilted suggests insecurity or change in your emotional life. If you are jilting someone in your dream, the dream probably suggests either guilt over treating someone inconsiderately, or a desire for more freedom in your life.

Journey *see also* Aeroplane; Boat; Car; Railroad; Travel

The journey is one of the most common symbols for our passage through life. As a result, dreams involving journeys are likely to take many forms. In general, the difficulty or ease of your dream journey tends to reflect the conditions of your current stage of life. For example, a dream in which you are lost and unable to navigate is likely to suggest a confusion or lack of direction in your life. A dream in which you emerge into a beautiful landscape is, by contrast, likely to express your optimism about what lies ahead. Like life itself, dream journeys are endlessly varied, reflecting a potentially infinite number of possible combinations. Use all the symbols in the dream to interpret the meaning.

Judas

The figure of Judas is one of the most basic symbols of betrayal. But Judas can also be a sympathetic character, who expresses our sense of being placed in a morally difficult situation in which we are pressured to betray our principles or tempted to do something we suspect is wrong. This dream could be inviting you to think carefully about your own actions or motivations in relation to those around you.

J

Judge *see also* Court

A dream of a judge is likely to symbolise our own tendency to judge others or ourselves. This dream could indicate a tendency on your part to be too harsh on yourself. It may also be a warning that your attitude towards others risks being unsympathetic, or overly 'judgemental'.

Juggler

The significance of this dream symbol is pretty clear. You are probably in a situation where you are conscious of having to keep a number of different balls in the air. If the dream is accompanied by a sense of exhilaration and accomplishment you are probably enjoying the challenge. It you are terrified of dropping something it may be a sign that you are overextending yourself and need to cut back on your activities or commitments. However you feel, the juggler in your dream

gives you the chance to look at yourself and your performance from a more detached perspective. Generally, if the
dreamer is uncomfortable with what they are juggling in the
dream it may be a subconscious message to lighten the load
in waking life.

Jump

Jumping in a dream can symbolise either a leap of faith, or
the need to make an exceptional effort if you are to obtain
something you desire. This dream can also be a sign of the
need to cross over or make a bridge between two contrasting or widely separated things—whether they are ideas,
activities or people.

Jungle

The jungle is a primitive symbol of danger and the struggle
to overcome obstacles. More specifically, it may suggest
'entanglements', whether in your romantic, family or professional life. If things are a little wild and unpredictable in
your life, proceed with caution.

Jury *see also* Judge; Court

This dream symbolises issues of fairness and judgement. If
a jury is judging you it could be a sign that you feel put
under pressure by others, or that your actions are under
scrutiny. If you are a member of the jury, the dream suggests
that you are being required to make up your mind about a
difficult issue.

J

K

Kaleidoscope

Dreaming of a kaleidoscope may express your desire to achieve pattern and harmony. However, it can also reflect your feelings about how you view the world around you. Is it broken up into many pieces or are different aspects of your life shifting too rapidly for you to be able to make a coherent whole? In childhood, a kaleidoscope has a magical quality, an altering perspective, which is extremely pleasant. The dreamer may wish to regain this type of feeling or see the world with magic and wonder.

Kangaroo *see* Animals

Karate

To dream of this martial art suggests that your aggressive impulses are well in control, and able to be expressed without hurting others.

Keepsake

If you are presented with a keepsake in a dream it is probably a sign that you feel in danger of losing something. Alternatively, this dream may be forcing you to remember a person or event that you have been trying to put out of your mind.

Kennel

A kennel in a dream may suggest 'doggedness' on your part or another's. Alternatively, it may be a sign that you feel yourself to be excluded or treated as if you were inferior. In this case the dog that has been sent off to its kennel, or is howling outside it, may be drawing attention to your unsatisfied needs.

Kettle

Like a hearth, a kettle is a symbol of domestic life and comforts. For this reason dreaming of one can symbolise your desire for a cheerful social or domestic life. However, if the emphasis in your dream is on the kettle boiling, it may suggest that your emotions have been building up and are about to reach 'boiling point'.

Key

K

The key in your dream may symbolise your attempt to find a solution to a problem or situation that has been bothering you. If the key breaks in the lock, or refuses to open it, the dream suggests that you can't see a way beyond your difficulties. In an emotional context, the appearance of a key in a dream may be a sign that you have been keeping your feelings too locked up. In this case the dream may be telling you that you need to release some of them. In traditional Chinese lore, the key is a symbol of discretion.

Keyhole

Freud regarded keyholes as symbols of the vagina, an interpretation that gave any dream in which they appear an automatically sexual meaning. More generally, keyholes can suggest our desire to spy on others, or to penetrate their privacy. For this reason if you dream that you are trying to look through one, it may suggest that you are indulging your curiosity about somebody's private life too freely, or are at risk of gossiping about his or her affairs. Alternatively, it may suggest that you yourself feel that your privacy is at risk from the curiosity of others, or that you fear being exposed to scrutiny.

Kicking

Being kicked in a dream suggests that you fear hostility or ill will from others. If you are the one doing the kicking, the dream may be acting out aggressive impulses that you have tried to ignore. A kick in a dream may also be reminding you of something you have forgotten. If the dreamer is aimlessly kicking, they are trying to break free from some constraint in real life. In this instance, kicking may represent self-preservation rather than just being a symbol of aggression.

Kidnap

Kidnapping symbolises loss of control and dependency. This dream, therefore, expresses insecurity, especially your fear that sudden changes may be about to occur in your life. The dream may also represent your fear that something precious to you is at risk of being lost or taken away from you, whether that thing is a relationship, a talent, or an occupation.

K

Kidneys *see* Body

Killing

The aggressive content of this dream could be a warning that you have been keeping your anger or resentment too hidden, and that it is doing you internal harm. This dream does not necessarily stand for aggressive impulses towards others. It may also symbolise your desire to eradicate some aspect of your own personality, in which case the dream suggests low self-esteem or a negative attitude towards yourself.

King

The king in your dream may stand either for an authority figure, such as a parent or boss, or for your own desire for prestige or homage.

Kissing

This dream tends to symbolise a desire for intimacy, whether erotic or domestic in nature. More symbolically it can also be a sign that you have accepted or come to terms with something or somebody. For example, if you are kissing a friend goodbye, it could be a sign that you have accepted the need to change something, or to move on to another stage of your life journey.

| K |

Kitchen *see* Building, parts of

Kite

Flying or watching a kite is usually a symbol of aspiration or of a new project or enterprise. Whether you are having trouble keeping it aloft or admiring it in flight will help you to assess the sorts of obstacles you face.

Knapsack

To dream of a knapsack signals preparation for a journey— perhaps a new stage in your life. The contents of the knapsack will help you to interpret the nature of this journey—whether you are preparing for a long haul, for instance, and many different circumstances, or travelling light. You should also pay attention to the emotion accompanying the dream. Is it excitement or anxiety?

Knave *see* Jack

Kneeling

Kneeling in a dream can have several meanings. It may suggest your sense that others require you to take a lower or secondary role. Alternatively, it may also indicate that you want something so badly you are prepared to beg for it. The emotions that accompany the dream should help you to interpret its meaning. The dream is indicative of a need for submission, particularly in those who find it difficult to take a supporting role.

Knees *see* Body

Knife *see also* Dagger

Generally speaking, dreaming of a knife symbolises your aggressive, active side. However if the knife refuses to cut, the dream is more likely to indicate your sense of frustration or impotence. If, by contrast, the knife cuts something easily, it could be a sign that you will soon overcome some difficulties.

K

Knight

A knight in armour tends to be a symbol of the desire for strength and protection. This dream could be a sign that you feel you need a protector, or that you have been called upon to go out and do battle either for yourself or on behalf of others. It may also suggest that under your tough surface you feel more vulnerable than you look.

Knitting

Knitting suggests the desire to make something grow. It can symbolise domestic pleasures or any slow but rewarding activity. However, if the wool is tangled or you can't form the stitches properly (for example, if they keep falling off the needles) then this dream represents your anxieties about not being able to make progress in your work or home life. If the garment being knitted has a complex pattern, what is desired will take careful consideration and patience.

Knob

A dream with a knob in it, such as a door handle, stands for anything in life that you may have been trying to ignore, but which keeps reminding you of its presence by sticking out. This dream may be telling you that you have to seize whatever it is, and explore it more thoroughly.

Knock

A dream in which you are knocking suggests that you want something, but are prepared to wait for it to be given to you, rather than simply barging in. A dream in which you hear knocking is probably reminding you of something or somebody whom you may have been trying to shut out of your consciousness. A knock is similar to a bell or alarm—it's an unconscious warning of the onset of someone or something new. The dreamer has the power to block it or allow it to enter his or her life.

K

Knot

Generally speaking a knot stands for a problem or problems, something you are having trouble unravelling. It may suggest that you are experiencing emotional confusion, or can't work out how to solve a problem. If the knot comes undone easily in your dream, it is a sign that you should proceed with confidence. However, if you are tying a knot in a dream it suggests either that you're trying to remember something, or that you are afraid of losing a person or object.

L

Label

Dreaming of a label is about self-image and how others see you. It may be that you are trying to establish a new identity or break out of a role that you are no longer happy with. If you dream of labelling things, it means that you are searching for order or wanting to establish some sort of order in your life. If you are re-labelling something, it could be that you miscalculated and 'labelled' someone wrongly.

Labour

For a woman to dream of being in labour suggests that there is a new plan, scheme or project about to emerge and come to fruition. Labouring and labourers traditionally symbolise prosperity through hard work.

Laboratory

Dreaming of a laboratory generally indicates the dreamer's need to be objective about some issue. If you are a specimen in a laboratory, it may be that you feel that you are being judged, monitored and controlled by those in authority around you. However, if you are a technician or a scientist, you have control over the experiment you are conducting. Depending on the outcome of the dream, a successful experiment usually suggests that whatever you've been working on will have a positive outcome. If the experiment is a failure, the dream may be trying to tell you that you need to be more objective and calculating in your approach.

Labyrinth *see also* Maze

A labyrinth is a confusing network of passages from which it is difficult to find a way out. If you are dreaming of a labyrinth, you may be experiencing confusion of ideas, emotions or beliefs. Exploring the labyrinth is a symbol of exploring our deeper selves, especially delving into our fears that we keep hidden from others and conscious selves. Depending on whether you are lost in the labyrinth or you reach the exit, take note of the outcome. Should you be asking for help to find your way out? Are you facing your fears or running away from them without a resolution, forever roaming the labyrinth of your mind to escape them?

L

Lace

Lace is a symbol of the feminine and the delicate parts of our natures. If you are dreaming of making lace, it may suggest that you need to be patient.

Ladder

A ladder usually suggests a direction the dreamer is about to take. Climbing a ladder indicates success in a gradual manner, or in many stages (step by step), in order to achieve your goals (moving up the ladder). It may be highlighting your insecurities about opportunities that are not easily attained. Falling down or climbing backwards on a ladder will have the opposite meaning—that you feel that you have failed to achieve your goals.

Lagoon/Lake *see also* Water

Dreaming of a lake or lagoon is the dreamer's connection to the unconscious. It is the inner world of our fantasies, emotions and feelings—usually not known to others. If you dream of looking into a lagoon, it may be that you are looking into yourself. Clear water indicates self-confidence and optimism while murky water indicates that you may be experiencing depression or a state of uncertainty.

Lamb *see also* Animals, Baby animals

A lamb is a symbol of innocence, dependency and the vulnerable part of ourselves. Are you easily deceived, 'like a lamb to slaughter' or 'as gentle as a lamb'? Depending on the outcome of the dream it may be communicating the need to either put these traits into use or to adopt a stronger approach.

Lame

Lameness indicates our awareness of the imperfections and weaknesses in our personalities. If you dream of lameness, you may be experiencing a lack of confidence and motivation (what is your 'lame' excuse?). The left side of our bodies represents the creative and intuitive parts of ourselves, whereas the right side is the active and rational. Work out whether it is your left or right leg that is lame. To dream of someone else being lame indicates that your plans are not solid and will not be attained at this stage.

L

Lamp

In traditional symbolism, the lamp represents the spark of life. It brings clarity and shows the way ahead. A brightly lit lamp denotes a strong sense of purpose and direction, while a dim lamp indicates uncertainty and disillusionment.

Lance

A lance has a similar function to the knife—it cuts and penetrates. It is regarded as a symbol of sexual intercourse, the lance being a phallic/masculine symbol. If you dream of lancing a boil or cutting something out such as a poison or foreign object, it may suggest that it is time to release some toxic feelings that have built up over some issue. Waiting for the body to expel it naturally may entail physical and emotional suffering that can be avoided.

Lane *see also* Alley; Backstreets; Road

The meaning of seeing a lane in your dreams depends on how the dream makes you feel. Are you lost and filled with a sense of danger? A lane can conjure up hidden dangers and a sense of mystery (not taking the main road). It also often indicates a short cut of some kind. This dream reflects how you feel about the direction you are taking in life and how you go about achieving your destination (aim).

L

Language

To dream that you are listening to a foreign or strange language and not understanding it denotes that you are finding it difficult to understand what someone around you is trying to communicate. This lack of communication may be affecting you in a relationship or at work. On a deeper level it may be your unconscious trying to communicate with you from within, speaking 'in tongues' in order to tell you something about yourself which you do not consciously understand.

Large *see* Size

Lark *see* Birds, Canary

Late *see also* Time

Dreaming of being late or running out of time is an indication that you do not feel totally in control of situations around you. You may feel the sense that you've left something too late and now you've missed out. This dream could relate to opportunities, personal choices, leisure or ambitions. If others are late, pay attention to your communications skills and avoid misunderstandings.

Laughter

Laughter is the best medicine and laughing or hearing laughter represents a sense of joy and a release of tension which makes us feel light-hearted. The dream may be telling you to 'lighten up' and not take life so seriously. If you are on the receiving end of the laughter, it may be more a case of it's 'no laughing matter' or 'a laughing stock'. We may feel embarrassed at being ridiculed as a result of saying or doing something that is not appropriate for the occasion or the audience.

Lava *see also* Volcano

Lava represents a situation in which deep-seated emotions erupt and come to the surface. This dream suggests that the dreamer has been covering up emotions for too long, with the result that an 'eruption' is likely. Lava can also be a symbol of sexuality or may indicate a medical illness such as high fever, as the body overheats during the dream cycle.

Lavatory *see* Toilet

Lawyer

Dreaming of a lawyer is associated with one-sided arguments and contracts. Lawyers often possess negative associations in a dream, acting as a psychological warning that

L

you are surrounded by people that are false, untrustworthy or hurtful. You should beware of committing to any legal agreement without professional counselling or proper understanding of whatever it is you are entering into.

Lead (metal)

Lead is heavy and so are our burdens. What is it that is weighing you down and making you feel heavy-hearted? Take note of all the symbols in this dream to help you understand its message. Don't forget that just as lead can be melted, so too can your present state, allowing it to be changed or transformed into a more positive one.

Lead (dog)

Dreaming of a dog on a lead or leash indicates the need to balance the animalistic nature in us with our better selves. If you are wearing the dog lead, you may be feeling controlled and restricted emotionally and creatively.

Leading/Leader

If you dream of being a leader and taking control of others, it suggests that you are taking responsibility and initiative in your life, or that you have a desire to do so. If you are being led, you are not taking responsibility for your actions. A leader is also an authority figure. Your attitude towards the leader in your dream may reflect your true feelings about a person with authority in your life.

Leaf/Leaves *see also* Tree; Seasons

Leaves indicate our natural cycle: from blossoms (embryo) to green leaves (young/fertile) and finally to withered leaves (old age). Leaves can also indicate the state of your emotions. In this case, green leaves represent hope and new opportunities, while dry leaves can suggest a period of no activity, of sadness or of giving up on some aspect of your life. Take the view that leaves are cyclical, that the tree regenerates and a new season will change the colour and texture of the leaves. In other words, your current situation is transient and will change in time.

Leak *see also* Water

A leak represents waste and loss. Consider whether you are wasting your energy in some way or being careless or reckless. If something 'leaks out' it means that it is revealed without authorisation. Be aware of your responsibilities and take action only when it's necessary. A leak could also be telling you that you are feeling 'drained'. Take care of your health.

Leather

We refer to someone being 'as tough as leather', suggesting that leather is a durable and protective material. A dream in which you are wearing leather may be pointing out your need for protection, whether it is physical or emotional. If you are wearing leather in a domineering fashion and have accessories such as whips or harnesses, it may indicate your desire for control.

L

Lecture

If you are giving a lecture in your dream it's likely that you wish to speak your mind on some issue that is close to your heart. If you are on the receiving end of a lecture, you may either pay attention and so gain knowledge, or feel reprimanded.

Leeches

Leeches are regarded both as medical wonders and as a way

of describing people who 'suck you dry' with their requests and demands. The interpretation that applies to your dream often depends on your view of these creatures. Medically, leeches have been used to cleanse wounds. Socially, however, being labelled a leech is not a desirable trait. Consider which of these two definitions best suits the circumstances of your dream.

Left behind

Dreaming of being left behind is a sign that you feel rejected and inadequate in some way. If you leave something or someone behind, it may be referring to the past—leaving the past, people or situations behind as you move forward to a new stage in your life.

Left *see also* Right

The left is a symbol of our unconscious. It represents the hidden part of ourselves, our internal world of values, emotions and intuition. If we are right-handed, it is our left hand that supports the activity of the right hand. If you dream of being positioned on the left of a person or object, assess whether the dream is representing your 'leftist' attitude (unconventionality) or suggesting that you have been assigned a supportive rather than a dominant role.

L

Legs *see* Body

Lemon *see also* Fruit

We associate lemons with something being 'bitter' or—as in the case of a car that is described as 'a lemon'—an object that has given us endless trouble and is defective in some way. Consider how these two definitions apply to what is happening in your life and how you feel about it.

Lending

If someone lends you something it is given to you temporarily and you must return it at some stage, usually with a little extra (interest). If you dream that you are lending money or an object to someone, you may be offering support but expecting to have it returned when you are in need. If someone is lending you money, you may need to look at how you are managing your resources and ask for assistance. However, this may only be for a short term until you are confident of handling your affairs on your own.

Lens *see also* Glasses

What needs to be more closely examined? A dream of using a lens indicates a need to pay closer attention to detail.

Leopard *see* Animals

Leper

Lepers were once known as 'the untouchables' because of the risk of contamination they posed. If you dream that you are a leper, you may be feeling rejected by people, or sense that an aspect of your life has been contaminated. Dreaming of seeing a leper suggests that you need to acknowledge imperfections in others around you.

L

Letter

A dream of a letter is about communication, news, expression and reaching out. This also applies to e-mails. An unopened letter may represent the dreamer not listening to his or her intuition. Opening a letter suggests achievement, self-awareness and receiving news. If you receive a love letter, it may be wishful thinking, but it could also be a symbol of people's love for you. A bill in the mail indicates that whatever action we take will have to be paid for. If we are sending a letter or e-mailing, it could be a reflection of our need to communicate more clearly.

Lettuce *see* Grass; Food

Levitation

If you dream of being levitated off your feet and into the air, the dream may be telling you that whatever is sweeping you off your feet or making you feel 'as if you were floating on air' in your life needs to be examined more closely. You may need to keep your feet on the ground and get back down to earth.

Library *see also* Buildings

Seeing a library in your dreams represents your total life experience. Each book contains the skills, the experience, and the knowledge that we have learnt throughout our life so far. The dream may mean that you need to research a subject more thoroughly (check out your information) before going ahead with a decision or plan. Alternatively, it could reflect your quest for learning. Are you in someone's 'bad books' or should you be studious and 'hit the books'? Returning a library book indicates that you are willing to pass on your knowledge to others.

Lice *see* Insects

Lifeboat *see also* Boat

You may be feeling a need to be saved in this dream. If you reach a lifeboat in time, it could indicate you'd be successful at the last minute.

Lift *see also* Buildings, Elevator

Lifts indicate our emotional highs and lows. Going up suggests that you are elevated, 'uplifted', given support, rising to success and tapping into your spiritual self. Going down in a lift is symbolic of going within ourselves, tapping into our unconscious state and discovering what is hidden there. If you feel trapped, or there is no way to control the lift, you need to work out what it is that is blocking your emotions.

Light

Generally speaking, light indicates awareness, being 'switched on' to things, being seen and being active. It means illumination and consciousness. If the light is very bright in your dream, it suggests that you are being 'enlightened'. Pay attention to what is being revealed to you. Old-fashioned lamps are symbols of wisdom and guidance from a spiritual source. The Hermit in the Tarot holds up a lighted lantern to guide us into spiritual awareness. If you see a spotlight or light from a torch, focus your attention on what is shown to you. You may finally find the truth in a situation or the answer to a personal issue that you have been searching for.

L

A flickering or dim light is symbolic of the life force being weakened. Take care of your health. It may also mean that you don't have the 'full picture' on some issue; in other words, you do not have all the facts. Light at the end of the tunnel suggests hope is at hand, and if you 'see the light' you've finally understood something that was unclear before.

Lighthouse

The purpose of a lighthouse is to warn ships that may be in

distress, or have lost their bearings, and guide them to calmer waters. Because it is positioned near water, it symbolises the emotional difficulties that lie ahead. The light guides the dreamer by helping him or her to see what type of danger is ahead so that it can be avoided.

Lightning

Seeing lightning in your dream denotes unexpected changes, which come about suddenly (in a flash). It is also a destructive force that represents the knocking down of your comfort zone and the need to rebuild a new lifestyle. Lightning is an enormous electrical charge, which can lead to your discharging the old outmoded ideas and values in your life to make room for new ones. If you dream of being struck by lightning it is a sign that life changes are occurring at lightning speed in your life. If a tree is hit by lightning, it represents an ending, or a death of some issue that has been holding you for a long time.

L

Lily *see also* Flowers

A lily is a symbol of innocence, purity, virginity and other aspects of the feminine self. Many prefer this flower above any other for funerals, as it represents hope and everlasting life.

Limp *see* Lame

Linen

Linen suggests the finer things of life. A linen tablecloth suggests fine dining and more formal family celebrations. Dreaming of a white, crisp tablecloth may suggest that you long for the finer things of tradition.

Lion *see* Animals

Lips

Lips are a sensual part of our bodies and are used to express love by kissing. Dreaming of lips may be an indication that you wish for this experience or may need more intimacy in your life. 'Giving lip' and 'lip service' on the other hand, suggest backchatting and insincerity. When someone's 'lips are sealed', it means that they will not divulge a secret. Your dream may be interpreted in many different ways, so take note of all the surrounding symbolism in order to make a more accurate interpretation.

Lipstick

Lipstick exaggerates the lips, making the sensual part of our nature a seductive one. Lipstick on a collar is associated with suspicion and distrust, particularly in a relationship. Reflect on whether it is your fears that are holding you back from expressing your sensuality.

Liquid

Any liquid substance in your dreams represents 'flow'. Are you 'going with the flow' or are you resisting change?

Little see Size

Liver see Body

Lizard see Animals

Lobster

A lobster is a mini armoured tank—a symbol of aggressive masculinity. You may want to be more like the lobster—protected in your impenetrable armour and able to defend yourself against your enemies. If you are lacking confidence and feeling victimised, this dream may be pointing out the need to take on these qualities to help you get through this difficult emotional period.

Lock/Locked *see also* Cell; Key; Prison

If we see a lock in our dream, it represents our desire to keep ourselves safe and protected and, in particular, to protect our emotions from other people who might be trying to 'get at us'. The dream's message may be that whatever we have locked away needs to be freed, so that the tension (possibly sexual) may be released. We may wish to be 'freed' and require someone to 'force' us to become more expressive and uninhibited. If you see a lock being forced, the dream may be drawing your attention to this meaning.

Looking *see also* Search

To look at something in a dream is to give your full attention or be aware of whatever it is that you are seeing. Whatever appears in the dream, you are giving some thought or feeling to it. Being looked at by someone else implies seeing ourselves from a point of view that is not our own. Looking out from windows or from high places suggests ambitions (unfulfilled at this stage) and looking towards the future in a positive way. Looking down on a person suggests being judgemental about an issue, whereas looking down on or into something indicates close examination and reflection.

L

Lorry *see* Truck

Loss/Losing something

The loss of something in your dream could be a reflection of what you actually believe yourself to have lost in your waking life. It may be a loss of spark (lack of vitality or motivation), loss of health or loss of a partner. To have suffered such a loss and dream of it may mean that you have also lost part of yourself and need to find a way to cope with the grief. To lose an object in your dream means that you are not in tune with what's going on and you've 'lost the plot'. Try to be more in touch with people around you and to communicate clearly. If you choose to take the dream literally, make sure that you label your possessions, especially if you are travelling.

Lost

Being lost means that you are feeling confusion, are lacking in direction and are unable to make clear decisions. If you are lost in an alien environment, it implies that you are feeling out of depth in a new situation in your life, whether it is work related or personal. If you are feeling lost in a familiar surrounding, it could be that you are suffering from a bout of insecurity and are feeling overwhelmed. Slow down and don't act until you get your bearings right. Pay attention to anyone who comes along and offers assistance. It may help you to get back on track.

L

Lottery *see also* Gambling; Games

Lottery is collective gambling, where large groups of people take a chance at winning their life-long dreams of riches and wealth. If you dream of having a lottery ticket, it is a symbol of your desires and dreams. If you dream you've won the lottery, it could indicate that you've achieved something but not as a result of your own efforts. Generally, dreaming of a lottery can be taken as encouragement to take a chance in the game of life—especially if you've been too cautious up until now. On the other hand, if you've been reckless in some undertaking, dreaming of playing the lottery or losing could be a suggestion that you will be disappointed in some way. Winning a lottery is usually a feel-good dream, particularly if the dreamer has financial problems. In this case the dream is offering the dreamer psychological relief from his or her financial woes. While dreaming of lottery numbers hasn't been proven to be successful, it probably wouldn't hurt to write them down as soon as you wake up.

Loudspeaker

Hearing a loudspeaker suggests that there is something or someone trying to gain your attention. Is it going in one ear and out the other? What is it that you don't wish to hear, despite the loudness? Perhaps others aren't hearing you and your best way of communicating may be to be more assertive and outspoken.

Love

The love you feel in a dream is a genuine emotion. You may be actually experiencing it in your waking life or it may be a wish-fulfilment dream (a reflection of something you desire but which you have not yet attained). There are times when we feel unlovable, or love has not shown itself in our lives, and we dream of love in some form. This dream is compensation for not receiving that love.

Lover *see also* Affair

Dreaming of a lover indicates a desire for intimacy or acknowledgement of a lack of it in your life (see Love). Sometimes the lover could represent parts of ourselves—do we love ourselves enough? Lovers also symbolise communication and partnership—not necessarily only in love relationships. The feelings associated with this type of dream are important. A negative feeling suggests temptation and duplicity in your dealings with a partner, while a positive feeling indicates the opposite.

Luggage *see also* Bag; Travel

Are you carrying any emotional baggage, that is, emotions and beliefs that you won't or can't get rid of? Luggage is a symbol of the things we take with us that we feel we need, despite the fact that we don't actually use everything we take. If you have been feeling the need to unburden yourself, the dream may be prompting you to travel light and only take what you need with you. Perhaps you need to leave excess luggage behind in order to make progress.

Lynx *see* Animals

L

M

Machine/Machinery

Dreaming of a machine represents our body's functions and drives: breathing, ageing, moving and our inner workings, such as emotions, wishes, desires—all those parts of us that motivate and move us. Machines also suggest that 'automatic' aspect of our lifestyles and the habitual things we do without using our creative force for the full enjoyment of life. You need to examine all the symbols of the dream in order to come to a conclusion about this dream. Are you taking the machine apart? Perhaps this indicates your need to try to get at something that isn't working. If you see a mechanic in the dream, he or she may represent a doctor (helping to fix the machine or body). Dreaming of a well-oiled machine means that you wish for things to run smoothly in your life, without any nasty surprises.

Madness

If you dream of acting in a mad or irrational manner, it may represent your fears of being confronted by what is irrational to you. You may be confronting the part of you that is uncontrollable and has not been allowed to merge with the rest of your unconscious. Dreaming of madness, whether in yourself or others, is often a sign you are experiencing intense emotional situations in waking life. If this is the case then the dream is indicative of your sense of being out of control. Seeing a mad dog or a mad person can symbolise the parts of ourselves that are unable to come to terms with a new situation in our lives.

Mafia

The Mafia, as portrayed by the media, is a symbol of family honour, organised crime, secrecy and corruption. Consider whether it is really these qualities that the dream is attempting to convey to you and what role they play in your personal life. Are you lacking in close family ties? Are you carrying some kind of moral burden?

Maggots *see also* Insects

Maggots reveal that parts of our bodies are in 'decay'. It could be the spiritual (our attitudes are not wholesome) or the physical (feeling ill about an issue). Pay attention to this dream, as it indicates your attitude towards something that you really can't handle or that you find distasteful.

Magic

When we dream of magic, we are attempting to connect with the deepest powers within us. It may well be that we wish to accomplish great deeds or control situations that are beyond our human control. This is a positive dream, highlighting our subconscious wishes for more control over our present situation.

M

Magician

The magician is a symbol of the self and of our potential or hidden talents. We are in awe of the magician who can make things happen that are beyond logic and explanation. The magician is also full of surprises and may suggest a craving for things that are not mundane and predictable. To dream of a magician can also be a subconscious signal of the need to put our hidden talents towards some practical project.

Magistrate *see* Judge

Magnet

A magnet has the power to attract or repel. This dream symbolises the effect or influence we have on others and vice versa. As it is a power, consider how you draw many things in your life—you may attract good things or you may be capable of drawing negative influences around you. Be aware that you have this energy. Focus on what it is that you wish to attract and what you want to repel.

Magnifying glass *see also* Lens

When something is magnified in our dreams, and appears larger than life, it is a good indication that we need to pay attention to it. If you dream of using a magnifying glass, be more attentive to the small details in your life. It may also be that you are exaggerating a situation that need not be so huge; that is, that you're 'making mountains out of molehills'.

Make-up *see also* Cosmetics

Wearing make-up is about creating an image you wish to project to the outside world. Dreaming of applying make-up suggests that you may be trying to cover up your imperfections and/or create a beautiful image. The important message in this dream is that we have the ability to change the effect or impression we make on others. Like sunglasses, make-up can also hide parts of ourselves we wish not to expose.

Man

A masculine figure that appears in our dreams indicates

| M |

parts of our personality—the things that we possess and those that we want. An older man can represent wisdom or a father figure. A man in a woman's dream can represent the masculine side of her nature—that is, the logical, strong, assertive elements that she requires to survive in the world. It may suggest that a woman wishes to get in touch with the masculine side of herself in order to cope better with what is at hand. A man dreaming of a man is in fact dreaming of himself. To understand how someone feels about the masculine side, consider these idioms: 'be a man', 'make a man of', 'odd man out', 'man to man'.

Maniac *see also* Madness

When we describe a person as a maniac, we generally label them as threatening. There are 'maniac' drivers (lacking in control) and there are those who are passionately driven by some possibly irrational desire. Depending on the context of the dream, it may indicate that you are afraid of this aspect of yourself or of a situation around you. You may be hoping for some calm, order and control in your life.

Mannequin

A mannequin suggests a detached form of beauty or ideal. Dreaming that you are a mannequin may indicate that you wish to seek attention from those around you. On the other hand, you may be feeling that you are on display and that you would prefer some privacy in your life. Think of 'role model' or 'model behaviour' and how it fits into your value system. Perhaps you are not a model parent or student, for example, and you feel that you can't live up to the ideal. This dream may also be highlighting your feelings of detachment and objectivity towards something or someone.

M

Mansion *see* House; Buildings

Map

Dreaming of a map indicates that you long for direction. What direction do you wish to take in life? How can you best move forward with your ambitions or goals? If you can't read a map in your dream, it indicates confusion. If you don't have a map, but you know you should have one, the dream is telling you that you lack information and that without it you can't make progress. If you can read the map and it leads to somewhere you wish to go, it means that you are your own guide and that you will reach your goals at your pace and by your standards.

Maple

The maple is the national emblem of Canada. Dreaming of a national emblem suggests the desire to get in touch with all that is good and worthwhile. Maples are also a symbol of fall (autumn) or of the change of season from warm to cool. In this respect dreaming of them may be an indication of your current emotional state.

Marathon *see also* Race

Running a marathon represents our participation in life ('the rat race'). How we conduct ourselves in the race is an indication of how we truly participate in life. If you feel that life is a slog, you will be dragging your feet in the marathon—a race that requires a steady pace and which tests your endurance. If you see yourself enjoying the marathon and participating willingly, you are ready for a challenge and able to take things in your stride. If you are a spectator or an official, note how these roles are relevant in your life situation.

Marble

On the positive side, marble is a symbol of great beauty and permanence. It is used extensively in sculpture and in architecture to create lasting beauty. For these reasons it can indicate your wish for more beauty in your life. On the other hand, as many statues are made of marble it is also associated with the human qualities of being cold, harsh, unfeeling and inflexible. Do you need to adopt a more active and emotional approach to some aspect of your life?

Mardi Gras

Dreaming of being in a Mardi Gras parade or watching one represents celebration, fun and exhibitionism. Are these qualities lacking in some areas of your life or personality? Traditionally, Mardi Gras is also an exaggeration of the unusual or a celebration of the grotesque or abnormal. In a dream it can suggest there is some part of the dreamer's personality that he or she would like to expose but is frightened to do so, for fear that it will be considered abnormal or deviant.

Marigolds *see* Flowers

M

Marijuana

As a symbol, marijuana represents any illegal activity. Because smoking or inhaling it can prevent you from thinking clearly, dreaming of it can also highlight the risk of making unwise decisions. Alternatively, perhaps you feel the need to relax and tune out. Generally, this dream depends on the context in which you view the drug. If you are a user, it may just be routine, but if you have never tried it, you should focus on what the experience is and how you may be able to attain it without addiction or illegality.

Market/Marketplace *see also* Fair

A market is a place of commerce and trading, and as a symbol represents 'public' space and dealing with people in general. Dreaming of a market may suggest that you need to be more commercial in your ventures and look for the resources that will allow you to pursue this goal. Dreaming of a stock market could be an indication that you need to carefully consider financial decisions.

Marriage/Wedding

Couples sometimes refer to each other as their 'better' or 'other half'. This indicates a union that brings about a wholeness or completeness. Dreaming of a marriage or wedding can represent the two aspects of yourself—such as the practical and spiritual, rational and emotional—and suggest how uniting these aspects would bring into existence new abilities and insights. Dreaming of a wedding dress suggests how you are feeling about your own marriage or relationship. If you are feeling negative or anxious about the relationship, your emotions in the dream sequence will indicate confusion, anxiety, or illness.

Marsh/Swamp

To dream of marshy or swampy ground signals that there is something that is making you feel bogged down or held. Losing ground, being stuck and lack of control are all issues that relate to difficulty in our emotional lives. If you want to move forward but can't, it could be that you are ready to move on to a new emotional level but that you either don't have the emotional support you need or lack self-confidence to do so. If this is a recurring dream, focus on the ways you can solve this issue in your life.

Martyr

A martyr is a glorified victim. Religious martyrs have traditionally been depicted as heroes/heroines who have gone to their deaths for their strong beliefs. Dreaming of a martyr reflects your admiration for this type of extreme behaviour in which you become a victim in order to prove your point. If you feel that you are a victim in the sense that everyone expects you to perform certain duties, but you perform them grudgingly, it may be time to review the role you have either taken on yourself or that others have given you.

Mask

Dreaming of wearing a mask indicates a disguise that you feel is needed if you are to face others. It is a façade—not always totally honest, but necessary at certain times. It can be a defence for the wearer, enabling the dreamer to conceal a vulnerable side from the public. On the negative side, wearing a mask can also indicate deception. Assess what it is that you are trying to conceal from the world and whether it is best to hide behind the mask or come out and show your true side—even if only to a chosen few.

M

Massacre *see also* Murder

Massacre is murder on a large scale. Dreaming of a massacre, whether you are a witness or take part in the killing, indicates a need for you to terminate or put an end to certain habits, values or attitudes that are no longer working for you.

Masturbation *see* Sex

Mat

If you see a doormat in your dream, take note of why you

are focusing on it. Is it out of place? Is it threadbare, dirty or worn out? Is it welcoming? All these suggest your attitude towards yourself. Consider whether you are being treated like a doormat and your reaction to this situation. Perhaps you're not so welcoming of certain people or standards entering your home. When interpreting this dream, keep in mind that the house represents you.

Mattress *see* Furniture

Maze *see also* Labyrinth
A maze represents a confusion of feelings and ideas that make it difficult for us to find our way or make progress. Beliefs and old values influenced by authority figures can block our ability to think clearly, making us feel as if we are lost in a maze of our own doubts and irrational fears. If you dream that you make it through the maze to the exit, it means that you will overcome your fears and become a wiser, more confident person in the process.

M

Meals *see* Food

Meat *see* Food

Medal
A medal is a symbol of achievement. As humans, we all want to be appreciated for our efforts, and winning a medal or award is an acknowledgement of our talents. Other feel-good emotions associated with a medal are respect and achievement. This may be a wish-fulfilment dream or it may be pointing you to the fact that you are not feeling appreciated and you need something that will prove your worth.

Medicine

Dreaming of taking medicine represents the need to undergo unpleasant experiences in order to achieve a positive outcome. It is a symbol of healing through unpleasant or unpalatable means that is ultimately good for us. 'Taking one's medicine' or experiencing a 'taste of your own medicine' are terms used to describe the need to accept your fate in order to learn a valuable lesson. If you choose to take the dream literally, have a health check.

Menstruation

A woman who dreams of menstruating but has ceased to menstruate may be grieving for the loss of youth and fertility, or unable to accept her new stage of life. If a man dreams of menstruating, it represents his urge for more creative pursuits in his life.

Mermaid/Merman

Mermaids are mythical creatures said to dwell in the sea, but able to breathe on land. This duality in their nature makes them symbolic of our desire to be able to connect the rational with the emotional, allowing us to be more at peace with our environment. To dream of mermaids may mean that the dreamer needs to let go of the rational and take a leap of faith.

M

Metal

Any metal in a dream represents the restrictions that we feel society imposes on us as individuals. We may feel that the world is hard, cold and uncaring towards us and that we can't break out of the metal shell we're encased in.

Meteor

If you witness a meteor landing on earth in your dream, you

may be expecting some sort of clash with someone from outside your comfort zone. This could be because you have an obstinate view of a situation and you are aware that your ideas will not change, despite the opposing force you will face as a consequence.

Microscope *see* Magnifying glass; Lens

Migration

Dreaming of migrating indicates your need to find greener pastures and achieve your goals in an environment where you will not be judged by old standards. If on the other hand the migration is forced, the dream may be expressing your frustrations at having to change your ways of thinking and abandon your comfort zone. Your attitude within the dream holds the key to the message it is trying to convey. In general, dreaming of migration reflects uncertainty about the steps the dreamer is about to take. However, it also suggests that beneath that uncertainty there is the promise of prosperity.

Military

The military represents discipline, enforced regulations and obeying commands for the good of all. If you dream of being in the military, you may want to integrate some of these qualities in your own life situation in order to achieve a desired result.

Milk

Milk is a symbol both of sustenance and kindness. Milk is given to babies as their first taste of food, and we relax better at night if we have a glass of warm milk. If you see the dream in this context, it may be highlighting the fact that you are not taking care of your basic human needs. However, milk can also manifest itself as a less desirable trait: being taken advantage of is referred to as 'being milked' and if you 'cry over spilt milk' you are meant to take the consequences that are a result of your actions.

Mill

To dream of a mill suggests difficulties in the dreamer's waking life. A mill represents the process of extracting what is important in your life. In order to extract and turn it into nourishment, the mill uses the potentially painful method of crushing. This dream suggests that your own experiences may be painful as a result of this extraction process, but that the pain will be worth it, as you will be transformed for the better. It suggests that you need to retain what is positive but throw out anything that is negative in your current circumstances.

Mine

'Working in a salt mine' is a saying we use to convey the repetition of the work place. Mines are a symbol of places where we work, but can also signal the process of going within ourselves and examining our potential. Are we a 'gold mine' waiting to be discovered? In general the mineral associated with the mining will reflect the meaning of the dream. For example, a salt mine suggests persecution or even dictatorship, while gold indicates that the dreamer's true worth is about to be discovered.

M

Mirror

Like water, mirrors symbolise the process of looking into the unconscious in order to discover who we really are. If you dream of looking into a mirror it suggests that you are concerned about your image—about what others think of you and how you 'face' the world. There may be anxiety over appearance, ageing, health and attitudes. Perhaps you are too anxious about your image and don't spend enough time reflecting on whom you are comfortable being. A mirror provides a reflection of ourselves, which is not necessarily a true representation of who we are inside. Rather, it symbolises what we would like to project onto others. If you dream of a mirror, your feelings within the dream will tell you whether or not the projection is an accurate one.

Miscarriage

A miscarriage represents a loss—one that is untimely and unexpected. It could indicate the loss of some aspect of ourselves that has disappeared through no intention of our own and that we now grieve for. It could also stand for the loss of work, a relationship or a new scheme that you never got the chance to see through. A 'miscarriage of justice' is an unfair result. If the dreamer is a woman and has suffered a miscarriage, it is an indication that she has not given herself enough time to grieve in order to be healed completely.

Mist *see* Fog

Mistletoe

Good fortune and health are qualities attributed to the mistletoe. Festivities, decoration and family togetherness are all associated with this Christmas plant. Because we associate mistletoe with kissing, it also represents the promise of intimacy.

Moat

A moat in a castle, usually medieval, is a symbol of our need to defend ourselves emotionally against intimacy. As the castle is a fortress—a defence system against anyone penetrating it—the drawbridge is movable. We choose to open our castle grounds when we are confident or to close up when we feel under attack or vulnerable. Because the moat has water, our emotions are what we are trying to protect.

Mole *see* Animals

Monastery *see* Abbey

Money

Money plays a very important part in our lives as it creates the conditions for our well-being. However, dreaming of money does not refer to the actual money in our lives, but to what we value. Time, energy and love are three things that are valuable to all of us and having enough of any is a concern. If you dream of holding onto money, you may be 'tight' or feeling emotionally insecure. Not having enough money makes us feel inadequate. It can also indicate a feeling of sexual impotency. Counterfeit or stolen money represents the belief on our part that we are being taken for granted and that we feel cheated in some way. Money also stands for power and our potential for success. Generally, this dream is asking the dreamer to pay attention to his or her values and to reassess them on a regular basis. Money also has to do with cost. What do your actions, which derive from your values, cost you?

Monk *see* Abbot

Monkey *see* Animals

Monster see also p.viii (Introduction); p.17 (Typical dreams)

A monster is a fear—one that is absolutely terrifying. The larger and more aggressive the monster, the greater our fear. The fear is usually one that we have allowed to sprout and grow out of proportion and which then comes back to frighten us. Fears depend on the individual and the image of the monster needs to be analysed by the dreamer. If this is a recurring dream, it is a good idea to try to work out what has you terrified. Also identify ways in which the monster gets at you and try to escape its clutches in the next dream. Perhaps this can free you from this fear. If you are feeling helpless, the dream is controlling your emotions. If you gain some power over it, you will slowly come to face the monster and shrink its size and importance in your life.

Moon

The moon has been a symbol of the feminine since early times. Traditionally it represents the unconscious, intuitive or mysterious sides of ourselves. The moon has also long been associated with love and romance. That is why so many romance novels and movies have a moonlight setting (slightly obscure, as opposed to the glare of the sun and given an air of unreality by the shadows cast by the surroundings). To 'reach for the moon' is to be unable to attain your desires while being 'over the moon' is to be emotionally ecstatic. The moon is not only symbolic of romance or mysticism, but can also represent intuition, particularly in relation to unforeseen doom and gloom. It is often an indication that the dreamer is concentrating too much on the uncertainty of situations in waking life, particularly where emotions are concerned. This dream may be telling you that you need to concentrate on the practical aspects of a situation, if you want to avoid setting yourself up for failure.

Morning

Morning represents youth or the part of our lives when we are most active. Dreaming of the morning is positive as we can still shape the day and its events through our thoughts and actions. It is a dream of vitality and optimism.

Mosquitoes *see* Insects

Moth *see also* Insects

The moth is a symbol of transformation. This dream suggests that we search for deeper truths (as moths are attracted to the light) and by delving into the hidden side of ourselves we change our perceptions.

Mother *see also* Family

The mother represents the nurturing and protective aspects of ourselves. How we relate to people in any relationship is symbolised by this figure. If it is a negative dream, the mother image may be possessive, jealous and lacking in emotional bonding. Assess whether the dream is indicating that you need to apply the positive maternal instincts to your life, or whether you need to acknowledge the negative aspects and integrate them for a more balanced outcome.

M

Motorbike

The image of the motorbike arouses feelings of adventure, freedom and escape and is associated with rebellious youth. Dreaming of riding a motorbike represents our physical energy and independence as well as sexual drive. If you are feeling confident and are in control of the motorbike, your daring and sense of adventure will pay off. If, however, you are not in control of the vehicle, it could be wishful thinking on your part to be free and daring, because you don't have the confidence to carry it off. You may be yearning for past youth or regretting the time you spent being 'responsible', or in mourning for your own 'reckless spirit'. Accept it and move on.

Mountain

To dream of a mountain represents the obstacles in your path that you need to overcome and any larger than life hazards ahead. To reach the summit is to achieve your goals, but how you go about doing this will be different for everyone. Being afraid of being at the top of the mountain indicates your fear of success or that you fear failure, as you stand alone above the rest. Work through this symbol, taking into account all other aspects of the dream and discover what the dream is asking you to overcome and how to do it.

M

Mourning *see also* Funeral

The process of mourning after a loss or an ending of an important facet of your life is one that is not easily practised in waking life. We put on a brave face and try to keep busy, however sad we feel inside. Mourning in your dreams, therefore, is a sign of your subconscious releasing the grief and of keeping the body healthy at the same time so that emotions aren't bottled up. Through dreams we can privately mourn and find ways to begin anew.

Mouse *see* Animals

Mouth *see* Body

Moving

Depending on how you move in a dream, each action has its own meaning. Moving quickly might mean that you are making swift advancements and are accepting of the flow. You are at ease with yourself. Moving backwards suggests that you are withdrawing from a situation, unable to confront what's ahead. Moving sideways symbolises avoidance. If you are stuck and unable to move, it indicates that you are being held back by your own fears and self-doubts.

Mud

The mud we see in a dream denotes emotions that cause us to feel 'bogged down'. When something is 'muddy' it means that it is not clear, so this dream is a warning not to go ahead with any plans until the muddiness turns clear. If you are sinking in mud, it means that you are feeling helpless. Dreaming of mud and feeling repulsed by it, represents your feelings—do you feel guilty about some issue? Are you mud slinging or is your name mud?

M

Murder/Murderer *see also* Killing

To dream of murdering someone is an expression of how you feel about someone or something in waking life. You want to get rid of the object or person so that you can be happy or have more control over your future. Work out what the person or object represents to you. It could well be that it's part of your own personality that you want to 'murder' or values represented by others such as bosses, co-workers, a partner or children. If you are murdered in the dream, it means that you feel as if you are being destroyed by some external force beyond your control.

Museum *see also* Buildings

A museum is a place where memories are stored and precious things are preserved. It represents the living past, family and heritage. Perhaps we are trying to connect with this past in order to come to terms with who we are and what our values are based on.

Music/Musical instruments

Music is an expression of our inner selves and how we connect with life. Music, like life, has its discords and harmonies, its highs and lows. Hearing music in a dream can be interpreted either as 'music to my ears'—that is, pleasant words—or 'facing the music'—taking responsibility. If you are playing music you are expressing yourself in your own individual way. If the notes are harsh and discordant, there is an underlying conflict in your waking life. Pay attention to the rest of the dream so that you find its source. A musical instrument represents the way we communicate with others. If you were to play an instrument which one would you choose to best express your personality? Percussion instruments are associated more with the earthy rhythm of life, while the string and wind instruments are to do with the mind.

Mutation *see also* Deformity

To see something that is not quite right indicates that you are not taking things at face value. If you see morphing, that is, a situation in which one thing flows into and becomes another, it may be a warning that a person or a situation is not what it seems.

N

Nail

Nails can mean a variety of things depending on the context of the dream. Dreaming of nails may suggest you feel cornered—'nailed against the wall' or 'nailed down'. It could also mean that you have had an insight or achieved a result: that is, you've 'hit the nail on the head'. Generally we associate nails with being 'bonded' and in that sense, we are holding together (particularly in a sexual relationship) or holding onto something. If you dream of being nailed to a cross, it suggests pain and sacrifice—once again referring to a relationship or your feelings towards some sort of critical situation. Perhaps you're feeling helpless, or see yourself as a martyr.

Naked *see* Nude

Name (of person)

If you hear your name being called in a dream, it suggests you should be paying attention to your individuality and personal nature. If your name has been changed, work out why you'd like to be someone other than yourself. Perhaps you sense a change in how you see yourself. Other people's names highlight our need to look at those qualities we admire or dislike in those people. In doing this, you may discover a new aspect to yourself.

Napkin

White dinner napkins are associated with formal dining and celebration. If they are crisp and clean, it is a positive sign that you are looking forward to an occasion. If the napkins are mismatched or soiled, it indicates that you may have problems in dealing with an occasion that requires you to be on your best behaviour or to put on a façade.

Narrowness

When we think of a street as narrow, we often mean that it is restricted and secluded. Usually we avoid these streets, as they make us feel unsafe. Dreaming of being in a narrow space denotes feeling restricted or having limited choices or views (being narrow-minded). The dream may mean that you wish to be free of these limitations.

Nausea

You need to expel whatever is making you feel sick—either physically or emotionally. Think of a person who is making you feel this way in your life and deal with the problem— either by removal or confrontation. On a physical level, this dream could be warning you of a potential health problem.

N

Navel

Our umbilical cord is a connection to the womb. As a result, dreaming of a navel suggests either our dependency on mother, or the way we connect to the outside world. The dream may be indicating that we need to be more independent and not rely on things or others around us to get us through life.

Navy *see also* Army

To dream of being in the navy suggests your desire for

organisation and structure in your life. Depending on what rank you see yourself or others, the dream reflects your status as you or others see it as well as your desire to improve on it. The navy also offers escape and travel. Is this what you are really longing for?

Nearness

If something is close to you in a dream, it means that you are close to achieving whatever 'it' is in reality. Being near-sighted, however, denotes that you are focusing your energies on a short-term goal rather than the future. Are you missing the 'big picture'? Pay closer attention not just to one objective but to the overall scheme of things.

Neck *see also* Body

The neck is the connection between the body and the head. Dreaming of it could indicate that you are facing a struggle between the two. The neck is also associated with risk—as in the expressions, 'break one's neck', 'risk one's neck'. The neck is also associated with gracefulness or elegance, which may be traits the dreamer desires. Alternatively, someone close to the dreamer may be acting like 'a pain in the neck'.

N

Necklace *see also* Jewellery/Jewels

Traditionally, a necklace is associated with power, honour and riches. To some extent, this is true, as it can represent a deep emotion on the part of the wearer or the giver of the necklace. As it is a piece that has the capacity to hold the most jewels, the necklace makes a grand display, visible to all for admiration.

Needle

A sewing needle in a dream may represent the power to

mend, bring together or patch things up. To 'needle' someone is to irritate them and 'a needle in a haystack' is something that is impossible to find. Needlework is regarded as an image of what you've 'made' of yourself—your achievements and failures. If you are finding it difficult to thread a needle, it may be that you can't get started with a project. Discover what the source of frustration is. The needle that is used on our bodies for medical purposes denotes a sickness in the body in the negative sense, and healing power in the positive. Freudians would classify a needle as a phallic symbol.

Neighbour

A neighbour reflects the qualities you see in your neighbour (or someone close to you) as well as your relationships with others. Dreaming of having a good neighbour is a sign of well-being and tranquillity. If your neighbour is fighting with you, take a look at what's causing the dispute and resolve it, as it usually reflects your own personal relationships with people around you.

Nephew *see* Family

N

Nest

'Nesting' is a term used when women prepare their homes, usually with a major spring clean, before they go into hospital to give birth. It is not surprising, then, that the nest is a symbol of the home. This is usually associated with safety and comfort: in other words, a sanctuary. It is also a sign of fertility. To see a nest in a dream with broken eggs suggests failure and loss. We speak of 'our nest egg' as our financial security and the 'empty nest syndrome' happens when all the children leave home and the parents are left alone. It is important to look at the significance of these sayings in order to discover the significance of the dream. The dream may be telling you that you are too dependent on your parents or warning you to make sure that you 'feather your nest': that is, that you build up your assets.

Net

If you dream of being caught in a net, consider which parts of your life are being stifled, held back or trapped, giving you the feeling of being ensnared or overwhelmed. If the feeling in the dream was pleasant, that is, you dreamt of falling in a net, the dream may suggest security, either financial or in relationships. These days we refer to the Internet as 'the Net', so consider whether communication is the issue you are trying to resolve.

Are you reaching out to as many people as you should? If there is a negative feeling associated with the dream, particularly if it is related to the Internet, it may be a sign that the dreamer is ignoring real life for virtual reality. Regardless of whether the feeling is negative or positive, dreaming of a net in relation to communications suggests that the dreamer needs to open up 'networks', whether they are real or not.

N

Nettle

When nettles appear in a dream, beware of being stung. You may feel stung by someone's remarks. It is best to avoid certain situations where you know this is likely to happen.

New

If you dream of 'something new', it usually indicates a new start or beginning. This type of dream can be inspirational for the dreamer as anything new brings hope.

New Year

Unless you are having this dream close to New Year's Day, it usually represents your new plans for the future. New Year is a time of hope and resolutions, so dreaming of it indicates a new potential, project, phase or relationship in your life. It may mean a fresh start for you.

Newspaper

Dreaming of a newspaper suggests becoming aware of some issue or news that was not known to you before. Usually, it indicates finding out something about yourself. Delve further to see what type of newspaper you dreamt of and which section you were reading. If the feeling associated with the dream is negative, it may mean that the dreamer feels as if his or her life has been sensationalised, or placed under some sort of scrutiny.

Night *see also* Dark

The night is the ending of the day and as such can reflect the end of something in your life. It can represent our unconscious or the areas of ourselves that we don't wish to show to anyone else. It is also a time of rest, when the body and mind can be rid of expectations, physical activities and constraints. In one sense then, dreaming of the night suggests a longing for freedom, sometimes expressed by dreams of running away from the house at night or breaking into a new place. In general, the night represents the darker side of the self, which it is safe to explore during a dream state.

Nightmares *see also* p.21 (Recurring dreams, anxiety dreams and nightmares)

If we are overwhelmed by emotions of fear and anxiety in a dream, it's a good indication that it is a nightmare. In a night-

N

mare you are usually trying to get away from a situation or feel stuck in a terrifying condition. It is the intensity of the fear that makes us remember this dream. There are typical nightmarish dreams that we all encounter but whose meanings vary for each individual. Understanding the cause of the nightmare can help us to deal with our real-life fears and obstacles.

Nine *see* Numbers

No
If you have difficulty in saying 'no' to people and their requests in your waking life, chances are you dream of giving this response to them in your dream. This dream reflects how you really feel. It is important that you take note of what you are saying 'no' to and apply it to your life situation.

Noon
The hours of the day refer to age and our sense of responsibility and pressure. Noon represents mid-life and it is a time when we are fully responsible for ourselves. Usually it is a time of great pressure and decision making.

Noose *see also* Rope; Hanging

N

Having a noose around one's neck is not the most comforting of dreams. It suggests a feeling of helplessness and vulnerability. It is also a dream of fear—fear of getting involved or 'hung up' on someone or something as well as dealing with repressed emotions.

Nose *see* Body

Novel *see also* Book; Reading
If you dream of reading a novel, try to remember the theme

or genre. Books generally try to introduce us to new points of view and provide us with escapism. If your novel was an adventure or romance, the dream may be suggesting that you should include more of those elements in your life. It may also indicate your need to investigate or probe further into issues and perhaps change your perspective or approach to a situation. This dream may also have a punning meaning, in which the dreamer feels as if he or she has produced or taken a 'novel' approach to something in life and, as a result, is an innovator.

Nuclear *see also* Bomb

We are living in a nuclear age, where we face injury and death by the use of nuclear weapons, particularly bombing devices. This creates anxiety about our safety and our future, as well as that of the next generation. This dream usually reflects those anxieties and fears, particularly after incidents are reported in the news.

Nude

Dreaming of nudity reflects our need for self-expression and desire to be seen for who we truly are behind our façade (clothing). If you dream you are naked and embarrassed, it suggests anxiety about how others see you and vulnerability if your weaknesses are exposed. It may mean that you feel guilty about harbouring some feelings about your sexuality or a trait that you don't like.

Numbers

Numbers hold a different significance for each one of us. A number may refer to a date of birth, a house number, your family group or other events significant to you alone. The numbers below are generally regarded as universal symbols;

N

however, you should interpret your dream with reference to all the numbers that have a special meaning to you.

One One represents being alone; the self; unity.

Two Two stands for duality, two sides of something (male/female; left/right; yes/no); also communication or relationship.

Three This number suggests a triangle and family unit—mother, father and child—and by extension, growth and fertility.

Four Stability and strength are signified by four: it is a solid structure and is associated with the four elements of fire, water, air and earth. It also represents the four seasons and, as a result, is both a balanced number and a cyclical one. The number four is often associated with logic.

Five Five represents the human body—five fingers, five toes and five senses. It can also denote impoverishment, whether mental or physical.

N

Six The number six is associated with balance and with approaching your goals.

Seven Traditionally a sacred number, it also suggests uncertainty and change, in which everything happens in cycles of seven.

Eight Eight symbolises death and resurrection. The symbol of the number 8 on its side means infinity. This is a magical number that can denote significant lifestyle changes.

Nine Representing pregnancy and childbirth, nine is also the end of the cycle and the start of something new.

Ten Ten represents the male and female as one; a new beginning. This number is also associated with the public arena and with communication within groups.

Twelve This number can stand for a full cycle of the year— twelve months, the twelve disciples, or the twelve astrological signs.

Twenty-four This is the symbol of the cycle of night and day (twenty-four hours).

Zero Zero symbolises the female.

Nun

A nun symbolises sexual restraint and morality. If you dream of becoming a nun, the dream may by expressing a wish to connect with the more idealistic side of yourself. However, depending on the mood of the dream, it may also represent your feelings of restriction or frustration.

Nurse

Nurses are depicted as the angels of mercy; dedicated to 'nursing the sick back to health'. Seeing or being a nurse in your dream represents a need for care and nurturing, in relation to your physical as well as emotional well-being. A nurse also represents the healing process, someone who 'revives' those on their way out of this world. This is generally a good sign. However, as with any symbols connected with health, it is a good idea to check your health.

Nut

If you refer to someone as a 'hard nut to crack' it usually suggests that the person has a tough exterior, but that if you do crack that shell, he or she is quite different and may hold excellent qualities. That is why it's important to find the kernel in the nut. Consider whether this image is referring to yourself or to someone else in your life that you haven't yet been able to fully understand.

Nymph

A nymph represents parts of ourselves, whether we are male or female, that are seductive, youthful and elusive. The dream may suggest that these are desired qualities you wish to make use of in your life.

N

Oak

The oak tree is associated with strength, long life and tradition. Its wood was traditionally used for building ships and houses as well as furniture. If an oak tree appears in your dream, or you dream of furniture made of oak, the dream may be telling you that some aspect of your life, such as your living situation or relationships, has strongly built foundations and is likely to endure.

Oar

An oar is a navigation device, so its appearance in a dream indicates a goal that you are trying to reach. It suggests that you will be able to guide your own destiny, but that doing so will require skill and care. If you lose or drop an oar in your dream, take it as a sign that you need to keep a firmer grip on your assets. You don't want to be 'up a creek without a paddle'.

Oasis

An oasis stands for any place of comfort and refreshment in a world that can sometimes feel desert-like. Dreaming of such a place suggests your desire to take time out, to be invigorated and nourished, and to stop struggling with your difficulties. You may long for your problems to disappear, or turn into a distant 'mirage' on the horizon. If, on the other hand, you dream that you are trying to reach an oasis but can't find it, it is likely that you are having trouble imagining an end to your current labours.

Oath

Swearing an oath in a dream suggests that there is an issue of commitment or loyalty in your waking life. More generally this dream may suggest the need to take something in your life more seriously.

Oats

As the basis of porridge and other simple but nourishing foods, oats are associated with nurturing, with homely pleasures and domestic comforts. Dreaming of them may signal your desire to be looked after, or to rebuild your energy in some way. The alternative significance of oats is sexual, and is conveyed by the phrase 'sowing your wild oats'. Perhaps you have commitment problems in a relationship, have been unfaithful or thought of being unfaithful to your partner, or are not yet ready to settle down.

Obedience

The significance of this dream depends on whether you are the one being obedient, or whether you are trying to get others to obey you. Either way this dream represents issues of authority and power. If you are demanding obedience from others, the dream could either be encouraging you to see your own behaviour towards others as 'despotic' or suggesting that you need to take more control in your life. Similarly, if you dream that you are obeying someone else, it may be a sign either that you feel exploited, or that you want the security that comes from following somebody else's orders.

Obelisk

An obelisk in a dream can be a symbol of your own inner nature and strength. This dream could be allowing you to assess the way your personality has been 'shaped', and the influences acting on it. The shape, size and decoration of the obelisk will help you to interpret the way you feel about yourself. An alternative meaning for this dream suggests that you are overly distant or cold (like a stone or a statue) in your personal or intimate relationships. This can represent the various inner depths of the dreamer, including the dark and cold side of one's nature. Such a dream may be a warning that you are using your strength or projecting yourself in a cold and unfeeling way in waking life.

Obituary

If you dream of reading someone else's obituary it is a sign that you are concerned about your relationship with them. If you are reading your own, the dream suggests your need to reflect on your life and achievements to date. Think about what you'd like others to say about you in your obituary. It may give you a better idea about the direction that you wish to take in life.

Obligation

Obligation relates to duty, so a dream in which you feel a sense of obligation can be either a reminder of a duty you have pushed aside, or a sign of your resentment at being made to do something you'd prefer not to. This dream prompts you to think about yourself and your actions in relation to the expectations and well-being of those around you.

Obscenity

If you have a dream that shocks you, you should not be too

O

alarmed. Dreaming is an activity in which the censors that operate in our waking life are often absent. Your dream may be representing urges or fantasies that you don't allow into your waking life, and it could be a way of releasing tension. This is healthy, as dreams enable fantasies to be explored without them being confronting or harmful. Dreams also often represent our attempt to process images and ideas that we encounter in our waking lives—in films, books or news broadcasts for example. If you repeatedly have dreams that shock you, however, it may be an indication that you have an overly controlling attitude to your sexual or aggressive urges.

Observatory

An observatory is a place designed to bring distant things into close view. Is there an issue or emotion that you have been trying to keep at a distance, and that you need to examine more carefully? Alternatively, dreaming that you are observing the stars through a telescope can suggest your aspirations to a higher intellectual or spiritual state. It can also suggest your desire to be promoted or to rise to a prominent position.

Obsession

A dream in which you are obsessed points to a source of anxiety in your life that needs to be worked through before it will stop bothering you. This dream could also be trying to draw your attention to some repeated activity or emotional situation in your life. Either way the dream calls for action in waking life.

O

Obstacle

Obstacles in dreams take many forms, all of which represent our anxieties and the things that prevent us making as much progress in life as we would like to. Paying attention to the nature of the obstacle in your dream, and the way you are overcoming it, can help you to diagnose the obstacles in your waking life and assess how well you are coping with them.

Occult

Dreaming of the occult suggests your desire to solve some mystery in your own life or to explore emotions that you usually keep below the surface. If you have a negative association with the occult, you are actually frightened of exploring those feelings that are just under the surface, or of solving the mystery.

Ocean *see also* Water

The ocean is a traditional symbol of both life and the emotions. Watching or swimming in a stormy sea can denote an awareness of the powerful forces of spirituality or emotion within you. If the sea is calm and tranquil, it suggests that you have come to terms with an issue or feeling, and can expect easier times ahead. If you are underwater in your dream, it may be a sign of your desire to delve deeply into your emotions on a particular subject.

Octopus

O

An octopus symbolises freedom of movement and adaptability. But if the octopus is threatening you, its eight arms may suggest that you are feeling 'strangled' or under attack from a number of different sources.

Odour *see also* Smell

Smell is one of the most imprecise but also one of the most evocative senses: the one that is hardest to translate into words. A powerful odour or fragrance could be prompting you to remember something in your past. A bad smell can symbolise disharmony in your current life and pessimism about the future, whereas a pleasant one suggests your desire to be in touch with pleasing emotions.

Offence

A dream in which you are offending someone suggests either that you need to pay more attention to other people's feelings, or that you are oversensitive to their opinions. Use the other elements within the dream, combined with your knowledge of your own actions, to interpret which meaning is most applicable to you.

Office

An office tends to reflect our feelings about our work or professional lives—especially if we work in one in our waking lives. Whether or not you feel comfortable in this office—whether the other workers are friendly, are ignoring you or trying to boss you around—may reflect how satisfied you feel in your actual work situation. Alternatively this dream may be a sign that you have too much responsibility at work, or that you have a project or problem that you can't leave behind when you go home.

Officer

Officers are authority figures, and as such may symbolise either another person in your life or the part of you that is responsible for creating order and discipline. This dream can signal a desire for guidance on your part; alternatively, it can suggest that you feel overregulated.

Ogre

An ogre is an authority figure seen in his or her most negative

O

light as overbearing, threatening or 'monstrous' in some way. If you dream of such a figure it may be a sign that you have a problem with an authority figure in your life—perhaps a parent or boss. The ogre may actually be you, so it may be a good time to reflect on how you are dealing with others.

Oil

Oil is a lubricant, and for this reason its appearance in a dream suggests the desire to smooth things over or make them work more efficiently. The meaning of this symbol depends on the kind of oil that appears in your dream. For example, engine oil suggests efficiency, especially at work, while massage oil may convey the desire to ease your problems away. On the same principle, cooking oil symbolises your wish for things to be easier on your home front.

Ointment

An ointment is a substance you rub on a wound to heal it, protect yourself, or make a problem go away. If you are using ointment in your dream, it pays to ask yourself what problem or emotion you are trying to solve. (A word that sounds rather like 'salve', another traditional name for ointment.) The rubbing action involved in applying ointment also suggests the desire to smooth or rub a problem until it disappears.

Old

Dreaming of something old or ancient often suggests your desire to connect with or re-examine something in your past; whether a person, an emotion or a situation. However, this dream may also be challenging you to think about your attitudes to time, or even death. The old person or object in your dream could be a symbol of your own fear of getting old, or of becoming irrelevant (an 'antique'). Sometimes such a dream is a subconscious message that the dreamer can learn a lot from the past or hasn't yet learnt what lessons the past has to offer.

Olives

An olive branch is a traditional peace offering, the symbolism of which may be reflected in your dream. Perhaps you have decided subconsciously that it is time to resolve a conflict or extend 'an olive branch'. Similarly, the olive's status as a source of valuable oil may make it a symbol of your desire to 'pour oil on troubled waters'. Olives are also associated with a healthy lifestyle. The message within the dream depends on what olives mean to you.

Onion *see* Food

Opal

In traditional gypsy folklore, opals were symbols of deceitfulness and bad luck. This interpretation probably drew on the characteristic colouring of the opal, which is various and can alter depending how the light touches it. A modern interpretation might take the changing colour of the opal as a symbol of emotional highs and lows. If the opal is cracked or flawed in any sense, then it will be associated with some sort of emotional rift or break-up in waking life.

O

Opera

An opera is an extravagant and dramatic spectacle that appeals to all the senses. Are you making a drama out of your own life? Or do you feel like a spectator of the soap opera of other people's lives? Perhaps your emotions are reaching 'operatic proportions' and the dream is your way of expressing them. This dream could be suggesting your desire to 'act out' your feelings more.

Operation

It is common to dream of an operation before going into hospital. In this situation the dream is allowing us to express our anxiety about an upcoming event. But if there is nothing physical to explain the dream, it probably has a symbolic or emotional meaning. Perhaps there is something wrong with your life or even your character that you would like to 'cut out' or have removed. Alternatively, it could be that you or someone around you is persisting in damaging behaviour, and needs to 'cut it out'.

Optometrist/Optician

An optometrist in a dream is often associated with your own need to see things a little more clearly, particularly on an emotional level. If you've been having difficulties with your eyes lately, take the dream literally. You may need glasses.

Oracle

An oracle tells the future, but often in a mysterious or riddling way that can be hard to interpret. A dream with an oracle in it suggests your desire to see what lies ahead of you, or to obtain information about the outcome of an action. But it is also a reminder that because we and others around us are responsible for making our futures, such information is difficult to obtain. Sometimes such a dream is basically telling the dreamer to focus on the present, not the future, in order to achieve present goals.

O

Orange *see* Colour; Fruit

Orchard

An orchard is usually a happy place in dreams, which may convey associations with childhood pleasures, fertility or plenty. Perhaps you are longing to enjoy the 'fruits of your labours'. Alternatively, this dream may be a sign of your desire to leave an urban environment and enjoy a life that is closer to the earth and to natural rhythms and pleasures. More symbolically, the fertility of the orchard may reflect a concern with your own fertility: perhaps you or someone close to you may be thinking of or about to conceive or give birth to a child.

Orchestra

An orchestra represents a large number of individuals working together in a disciplined but also expressive way to create a harmonious outcome. This dream could be a symbol that you are satisfied with your work and fellow employees, especially if you work in a creative or expressive field. Conducting an orchestra in your dream tends to symbolise your attempts to direct your own life. Take note of what the orchestra is playing in your dream. The tune may be associated with a time or event in your life where the notes were first heard.

Ore

O

Ore stands for the dreamer's potential and for his or her talents, skills or creativity, which often lie beneath the surface. As a result this dream suggests the need to 'dig out' and bring to the surface something of value to the dreamer. It indicates that your talents are there, no matter how deeply buried or in need of refining they may be. If you experience this dream, you could be about to enter a more creative or rewarding portion of your life.

Organ

Organ music is associated with churches and religious ceremonies. It may suggest your desire to explore your spiritual or religious impulses, or it may stand for an activity that takes place in a church—such as a baptism, wedding or funeral. The word organ also refers to the different 'organs' of our bodies, such as our sexual organs, kidneys, heart, etc. (*See* Body for their individual meanings.)

Orgy *see also* Sex

An orgy is an occasion for the release of pent-up energy, especially of a sexual nature. This dream could be compensating for an excess of self-control in your waking life. But it can also be about the way you relate to people in a group, especially where issues of inhibition or self-expression are concerned.

Orient

In the West, the Orient is associated with the exotic, with ancient wisdom and mystic tradition. Some dream interpreters go so far as to associate the Orient with the dreamer's unconscious. A dream of the Orient or of an Oriental person may signal your desire to explore any of these areas. Alternatively—especially if a compass is involved—the dream may signal your desire to 're-orient' yourself in a relationship or work situation.

O

Ornament

Ornaments can be both valuable (in the case of jewellery) and inessential (not part of your basic clothing or furniture). The ornament in your dream may stand for some aspect of your life or personality that you don't use much, but which you value nonetheless. Perhaps it is a sign that you need to acknowledge this aspect—to make it more central and less 'ornamental'.

Orphan

Dreaming of an orphan signifies your fears of being abandoned, unloved or rejected. This is a dream that suggests vulnerability and uncertainty about your place in life. It is probably a sign of the dreamer's desire to be loved and accepted. If you dream of adopting or taking care of an orphan, it probably signals your desire to nurture or protect a part of yourself that feels vulnerable or unloved.

Ostrich

Because ostriches are famous for burying their heads in the sand, the appearance of one of these birds in a dream is a sign that you are trying to avoid something by refusing to look at it. Your dream may also be reminding you that this method is not going to solve your problem. As the ostrich is a flightless bird, such a dream can also indicate you are grounded by present circumstances and are unable to see a solution because you're not looking.

Otter *see* Animals

Ouija board *see also* Seance

This device used to be employed by mediums to try and channel messages from the spirit world. As a result dreaming of one symbolises your desire to access your 'other side' or unconscious, and to bring back a message of value. It suggests that you are looking for answers or advice on some issue in your current life. If feelings are negative in such a dream, it's a warning that you're messing with something you know nothing about and you're apprehensive about the consequences in waking life.

Outlaw

The outlaw in your dream probably represents the law-breaker in you—the reckless, rebellious or freedom-loving part of yourself that wants to throw off restrictions, whether they are legal, moral or social. This dream suggests that you want to reach the top, but don't want to go through all the red tape or legalities to get there.

Outside *see* Buildings, parts of

Oven

Ovens are associated with heat, and also with domesticity and the things that sustain us. The oven is also a source of amazing transformation: an appliance that changes unappetising, raw food into something delicious. In this context, the oven in the dream may suggest your own potential for transformation or change. The expression 'a bun in the oven' is used to describe pregnancy, giving the oven the added association with sexual creativity and new life.

Overseas *see* Abroad

Oyster

The oyster's tough shell is associated with things that are difficult to reach or have valuables inside. This aspect of the oyster represents something you greatly value or desire, but that is surrounded by obstacles so that it can be protected against intruders. More positively, the phrase 'the world's your oyster' suggests a more optimistic attitude towards getting what you want from life.

P

Packing

A dream in which you are packing a bag or suitcase can have several meanings. At the most basic level, this activity suggests a desire to put order into your life, perhaps even to perform some kind of stock-take of your 'possessions' or talents. But because packing is something we tend to do before taking a trip, this dream also suggests preparation for the next stage of your life journey. This dream may signal your desire for independence. It may also be prompting you to think about the things that are most necessary to you in life. If you are being forced to pack in a hurry, it suggests that you are not quite ready for change. If you are having trouble fitting everything into your suitcase, you may be having trouble deciding on your priorities. To 'send someone packing' suggests the desire to remove them from our lives, while 'packing one's bags' can be a metaphor for moving on from a bad situation.

Padlock

A padlock suggests the desire to secure something—whether it's a person or an emotion. Perhaps you fear losing touch with a friend or partner, or there is an emotion you don't want to look at too closely. Alternatively, you may feel silenced. If you are opening a padlock in a dream, it suggests that you are trying to get in touch with emotions that may have been 'locked away'. Perhaps you are open to new experiences, or are preparing to 'speak out'. The dreamer definitely needs to unlock the padlock and explore those feelings.

Pain

A dream in which you experience pain may be a sign that you are hurting yourself in some way or that you feel punished by others. If you see someone else in pain, the dream may be forcing you to think about how your actions could be harming them.

Painter/Painting

Dreams involving paintings can have several meanings. On the one hand, painting is associated with self-expression and creativity, so a dream in which you are painting or watching someone else paint may be a reflection of how successfully you express yourself. A painting can also be a subconscious 'picture' of the way things are in your life. If you are painting a room or a house, as in decorating, the dream suggests a desire for change and renewal. The expression 'paint the town red' suggests the desire to celebrate. The colours of the painting in your dream may also be a reflection of your current mood or situation—is your picture predominantly dark, or rosy?

Palace see also Buildings

Dreaming of a palace suggests your desire for advancement, increased prosperity or an improvement in living conditions. If you are comfortable in the palace, it may be a sign that these things are within your grasp. If you feel out of place, however, or the people in your dream are ignoring you, it may be a sign that you lack the means to turn this dream into a reality, or don't feel that you deserve it.

Palm trees

Palm trees are associated with tropical climates, beaches and holiday resorts. This dream could be an indication of your desire to relax and take time out. But if you are trying to climb a palm tree or pick its fruit, the dream suggests that you are striving for something that may be out of reach.

Pan

A saucepan is likely to symbolise either your creative life ('what's cooking') or your domestic situation. If the pan is 'bubbling over', there's a good chance that your creative or home life is also full of energy and ideas. If you can't get the pot to boil, however, some crucial ingredient or motivating force may be missing. We use the expression 'flash in the pan' to describe an inspiration that is unlikely to last. There is also the expression 'out of the pan and into the fire', warning the dreamer to be more cautious in present situations.

Pancakes

Dreaming that you are eating pancakes or watching someone making them suggests a desire for emotional nourishment or fulfilment. It may be a sign that these things are lacking in your current relationship or home life. If you are pouring syrup on the pancakes, it may be a sign that you need more 'sweeteners' or inducements in your life.

P

Pantry

As you might expect, a pantry symbolises the things that nourish you and keep you going. In a dream a pantry is likely to represent the emotional resources that you are able to draw upon, both from within and from those around you. In this context, interpreting the dream requires you to take note of the condition of the pantry: is it well stocked, or are there empty shelves? Because pantries tend to be a feature of old-fashioned kitchens, this dream may also have significance in terms of your childhood. For example, the pantry in your dream may represent the nourishment or basic resources that you received from your parents and family when the foundations of your current life were created. An empty pantry would suggest that they have given all they have to give. It's basically a warning that the dreamer needs to restock resources.

Paper

Paper symbolises communication and self-expression. If the paper in your dream is blank, it may suggest problems in these areas. Similarly, if it is covered in illegible writing, it is likely that you are having trouble either communicating with others, or expressing your own needs. Wrapping paper tends to symbolise the way you present yourself to the world. But if you are having trouble removing the paper, some deeper issue or emotion may be escaping your attention. An alternative meaning is associated with the term 'paper-thin'. This would indicate that the dreamer doesn't feel secure, that things can easily be torn, secrets can readily be discovered and so forth.

Parachute

Parachutes represent protection, especially against falling or failing. Dreaming of one may signal that you are ready to tackle a new challenge or activity, or that you seek greater freedom in your life. If, however, you dream of falling and your parachute refuses to open, the dream symbolises your fear of failing in an important enterprise. Perhaps you are insufficiently prepared, or don't trust those around you to offer support when you need it. The dream may be also be suggesting that you are putting up too many protective mechanisms. Isn't it time to take the jump?

P

Parade

If you dream that you are 'on parade', it could be a sign that you feel anxious about having to present yourself in your best light or take on a public role. It could also suggest that you have been 'parading about': overexposing or boasting about yourself to others. If you are watching a parade from the sidelines, it is possible that you feel shunted to the side or not allowed a big enough role in a current activity or relationship.

Paradise

A dream of paradise is likely to be compensatory; offering us pleasure and consolation when our waking lives are less than perfect. As an ideal image of harmony and plenitude this dream can be a reminder of the goals we are striving for, and a message to not give up on our attempt to achieve them.

Paralysis

Paralysis in a dream is likely to symbolise some situation in our waking lives in which we feel helpless and unable to act. What circumstances in your life are preventing you from functioning as you would like? This dream can also indicate that your vital functions have been blocked or 'paralysed' by emotions such as fear or guilt. Examining the source of these emotions may help you to make them less paralysing.

P

Parasites

Parasites in dreams represent the way we feel about people or things that cling to our emotional lives, drain our energy or confuse us. If, in the course of your dream, the parasite leaves your body, it may be a sign that you are ready to leave these negative emotions behind you. The dream is telling you that if you have people around you who are acting like parasites, it's time to leave them behind.

Parcel

A parcel is a mystery, and can also be a gift. It can stand for some hidden potential within yourself that you have not yet fully explored or 'unwrapped'. Alternatively, the parcel in your dream may symbolise an event or emotion that has taken place, but which you have not yet explored the importance of. Either way, the parcel in your dream is an invitation to unwrap something and see what is inside. If you are sending a parcel it may symbolise that you are trying to offer something of yourself to another.

Parents

Dreaming of your parents usually symbolises your attitudes towards authority. This dream may signal a guilty conscience, or your resentment or acceptance of some authority figure or figures in your life. Because our parents played a crucial role in protecting us when we were children, their appearance may also be a warning that you need to take care in a particular life situation. Your attitude towards the parental figures in your dream, and theirs towards you, will help you to interpret the meaning of the dream. Some dream interpreters believe that parental figures in dreams stand for the 'male' and 'female' parts of ourselves. In this context, the father in our dream traditionally stood for discipline, power or social authority, while mothers represented love, encouragement and the things that nurtured us.

Park

A dream that suggests your desire to escape some confining

situation, to explore the wide open spaces or to enjoy more play in your life.

Parliament

Dreaming of a parliament tends to symbolise the process of decision making. If the different members of the parliament are having trouble agreeing, it's likely that you are also having trouble making up your mind about an issue. To dream about a parliament also symbolises accountability to others. The dreamer is responsible for any decision that he or she makes.

Parrot

Parrots are associated with mimicry. For that reason they can represent anxieties about originality or self-expression. Do you feel as if you are required to 'parrot' somebody else's words or ideas rather than develop your own? If so, this dream could be a message that you need to consider striking out on your own and finding your own voice.

Party

Dreaming of a party is associated with our feelings about the ways that we socially relate to others. It also relates to how we are able to relax and enjoy ourselves. As in waking life, parties in dreams can be a source both of pleasure (if we are 'the life of the party') and anxiety (if we feel uninvolved, ignored or nervous about our social skills). This dream could be helping you to assess the way you feel about being around large groups of people. It could also be enabling you to relieve your fears about demanding social situations. Perhaps it's about time you got out more.

P

Passion

A dream in which you are experiencing intense passion probably points to a lack of it in your waking life. Perhaps you tend to be emotionally inhibited, or your situation isn't giving you many chances to experience passion. This dream could be a sign of your desire for a new relationship, or of the need to renew an existing one. Alternatively, it could reflect the fact that you feel stale and uninspired in a job or project.

Passport

A passport is the proof of your identity. It is also the document that gives you entry into different places. As a result, dreaming of a passport may signal doubts or anxieties about 'who you really are'. It may also represent a desire to travel or to gain entrance to something. This doesn't have to be literal but may represent any aspect of the life journey (such as 'social mobility'), in which case the document in your dream may stand for those things or qualities that offer you a 'passport' to a different or better life.

Path

How does your path in life appear in your dreams? Is it difficult, winding, full of dangers and obstacles? Or is it smooth and well-trodden, shaded by trees, or surrounded by attractive gardens or 'prospects'? These details suggest your current state of mind about your overall progress in life. Are you playing it safe by following in others' footsteps and sticking to a familiar route, or are you prepared to venture into uncharted territory, where the way is less certain but may also be more rewarding?

P

Pawnbroker/Pawnshop

Dreaming of a pawnbroker or pawnshop usually symbolises

anxiety about lack of means. These may not only be financial, but also to do with time or energy. This dream may suggest that you feel obliged to temporarily give up something you value, such as a talent or a hobby, until you find yourself in a situation where you can reclaim it.

Peacock

Peacocks are traditional symbols of vanity, especially of the male variety. Are you trying to impress somebody with your exaggerated behaviour or fine clothes? This dream could signal anxiety about your need for approval and admiration. Alternatively, the peacock in your dream could symbolise someone who is trying to impress you. Your dream may be a sign that you don't entirely trust them, or that you suspect them of too much vanity or self-love.

Pearls

In gypsy dream lore pearls represented tears. For this reason a dream in which they appeared foretold sorrow to the dreamer. Today the expression 'pearls of wisdom' associates pearls with valuable insights.

Pears *see* Fruit

Peas

The ancient Greeks interpreted a dream of peas as an omen of business success. Today the expression 'alike as two peas in a pod' tends to associate this vegetable with things that look alike, or share common characteristics. This dream could be prompting you to think about someone you resemble, such as a family member or close friend. It could also reflect your anxieties about being too conformist, or fears of losing your individuality in a social group or relationship.

P

Pen/Pencil

These implements are used for writing or drawing, so they suggest issues of communication and self-expression. A pen is more likely to symbolise the former and a pencil the latter, although these meanings will depend on your own circumstances. Pencils are also associated with childhood, the period when we first begin to learn how to write and are anxious to prove ourselves. Freud interpreted the pen as a symbol for the male sexual organ. According to this reasoning, if you are a man and you dream either of losing a pen or being unable to write with one, the dream suggests that you are anxious about your potency or ability to perform adequately in a social role or relationship.

Pendulum

Because pendulums are most commonly associated with clocks, dreaming of one probably indicates a concern with time issues. Perhaps you feel as if you are 'marking time', rather than making progress, or you are worried about time running out. But because pendulums swing from one point to another, they are also symbols of ambivalence or of not being able to make up one's mind. In this respect the dream may represent your feeling that you are poised or suspended between one thing and another, unable to decide between the two.

P

People

Sometimes the people in our dreams represent actual people in our waking lives. At other times they stand for something or somebody else: disguised versions of people we do know, or aspects of ourselves. You may be able to 'unmask' the true identity of the figures in your dreams by paying attention to the clues or features that link them to their origins. For example, someone who treats you in a harsh manner in your dream could represent a person in your life who has treated you this way.

In general we tend to dream about the people in our lives for whom we have strong but mixed feelings. The figures in your dreams may also stand for your own thoughts or feelings. In this case their interactions within the dream may be helping you to explore your feelings about a particular issue. If one character in your dream merges into or becomes another, it is likely that they represent aspects of an idea or feeling. When interpreting dreams of people you should try to analyse who or what they stand for in your life. For example, if you dream of an actor, it is likely to reflect your feeling that you or someone close to you is behaving artificially. Are these people drama queens? What are their genuine selves?

Similarly, dreaming of distant relatives such as grandparents may refer to issues belonging to your family background or roots. These figures might also be disguised versions of people closer to you, such as parents. Dreams of authority figures can indicate an issue either with an actual authority figure in your life (at the most basic level, your parents) or with your internal qualities of conscience, sense of responsibility or discipline.

Pepper

P

Dreaming of this pungent spice may suggest that things are about to become livelier ('pep up' your life). But because pepper can make us sneeze, it may also signal irritation with a person or situation.

Perspiration
A dream in which you are perspiring could have a physical

cause—indicating that you are too hot in bed. More symbolically it can suggest that something in your waking life is causing you to perspire—whether it's fear, anxiety or some other form of tension.

Pest

In dreams, as in waking life, pests are things that bother us and won't go away. The person who is pestering you in your dream may stand for an actual person, but could also represent a thought or emotion that has fastened onto you and won't leave you alone. If something or someone is pestering you in your dream, it's worth thinking about the things in your life that exert a negative influence, or the thoughts you are having trouble dismissing.

Pet

Dreams of adopting or looking after a pet symbolise the dreamer's desire to give and to receive love. If a pet is following you around trying to get your attention, it could be a reflection of your awareness that someone around you is vulnerable and needs care. The way you feel about the pet in your dream will reflect your attitude to this person and his or her demand. The pet could also stand for your own vulnerable aspects, in which case it suggests your need to be protected and loved.

P

Petrol

Petrol is the basic fuel we use to 'drive' ourselves from one place to another. If you dream that your petrol tank is empty, it could be a sign that your reserves of energy are low or that you lack the basic motivation to perform a task. If you are filling your tank with petrol, it's a sign of your desire to really 'go places'.

Photo

In dreams, photographs often stand for the dreamer's memories. If you are looking at family photographs, it could be a sign that you need to take stock of the influences of your family environment or childhood. Taking a photo, on the other hand, may signal a desire to reach some insight or realisation about a current situation or emotion. Looking at a photo of yourself, or being photographed, is more likely to reflect your concerns with your self-image. If you are developing photographs in a dream, it is likely that you are trying to shift some perception from your subconscious to your conscious mind.

Piano

A piano is a symbol of creativity, although it suggests that accessing that creativity requires discipline and practice. If the piano won't play in tune, something in your life may be 'off key' or lacking in harmony. In Italian, piano means soft or gentle, so this dream could also be suggesting that you need to tread softly or carefully around a person or issue.

Picnic

The picnic in your dream probably represents your romantic or social life. Is your life like a picnic? When interpreting it you should take note of the circumstances that determine whether or not you are enjoying the experience. These things could include the weather, the company, the food, and the presence or absence of irritating factors such as ants or mosquitoes.

P

Picture

Looking at a picture in a dream symbolises your attempt to examine some issue in your life or aspect of yourself. In this respect the dream is allowing you to take a more objective or detached view on a situation or feeling. Factors such as the colours and patterns in the picture will help you to determine the emotions that are 'colouring' your attitude to what is concerning you. Got the full picture?

Pie

In traditional gypsy interpretation, a dream in which the dreamer was making pies foretold happiness and prosperity. Today we are probably more inclined to interpret this dream as a sign that you want to get at the 'meat' of an issue. If the pie is too hot for you to eat, it probably symbolises your frustration that something is preventing you from getting your teeth stuck into an issue or activity. It also depends on what kind of pie; for instance apple pies are associated with all things good and wholesome. Eating an apple pie might indicate that you are looking for the good in something.

Pigeons *see* Birds

Pigs *see* Animals

Pillar

A pillar or column can symbolise our spinal column or backbone. In this context the condition of the pillar reflects the support available to you, or your ability to remain upright in difficult circumstances. It may even suggest your desire to be a 'pillar' of your community. The other symbolism of the pillar relates it to the male sexual organ, and describes it as representing the driving or forceful aspects of your personality.

Pill

In general, taking a pill is something we associate with

P

duty rather than pleasure. For this reason it tends to stand for something we do because we know it will be good for us, rather than from inclination. This dream may suggest your need to take some action—perhaps suggested or 'prescribed' to you by another—to prevent a situation becoming worse. The phrase 'a bitter pill to swallow' associates the act of taking a pill with coming to terms with an unwelcome realisation. Traditionally, the word 'pill' was also used to describe a worthy, but boring or unimaginative person. Perhaps someone around you is behaving in this way.

Pillow

The pillow symbolises comfort, support and rest. The pillow in your dream may represent your desire for one or all of these things. Alternatively, it may stand for an actual person whom you rely on to support you through difficult times. If you want a pillow but can't find one, the dream suggests that you may be denying yourself basic forms of comfort or support. This dream suggests that you need to take more care of your emotional needs.

Pilot

Dreaming of a pilot suggests either confidence about your direction in life, or an active search for guidance. It can also symbolise the dreamer's desire for protection. Are you looking for a 'safe harbour', or are you concerned about landing safely?

P

Pimple

If you are self-conscious about a pimple in a dream, it's probably a sign that you worry that others will notice the 'blemishes' in your personality. As a result this dream tends to symbolise issues with self-esteem and your concern about the way you appear to those around you. The pimple may also stand for some issue or aspect of your personality that has swelled out of proportion and is threatening to mar your social life. Squeezing a pimple in a dream (something we're all told not to do) may suggest the desire to get rid of some negative emotion.

Pine cone

In gypsy lore dreaming of a pine cone foretold good health. This was probably because the pine cone, with its many seeds, is a traditional symbol of life and abundance.

Pipe

This dream will have different meanings depending on the kind of pipe that appears in it. A water pipe relates to the way you 'channel' your emotions, while a tobacco pipe tends to symbolise your desire for relaxation or escape. A musical pipe suggests your desire for self-expression and, through its association with breath or wind, connection with natural forces. For Freud, the pipe represented the phallus.

Pirate

P

Being captured by pirates usually symbolises feelings of lack of control and vulnerability. For a woman this dream may represent a fear or anxiety about the aggressive behaviour or controlling attitudes of the man or men in her life. On the more positive side, pirates are also associated with adventure and action. If you dream of being a pirate it may suggest that you want a more active role in life, perhaps even one that is outside social conventions or the norms of what is expected of you.

Piston

A piston is a symbol of drive and energy, especially in a sexual context. The way the piston is working in your dream will help you to assess your energy levels in waking life.

Pit

Dreaming of a pit is an obvious reflection of the dreamer's fear of falling or becoming trapped. The expression 'pit of despair' denotes an emotional situation that is very difficult to climb out of. In this respect the dream may symbolise the dreamer's need for outside help and support if he or she is to escape a negative emotional situation. Pits can also symbolise fear of death—not necessarily physical, but the symbolic 'death' of some relationship or phase of your life. A pit also represents the ruts or holes we make in waking life.

Pitchfork

A dream in which you are using a pitchfork suggests your desire to shift obstacles out of your way. It is a dream that symbolises the need for hard work if you are to achieve a desired goal or end.

Pity

If you feel pity in a dream, it may be yourself rather than another who is the object of the emotion. This dream should prompt you to ask why you feel in need of sympathy.

P

Plague

Dreaming of plague suggests that some force or emotion is out of control in your life and threatens to render you helpless. It may also suggest that you feel threatened by some misfortune or by the ill intentions of another. Often a plague suggests that there are negative people or circumstances around you, which are beyond your control. Don't try to change things—just protect yourself.

Plank

A plank is a symbol of support, often something that we use to create a bridge that will carry us from one situation to another. If, however, you are 'walking the plank' in your dream, it suggests that you are about to venture into an emotionally risky situation.

Plants

In general, plants are symbols of life and growth. The plants in your dream may represent emerging aspects of yourself such as talents or enthusiasm. If you dream of withered or dying plants, it suggests either a lack of emotional nourishment, low energy levels, or neglect of a relationship.

Plaster

A plaster ceiling can symbolise your aspirations, or what you look up to in life. Plaster falling on your head suggests insecurity about the things that are 'above you' such as authority figures or future events. A sticking plaster (Band-Aid) symbolises the desire to patch a relationship or emotion, or to protect a vulnerable part of yourself from getting hurt.

P

Platform

Generally, a platform provides us either with a jumping off place to something new, or a chance to look around and view our surroundings from up high. This dream can suggest preparation for a change or a desire to assess your current situation from a more objective point of view.

Because platforms are associated with height, this dream may also suggest your feelings about being promoted or 'elevated' above others around you. Depending on your feelings in the dream, this situation could be a source either of nervousness and anxiety, or of excitement.

Play *see also* Stage

Like pictures, plays usually represent aspects of your life situation, and suggest your need to observe these from a more detached perspective. How you feel about your current situation will be reflected in the kind of play you are watching—for example, is it a comedy, a tragedy or a mixture of genres? The audience reaction to the play will provide a clue as to whether you approve or disapprove of the role you are currently playing.

Ploughing

Because ploughing prepares the ground for sowing seed and makes it more fertile, it is a traditional symbol of sexual intercourse. However, this dream may also represent your desire to bring other things to fruition, like ideas or creative projects. In general, it symbolises the hard work that needs to be done if you are to make something in your life 'grow' and flourish.

Plumbing

If you dream of problems with your plumbing, chances are that there is a 'blockage' somewhere in your emotional life. This dream could be a sign that you are bottling something up; or that the different aspects of your emotional life are not balanced or are out of sync. If you are calling a plumber in your dream, it suggests your desire to solve a problem or remove an obstacle. The expression 'to plumb the depths' suggests going to the heart of a matter, even if it is difficult or unpleasant.

P

Plums *see* Fruit

Plunge

The expression 'about to take the plunge' associates this action with the start of a new project. It also suggests this enterprise or activity (whether it's taking on a new job or asking somebody out on a date) is one that requires courage, and may involve the risk of failure or getting hurt. This dream may be preparing you to take a decisive step towards something new.

Pocket

A pocket is a place we store things to keep them safe, and it is also a hidden place. For these reasons a pocket in your dream can symbolise secrecy: those thoughts and feelings you keep hidden from others, and the possessions you want to keep safe. Pockets are also associated with sexuality, and this meaning could be reflected in your dream. Being 'out of pocket', on the other hand, suggests lack in some area of your life, while 'lining your pockets' indicates that you are seeking to provide for your own advantage, perhaps at the expense of others.

Point/Pointing

If you or someone else is pointing to something in your dream, your subconscious is trying to draw your attention to something you have been ignoring. Expressions such as 'getting to the point' suggest the need to arrive at some meaning or decision. A 'pointed remark' is an insight that can hurt, but that also contains a revealing truth.

Poison

The poison in your dream is likely to stand for a harmful

P

emotion or attitude, whether it originates in yourself, or comes from others. Interpreting the surrounding symbols in your dream will help you to decide what this is, so you can 'neutralise' it.

Poker *see also* Games
The card game of poker is associated with gambling in its aspects of both luck and skill. Perhaps you are about to take a chance on something, or you are thinking about the cards you have been dealt in life. A 'poker face', on the other hand, is one that doesn't give away what the player is thinking or feeling. In this context you should think about whom you are reluctant to share your feelings with.

Pole
The meaning of this dream will depend on the type of pole that appears in your dream, and what it is being used for. Pole vaulting, for instance, suggests the desire to soar over your obstacles, while a flagpole can be a focus for our sense of identity or belonging. In Freudian dream interpretation, the pole is a symbol for male sexuality.

Police
If the police appear in our dreams, we may have subconsciously called them to report a crime against us, to punish someone who has injured us, or to retrieve something that we have lost. More negatively, the police can appear in our dreams in response to our own sense of guilt about having behaved badly or 'broken the law'. Police can be frightening figures who often relate to childhood fears of authority, or suggest that we still carry some unconscious guilt for something that happened in the past.

P

Pomegranate *see* Fruit

Pond/Pool

Ponds tend to symbolise our own need to reflect on or consider our emotional life in a state of tranquillity or calm. However, if the pond is stagnant or filled with weed, our own emotional lives may also have become bogged down in some way. If this is the case, we need to introduce some new element into our lives or find a new emotional outlet that will allow things to flow more freely again.

Popcorn

A dream in which you are eating popcorn may reflect your wish for more excitement in your life. This dream may occur before you are due to attend an event or entertainment.

Poppy *see* Flowers

Post office

This is a dream of communication—probably long distance. Dreaming of a post office could symbolise your desire to get in touch with someone who is far away, either because they are in a different country or city, or because they belong to your past. Alternatively, it could be prompting you to make contact with something or someone that you have pushed away from your conscious mind.

P

Potatoes

The meaning of this dream is probably going to depend on the way you feel about this vegetable. For most of us, however, the potato is a staple food—not glamorous, but nourishing. For this reason it tends to represent a domestic situation that is secure and comfortable, but not necessarily exciting.

Poverty

Dreaming of poverty doesn't necessarily symbolise money worries. It can also suggest that you feel emotionally or spiritually 'impoverished'. Perhaps a relationship is failing to provide you with the emotional sustenance you need. Poverty is more indicative of emotional deprivation in waking life. The dreamer is feeling lonely and perhaps a little bit of a failure. It's a warning that you need to reach out and talk about your feelings.

Prayer *see also* Body, Knees

A dream in which you are praying has several possible meanings. It may signal your desire to overcome uncertainty and find definite answers to a problem. It may also represent your need for guidance on an issue that you are concerned about or a desire for approval from those in positions of authority.

Pregnancy

A dream in which you are pregnant can reflect either your desire for a child or your fear of falling pregnant. If you are actually expecting a child at the time of having the dream, it is probably the way your subconscious expresses and relieves the feelings of anxiety associated with birth and looking after a baby. More symbolically, a dream of pregnancy may symbolise any new project or area of your life that is opening to change or growth. For example, it may suggest that you are about to give birth to a creative project or idea.

P

Present

To dream of being given a gift suggests your openness to what others have to offer. It can also mean that you feel supported or approved of in your waking life. If you are giving a present, the dream suggests your desire to connect with someone around you. The emotions surrounding the dream will indicate how well the dreamer feels that his or her efforts are appreciated.

Priest *see* Abbot; Religion

Prince

A prince is an archetypal symbol for a young man, so the prince in your dream probably represents one of the important males in your life, whether a brother, lover or friend. If you are a male and have this dream, your prince may also symbolise the aspects of yourself that you feel most positive about.

Princess

The princess is the female equivalent of the prince. This figure represents either your own characteristics, or those of a young woman to whom you are close.

Prison *see* also Cell

The prison in your dream may stand for a situation you've created yourself. In this respect you can be both prisoner and jailer. This dream may be prompting you to think about any emotional traps you have created for yourself in your waking life, or patterns of behaviour that are preventing you from moving forward.

P

Prize

Dreaming that you are receiving a prize or watching someone else receive one usually suggests a desire for recognition or rewards. This dream may also indicate an improvement in your well-being or self-esteem.

Promise

A dream in which the making of a promise occurs is probably reminding you of an obligation you may have consciously forgotten—whether you owe something to another, or they are obliged to do something for you.

Propeller

Like engines, propellers stand for our drive, our stamina and the energy with which we make things happen in our life. Propellers are associated with flight, which suggests that our energies in this instance may be required to 'lift' us beyond our present obstacles or situations.

Property

Property stands for our inner resources—the qualities that we have available to help us make the most of ourselves. A dream in which you are selling property suggests your desire to obtain recognition for your achievements, or to market your talents in some way. If you are trying to buy property, it may mean that you are keen to develop your inner resources, or to establish yourself more securely.

Prostitute

A dream with a prostitute in it will mean different things depending on the circumstances of the dream and the dreamer. More symbolically, this dream can suggest that the dreamer—male or female—feels 'prostituted' or used in some way: a dream that probably denotes dissatisfaction in a job or relationship. For men, dreaming of a prostitute can signal a desire for sex or taking what they want in a way that isn't complicated by emotional ties. For a woman, it may signal either a desire to express her sexuality outside traditional moral restrictions and roles, or a desire

P

to gain power or money. It may also indicate some guilt about her sexual desires or the fear that others don't respect her.

Psychologist

If you dream of a psychologist, it's a sign that you feel the need for 'counselling' of some kind. In this respect the psychologist in your dream is most likely to represent your own capacity to interpret your current emotional state and devise strategies for improving it.

Public house

If you dream of being in a bar or a public house, it suggests that you need people around you for socialising. Perhaps you are feeling isolated in your private life and need to make new friends. Generally a dream about this public place is to do with how we relate to group situations.

Puddles

Puddles can symbolise the obstacles that force us to take more roundabout routes towards our goals. Their watery content suggests that these issues are of an emotional nature, and our desire to avoid them can also suggest that we are afraid of involvement. If you are afraid of getting your feet wet, you may be forcing yourself to take a detour so that you won't have to directly face up to or 'wade' into a troubling problem or situation. The muddier the puddle in your dream, the more confused you feel about a certain issue in your waking life.

P

Pulse

Our pulse is a vital sign and symbol of life. For this reason, being aware of your pulse in a dream is likely to reflect an anxiety about death or sickness. If you dream of taking someone else's pulse, it could be a sign that you are worried about losing them.

Pump

Pumps are generally used to channel a resource such as water from its source underground to the surface. Perhaps there is some issue or emotion that you need to bring to the 'surface'. Alternatively, you may have a talent that you are trying to uncover. In this case the action of pumping suggests that achieving this will require some effort.

Pumpkin

This bright orange vegetable is associated with Halloween and with autumn. In your dream it may symbolise the coming to fruition of a plan or idea.

Punishment

If you dream of being punished it is less likely to symbolise the desire of others to punish you, than your own selfcritical or unforgiving attitudes towards yourself. Perhaps you are unable to live up to your own expectations. This dream may relate to a conflict or situation that dates from your childhood, a time when we often feel guilty or responsible for actions that may not be our fault.

Puppet

P

Puppets don't have control over their own movements, so if you dream of one it is a sign that you feel either manipulated, or driven by forces that are beyond your control. By dramatising your feelings of powerlessness, this dream could be trying to tell you to take back control.

Purse

Traditionally, the purse is a symbol of femininity. Thus, if a woman dreams of a purse it may represent her feelings about some aspect of her sexuality. More generally a purse can also stand for the things that are valuable to us, such as money or relationships. Losing or mislaying a purse may suggest a fear of loss in these areas, while the action of putting something in a purse symbolises your desire to protect or secure something.

Pus

This bodily substance is associated with wounds and indicates that infection is present. Therefore, it can symbolise the presence of the negative emotions—such as envy or unhappiness or self-doubt—that infect our thoughts and undermine our self-esteem. However, pus is also associated with healing, so its presence may signal your desire to resist these negative emotions or to recover from a hurt or wound.

Push

This is a dream that symbolises the pressures that surround you. If you dream that someone pushes you, be alert to the circumstances in your waking life in which you feel prodded into action. If you feel resentful towards the person in your dream, it may be a sign that you are reluctant to accept change, or are taking an action unwillingly. If, on the other hand, someone is pushing past you in your dream, the dream may be more about your worries of being left behind.

Puzzle

If you find yourself trying to solve a puzzle in your dream, there's a good chance that something is also 'puzzling' you in waking life. The way you go about solving the puzzle in your dream may give you a clue that helps you to resolve this issue.

Pyramid

Pyramids are associated with death, mysticism and the focusing of mental and spiritual energy. This dream may reflect your thoughts on questions of death and the afterlife. Alternatively, it could indicate your desire to focus on and integrate the different parts of yourself. Pyramids are also associated with preservation. In this case, it may be a subtle warning that the dreamer needs to centre their spiritual and material selves in order to find balance in the waking world.

P

Quagmire

If you dream of a quagmire it is more than likely that you feel seriously 'bogged down'. Perhaps you are stuck in a rut, and need an injection of energy or new ideas to get yourself moving again. This dream could apply to a relationship, an activity or a business.

Quail *see* Birds

Quarantine

A dream in which you are forced to put a pet into quarantine probably suggests your fear that you are unable to take proper care of something or someone in your life. This could be a dependant, such as a child or partner, or a vulnerable part of yourself. Another meaning of quarantine is isolation. Either you feel unable to stay in touch with others, or you fear that they have reason to avoid you.

Quarrel

The quarrel in your dream probably symbolises a conflict within yourself. Perhaps your emotions are pulling you in different directions, or you are having trouble reconciling your head and your heart.

Quarry

Dreaming of a quarry suggests the work that has to be done if you are to access the valuable insights that you hold in your subconscious. Alternatively, the desolate, abandoned appearance of a quarry may suggest that you feel exhausted or overextended: stripped of your resources. In this case the dream suggests that you need time to recover if you are to recoup your vital energies. If the dreamer is working in a stone quarry it can be indicative of feelings that he or she is nothing but a slave to others' needs in waking life. In this case, the message is to be good to yourself.

Quartet

Like most dreams involving music or musicians, this dream symbolises a desire for harmonious relationships and cooperation between individuals. In contrast to an orchestra or band, a quartet usually plays 'chamber music', so this particular collection of musicians may suggest that the dream relates to your private life and intimate relationships. The key symbolic meaning here is logical harmony—a desire for elements in the dreamer's private life to come together in practical and harmonious ways.

Quartz

Dreaming of quartz suggests that a new idea or project may be about to 'crystallise' in your life. More generally, the crystalline structure of quartz may suggest a desire to see through a difficult matter, or to achieve some form of clarity. The association of quartz with crystals may also indicate that the dream relates to healing.

Quay

Quays or docks are strongly associated with meetings or

departures. For this reason dreaming of one is likely to suggest either the process of leaving something behind, or the desire to begin a new phase in your life. The circumstances within the dream will help you make sense of its meaning, while your emotions will reveal your attitude towards this change.

Queen

In some dream interpretations the figure of the queen is regarded as an archetypal symbol of the dreamer's mother. But the public role of a queen also suggests that this dream may be about your desire for public recognition, admiration or respect. Traditionally, dreaming of a queen was believed to foretell success for the dreamer.

Quest

The quest is one of the chief archetypal symbols of the life journey. While a dream quest can take many forms, they all tend to relate to the dreamer's need to progress. In this context the obstacles and difficulties facing you in your dream quest will help you to interpret the fears that hold you back in your waking life.

Question

If you have a dream in which you or someone else is asking a question, it is a sign that your subconscious is trying either to resolve an issue or acquire more information. This dream suggests doubt within some area of the dreamer's life. It may also indicate the desire for self-knowledge. Sometimes our dreams can provide an answer to a problem in our waking lives. Because of this, some dream interpreters recommend that we think about an issue or problem before going to sleep, so that our subconscious is more likely to supply the answer in the form of a dream.

Queue

This is a classic frustration dream, in which your sense of being held back from the things you want to achieve or acquire is symbolised by the everyday experience of being forced to stand in line behind others. Perhaps you long for a promotion at work, but are being forced to 'wait your turn'. You may even feel as if others are being given preferential treatment over you. More positively, this dream may be prompting you to accept a slower pace of progress, on the principle that you will eventually get your chance.

Quicksand

Sinking in quicksand is a typical anxiety dream. The terror we feel when the ground beneath our feet no longer supports us but instead sucks us into its depths, symbolises our fear that the foundations of our life may be similarly overturned, with threatening or painful results. The quicksand may also represent your own self-doubts. Can you remain firm or grounded in the face of your insecurities? If, on the other hand, you feel no fear during this dream, it may be telling you that you have come to terms with your insecurity, and accept the need for change.

Quicksilver

Quicksilver is mercury, and this substance can stand for the dreamer's own shifting or 'mercurial' emotions. Perhaps you or someone close to you is overly temperamental, or can't be relied on to provide emotional stability. This dream could be symbolising a stage of your life where emotional consistency is impractical, and you are being forced to adapt temperamentally to changing conditions. More generally, it may simply represent change or instability in the external circumstances of your life.

Q

Quilt

Dreaming of a quilt represents your desire for emotional warmth, comfort or security. Specific quilts may carry special associations for the dreamer. For instance, if you dream of a quilt that you remember from your childhood (either your own, or one belonging to family members such as parents or grandparents) the dream suggests a desire to recapture the security and love you associate with your childhood. If the quilt in your dream is torn, soiled or on fire, it is a sign that you fear change or loss in your emotional or domestic life.

Quip

A quip is a joking or clever remark, usually uttered 'off the cuff'. A dream in which one occurs can have several meanings. It may indicate that you feel vulnerable to being joked about or becoming a victim of the quick wit or insights of another. However, the quip in your dream may also stand for your own ability to provide insight on your behaviour or social situation. Related to this, the dream could be encouraging you to acknowledge your own quickness of wit or intelligence.

Quiver

Quivering can be a symptom of being cold, and also a response to fear or excitement. In either case, it signals a state of physical or emotional vulnerability. Perhaps some situation in your waking life has left you 'a-quiver'. In this case the dream may be either drawing your attention to your heightened emotions or, if these emotions are something you are attempting to downplay in your waking life, encouraging you to adopt a more emotionally receptive state. A quiver also has significance in archery, as the pouch in which arrows are stored. In this context it stands for our 'armoury' or the resources we have available to help us aim for our goals. If you dream of an archery quiver, take note of how full or empty it is.

Quoits

In the game of quoits, players are required to throw a ring over a peg or pole. It is a game that requires the need for accuracy and the ability to judge distances. Dreaming of it may symbolise the need for similar skills in some situation that is taking place in your waking life. But because quoits is also a game associated with childhood, summer and situations such as luxury cruises, dreaming of it may also signal a desire for relaxation or recreation. Playing a game of quoits generally reflects a need for the dreamer to be accurate in waking life but he or she may also be taking the fun out of life. The subconscious message in this dream is to find fun in whatever you do.

Quotation

A quotation is usually presented within punctuation marks that make it stand out from the rest of the text. For this reason if you dream of uttering or listening to a quotation, it's probably a sign that your subconscious is trying to draw your attention to the words or meaning of the remark. Alternatively, someone close to you may want you to pay attention to something they are saying. A quotation also has another meaning as an estimate of cost. Dreaming of a quote in this context may indicate that you are trying to anticipate the consequences of an action. It may also stand for your efforts to make an assessment of your own talents or skills.

Q

R

Rabbit *see* Animals

Race *see also* Marathon

If you dream of taking part in a race it suggests rivalry or competitiveness. It also points to how you feel about your 'position' in life, either socially or professionally. Ask yourself who you are competing with and why.

Rack

Do you need some order in your life? A dish rack or clothes rack indicates the need to sort out small, domestic issues. To be 'on the rack' is a dream that indicates a guilty conscience. Are you doing something that is harming yourself? Perhaps you are not eating well or exercising as much as you should be.

Radar

A radar represents intuition, so if you dream of it, you are picking up on signals other people are giving out.

Radiance *see also* Light

Brilliance or light in a dream is asking the dreamer to look at something more closely with wisdom and 'clear' thought. Take note of what object the light is focusing on.

Radio

The radio is a symbol of communication, or even 'intu-ition'—that is, your ability to pick up feelings 'in the air'. The radio also represents the voice of authority, so listen carefully to what is being said and see whether it can be applied to some issue in your life. If you are speaking on the radio it indicates a wish to feel valued and 'listened to'.

Raffle *see also* Gambling; Games

If you dream of taking part in a raffle, you probably feel that it's time for luck to come your way. However, like gambling, it still involves a risk. In traditional gypsy folklore, a raffle was regarded as an indication of uncertainty.

Raft

Dreaming of floating on a raft represents temporary safety until rescue is at hand. Water is a symbol of emotion; there-fore, being on a raft at sea highlights your present emotional state—one that is filled with difficulty and uncertainty. The raft will only suffice for a while until you have the means to build a more solid vessel to take you to your destination. If you reach your destination unharmed then you will achieve your goal and overcome your emotional upheaval. If the raft comes apart, it is a warning to be careful and not move on until you have 'mended' the raft.

Railroad *see also* Journey

Generally a railroad or railway represents your life journey or the direction that events in your life are taking you. You may be wondering whether you are on the 'right track'. If there's only one track in your dreams it may indicate that there is only one option in your life or that you are inflexible in your thoughts. If there is more than one track you need to

R

make a decision which way to go. A railway station means that you're about to move into something new in your life and leave the old behind. You may be leaving a relationship or moving into a new environment.

Rain

Traditionally rain was associated with troubled times ahead, depending on the extent of the rain. Sayings such as 'save for a rainy day' and 'it never rains, it pours' reflect these associations. However, today we see rain in a more positive light. It refreshes us in times of drought and releases pent-up emotions that we've held in for too long. This action serves to heal us and make us feel better. Therefore, dreaming of rain could be a sign of your longing for release and new life in a situation that is stagnant at the present time.

Rainbow

A rainbow is a sign of good things to come—usually a change that you've been hoping for. The dream is also pointing out the beauty and value of life, despite difficulties.

Ram *see* Animals

Rape *see also* Sex

Most rape dreams are about power struggles—usually between the male and female parts of ourselves. You may be feeling threatened by your sense of helplessness over some issue. When interpreting this dream, be honest about how you feel about your sense of self. The dream may also be about a violation of space. You may feel that your territory has been 'raped' or that whatever is valuable to you has been forcibly taken away. Take care with contracts and business dealings. Rape dreams can also be a pure sexual fantasy

R

with no deep-seated meaning. If you have this dream, don't be disturbed or think that it means you have a desire either to be raped or rape. Rather, you should regard it as a natural way for the subconscious mind to explore sexuality.

Raspberries *see* Fruit, Berries

Rat *see* Animals

Raven *see* Birds

Reaching out

If you reach out for something or someone in your dream, it suggests your desire to grasp or manipulate something for your own gain. Study carefully what it is that you are reaching for, so that it is clear to you in your waking life. If people are reaching towards you, you may be feeling that there are too many demands on you at the moment. Generally, whether you are reaching out to others or they are reaching out to you, this dream indicates your need for help; either because there are too many demands being made on you, or because you feel shut out or isolated.

Reading *see also* Novel

Reading involves a search for knowledge and information. This may be from an external source such as a book or on a computer screen, but it may also take the form of an internal scanning that helps us to understand ourselves better.

Reaping

R

If you hold to the belief that you 'reap what you sow', this dream is indicating that you need to work hard to get the results you want. On a more negative side, the 'grim reaper' is the image of death that is pictured with a scythe ready to reap in the dead. Don't take it literally. Death in this instance is symbolic of the things in your life that you no longer need but which you still are holding onto.

Recurring dreams *see also* p. 21 (Recurring dreams)

It is common to have recurring dreams: dreams that perhaps start in your early years and then recur at different stages of your life. These dreams are always similar or have familiar outcomes. Unless the dreamer changes his or her method of handling a situation that is obviously causing emotional turmoil in waking life, this dream will continue to recur. Change your attitude, or the way you respond to certain emotional challenges that occur at regular periods in your life, and your recurring dreams will stop or change.

Red *see* Colour

Reflection *see also* Mirror

Seeing a reflection of ourselves represents our self-image. If you catch a glimpse of your reflection and it's not the way you usually see yourself, it could be your subconscious pointing out other ways to see yourself or how others see you.

Refrigerator *see also* Frost

Consider whether you have stored up resentments that have resulted in cooling your emotions (you may appear 'cold-hearted'). Perhaps you have put something in cold storage until you are ready to take it on. Usually, a refrigerator represents self-preservation. When we are hurt, particularly if we are women, we withdraw our warm emotions and give the 'cold shoulder' as a way to protect ourselves from further heartbreak.

R

Refugee

If you dream of being a refugee, it suggests your feelings of being out of your comfort zone (eviction) and an urgent need for acceptance. Do you feel like a stranger in some situation? Perhaps you are trying to adapt in order to survive.

Relatives *see* Family

Religion

Religious symbols and imagery appear in dreams when the dreamer begins to question his or her spirituality, morals, responsibilities or to search for some universal truth. Depending on the culture and religion, each religious image will have a specific symbolic meaning.

Angel Angels represent pure beings, messengers from the spiritual world or our ideals.

Baptism This is a rite of initiation and therefore symbolic of a need to be accepted into the community or group. Baptism can also symbolise a process of cleansing or decontamination.

Bible The Bible is a resource for us to use in times when we need reinforcement of moral codes and standards.

Churches, temples and places of worship These represent a place where we feel at peace—our sanctuary from the outside world.

R

Crucifixion/Cross This represents a giving up or sacrifice for the sake of others' well-being.

Demon/Devil/Satan A devil symbolises evil and temptation, and also suggests suppressed 'bad' feelings and sexual urges.

God A dream of God concerns a higher power that takes care of us. It is usually associated with feeling protected as we acknowledge our human weaknesses.

Nuns, priests and church officials As authorities of the church's teachings, these represent a moral code.

Rent

Dreaming of paying rent represents paying for what we want in waking life. In other words, we pay our dues or our personal responsibilities. Collecting rent, however, is about what we are getting from others.

Reptiles *see also* Animals

Generally reptiles are a symbol of our basic instincts—for example, reproduction, the need for food, flight or fight—all of which are necessary for survival. We connect with the reptile in our dreams through our survival instincts stemming from some ancient parts of our brain. As cold-blooded creatures, reptiles are also associated with emotional coldness. In this respect, the reptile in your dream could represent someone around you who is acting in a cold or calculating way. Alternatively, it could represent these qualities within yourself.

Rescue

R

If you dream of being rescued, you may feel a need to be rescued from 'yourself' or from some situation in which you play the role of victim. This event brings about change of some sort, even if it is just an emotional change in which you feel indebted to your rescuer. Rescuing someone else relates to our desire to do something noble and therefore have some sort of power or recognition. To interpret this dream, look carefully at all the surrounding symbols that occur in it.

Resign

To resign is to give up. Is it because you can't take the pressure or that you choose to seek an alternative lifestyle? Whatever the reason, you need to work through your emotional response to this dream. It may be telling you to try harder and not give up or be reinforcing the view that you have done as much as you can and there's no more to give.

Restaurant

A restaurant or café represents our need for company. We may be searching for emotional satisfaction or need to have an intimate relationship. The association with food suggests the need for emotional nourishment.

Rice *see also* Food

Rice is a symbol of sustenance and abundance. It is thrown at weddings to bring the new couple good luck and fertility. Does rice have a special significance in your life?

Riding

Riding has many connotations depending on the dreamer's use of this word. You may be feeling that you are in 'for a rough ride', or that you need to 'let something ride' for the time being. Search carefully for further clues that will help you to understand this dream.

R

Rifle *see also* Gun; Weapon

A rifle represents protection and because of its long shooting range is more likely to be associated with distant dangers. It may mean that the dreamer is afraid of being attacked from a vulnerable position and needs a sure 'weapon' for self-defence.

Right *see also* Left

The right is our dominant, conscious and moral side. We 'have rights', can be 'the right hand man/woman', or 'start on the right foot'. These all relate to the external parts of our world in which there is action and activity. This is the opposite of the left, which represents our internal self.

Ring

Seeing a ring in our dreams reflects our 'wholeness', and therefore a relationship of some sort. An engagement ring symbolises the state of a present relationship—promise not yet fulfilled. A wedding ring, on the other hand, represents commitment and ownership. A family heirloom symbolises tradition and the influence of the family.

Riot

To dream of witnessing a riot or being part of one denotes uncontrollable emotion in the dreamer. It may symbolise a need to overthrow oppression even if it means breaking laws in order to achieve a worthwhile aim. Consider what is causing you to feel this way in your life.

River *see also* Water

R

The river in our dreams represents the emotions that flow through us. We can go with the flow of the river, which means that we are at ease with ourselves and confident about where life is taking us, or we can drown in it—that is, drown in despair and a sense of being overwhelmed. Think about whether you are just floating along in your life journey, being tossed about or are taking control.

Road

Like a path, a road in your dream describes your direction or approach to something in your life. Dreaming of being at a crossroad represents the choices confronting you. If you see the road behind you, it symbolises your past, whereas the road ahead is your future. An unpaved road is 'off the beaten track' or the 'road less travelled'. This means it could just be sidetracking you from your true path. On the other hand, it may be a difficult road, but in the end more rewarding. A narrow winding road with lots of bumps and holes is a symbol of hardship and difficulties along your way. Change your existing conditions and the road will be easier to travel on. Going the wrong way up a one way street is an anxiety dream. It suggests that you are up against the norms of society. How long can you last without running into some problem?

Robot

In today's age of automation it's not uncommon to dream of robots. A robot is a symbol of efficiency, emotional detachment and control. These may be qualities that you feel are missing from your life and wish to incorporate more into your daily schedule. On the other hand, a robot's job is repetitious and unappealing. Perhaps you feel stagnant and unappreciated either in your job or at home. Consider which of these meanings are closest to your situation. This dream may also be warning you that you are living a 'virtual life', and that you need to reconnect with family and friends.

R

Rock

The rock evokes many images. It conjures up the qualities of strength and reliability (solid as a rock). Are we looking for a more solid foundation in our lives? The dream may be highlighting a need to see the rock within yourself and all the qualities it embodies such as rigidity and coldness, as well as dependability. Are you somebody's 'rock'? Perhaps you need a break from this role.

Rocket

The position and shape of a rocket suggests male energy and sexuality. As such it is regarded as a symbol of power. A rocket also suggests the need to probe. The dreamer may want to access the energy that the rocket represents.

Rocking

Rocking is associated with babies, sleep and comfort. Dreaming of rocking, therefore, is to do with a desire to return to this blissful state. Rocking the boat, however, refers to disturbing the peace or bucking the status quo.

Roller coaster

When we talk of being on a 'roller coaster ride', it refers to extremes in emotions (our highs and lows). Although the roller coaster is found at an 'amusement' park, it is quite a frightening but exhilarating experience to ride on one. Consider whether there is some of this fear/pleasure element in some aspect of your life that you are trying to come to terms with.

R

Romance

Dreaming of romance or the feelings associated with a romantic encounter could be the dreamer's way of expressing an emotional need. Despite the fact that romance is an illusion, we crave the passion and desire it brings out in us. The dream may be suggesting that you are neglecting the romantic part of your nature and that through expressing your needs more clearly you can achieve the buzz created by romance.

Roof

The Himalayas are generally referred to as 'the roof of the world'; that is, the summit or highest point that man can reach. The roof represents the peak or our view from the lofty summits, high up, removed and totally objective. We utilise this objective state of mind to either reach spiritual growth or to protect ourselves against emotional involvement. To dream of being under the roof suggests that you are protected. However, if the roof is leaking watch out for possible dangers. The leak may imply that you are emotionally vulnerable.

Room *see* House; Buildings, parts of

Rooster

A rooster represents virility and self-confidence (cockiness). You may have 'something to crow about' as you tell everyone about your achievement by crowing loudly. The dream may also be suggesting that you need a 'wake-up call'. Take care of your health or listen to any warning that people pass on to you.

Root *see* Tree

R

Rope

The rope is a complex symbol of strength and power that can be used either positively or against us. If you are tied to a rope, it is obvious that something/someone is holding you back. In this situation the rope represents the restraints you encounter in your everyday life. If you are tied up to some object, you need to examine the relationship between you and what you are tied to. For example if you are tied to the kitchen sink, the dream is clearly suggesting that you feel bound by domestic duties.

Traditionally, rope is also associated with the umbilical cord and, therefore, our attachment to a mother or maternal figure. The saying 'give a person enough rope and they will hang themselves' associates rope with being out of our depth. Perhaps you are at risk of getting this way in some project or situation in your waking life.

Rose *see* Flowers

Rowing

If you have no difficulty rowing and the boat is not upset, life ahead is looking positive. If this is not the case, you need to be more organised and coordinated to achieve your goals.

Ruins

If we see ruins it is usually as a result of vandalism or a natural disaster. If it is due to vandalism or carelessness it points to our own destructive urges. How did we create this state? If it is not of our own doing, but we need to pick up the pieces, then we must accept it and move on just as we do with all of nature's disasters.

Running

A running dream usually involves escape from a certain situation or person. Running away symbolises our desire to avoid problems, emotions or sexuality. If you succeed in running away or elude the person chasing you, it indicates that you may be able to change things in your life that have you 'on the run'. If you can't run because you're stuck, paralysed or in slow motion, it is because you are facing a great fear or anxiety. Review all the symbolism in this dream to find out the areas in which you are afraid of not being in control. If you are running towards something, it may represent an object or situation that you wish to reach. At times it could be that you 'run into danger'. When interpreting this dream, pay attention to all the sayings about running.

Rust

Being 'rusty' refers to being out of condition or practice. It can also mean neglect and lack of interest in life generally. Is there something in your life that needs to be polished up? Rust isn't attractive and prevents machinery from working. The dream may be telling you to clean up your act if you want to make any real progress.

R

S

Sabre *see* Weapon

Sack

Dreaming of a sack represents an ending or termination ('getting the sack'). It may also be to do with rest (to 'hit the sack') or sexual advances ('hop into the sack'). One way of interpreting a sack is as an image of the womb. Generally, this dream indicates a withdrawal from external pressures—whether this is from a job or from some other source.

Saddle

If you dream of being in a saddle, it suggests that you are in control of your own life. However, if you are 'saddled down', it means that you feel burdened and pressured. If you are thrown from a saddle, unexpected events will destabilise you and cause you to lose control. This dream is about control and your own sense of authority.

Safe (locker)

A safe filled with valuables suggests security and abundance. If the safe is empty or has been broken into, it may indicate a concern with loss. What is valuable in your life? What do you fear losing?

Sailing

Sailing represents the way we take charge of our life. The meaning of this image will depend on the direction of your goals and how you face life's decisions. Do you 'sail against the wind'? That is, do you fight and struggle to get what you want? Perhaps everything is 'plain sailing', in which case you tend to go with the flow to achieve your aims. Sailing is also about freedom and in this context your dream may be alerting you to your desire to break free from restrictions.

Sailor

The sailor represents ease of movement and our ability to weather the storms of life, particularly those involving emotional turmoil.

Sails

If sailing is about taking charge, sails symbolise the energy and power that move us.

Salad

A craving for a salad in a dream indicates your body's need for the vitamins provided by the variety of ingredients in the salad. Pay attention to the vegetables and their vitamin groups. On a broader level, dreaming of food denotes a desire for nourishment in general. Eat well and be prepared to pamper yourself a little.

Salt

Salt makes a difference to our lives, adding zest to our food and pleasing our palate. It represents the finer qualities that we incorporate into our daily grind. Salt is a staple food, which spices things up but can also be an aggravation (as indicated by the expression 'rubbing salt into a wound'). Salt

S

can symbolise status or goodness, as in the saying 'salt of the earth'. It may represent these qualities either in ourselves or in someone around us.

Sand

Sand is shifting and therefore unstable. Dreaming of sand in this context tends to refer to a lack of security ('a house built on sand'). Are your emotional or financial foundations unstable and liable to shift? Sand in an hourglass represents the passage of time, an image that may be highlighting your need to be more actively involved in shaping your life. Don't 'bury your head in the sand'. Live your life more fully before you become worn out.

Sand dunes

Sand dunes represent your longing for protection and shelter from the elements. If you have this dream you should work out what you need protection from and how you can feel secure.

Satan *see* Religion

Satellite

A satellite is a sign of communication. As a global means of communication it represents the desire to communicate on the most extensive scale. This dream may be suggesting either that you need to get in touch with a deeper or more universal level of yourself, or to reach out to more people.

Saw *see* Tools

Scaffold

A scaffold is a sign of a change that is about to enter your life. Given that a scaffold is a temporary structure, this may only be a temporary or short-term change. However, it will be a change nevertheless.

Scales

In the zodiac, the scales represent the sign of Libra, which symbolises the need for balance and order. Depending on the dream, scales can represent either a person who is a Libran or the dreamer's need to acquire more self-control or to make a decision. Scales also represent justice or fairness of dealings. The dreamer could be weighing up the pros and cons in preparation for making a fair or 'balanced' judgement.

Scar

If you see a scar on yourself or on another person in a dream, it denotes past hurts and injuries. Whatever has happened in the past still pains you today and perhaps this permanent memory has 'scarred you for life'. Try to deal with this emotional hurt so that you can heal and move on.

Scarecrow

A scarecrow is a decoy. Who are you trying to fool and why? Alternatively, there may be someone out there trying to fool you. Be on guard.

School *see also* Education

Dreaming of school, most likely your old school, represents your learning and knowledge. Not only do we gain an education at school, however, but we also learn about group pressure, authority, social acceptance, competitiveness and all those things that shaped us as we were growing up. It is common to dream about school when you are about to

S

undertake a new learning process. If you have this dream ask yourself whether you are preparing to embrace new attitudes, groups or knowledge.

Scissors

Scissors are used for cutting and are associated with sharpness, both concepts that occur in a range of idiomatic expressions. 'Cutting remarks' hurt us, as does a 'sharp tongue'. In a physical sense, this dream may suggest the feeling of being cut off from other people or certain feelings. It may also be telling you to cut out the things from your life that you no longer require.

Scrapbook

A scrapbook contains our most precious memories and mementoes. Usually the contents of the scrapbook are meaningful only to the dreamer. More generally however, this dream can suggest the process of holding onto an old memory. Perhaps it is time to close the book and move on in life on the principle that you can't go back to the past. A scrapbook can also give a distorted picture of the past, as it tends to project only the good. In this context the dream may be a warning that the dreamer is hanging onto the highlights of the past and not facing up to the whole truth of what really took place.

Screw

The word 'screw' has a variety of meanings depending on the context of the dream and the dreamer's culture. It stands for sexual intercourse as well as a prison officer. Having a screw loose or missing a screw means that you do not have full use of your mind or common sense.

S

Scroll

A scroll is an ancient form of knowledge. Dreaming of a scroll indicates that you have tapped into a hidden knowledge—perhaps about yourself or indicating some new insight.

Sculpture

Dreaming of a sculpture means that you are connecting with your artistic side. As a sculpture is permanent and can be viewed from all angles, the dream may be telling you to examine a work from every perspective before deciding how to evaluate it. If the dreamer is creating the sculpture, the dream may symbolise a desire for beauty and perfection.

Sea *see* Ocean; Water

Seal (animal)

Dreaming of a seal symbolises our ability to be in touch with the elements around us, while not straying too far from our safety zone. Like seals, we need rocks (stability) to rest, form relationships and for recreation. This dream may suggest that you feel ambivalent about a new situation that requires you to venture into new waters.

Seal (document)

A seal on a document can represent power, authority and knowledge. If we own the seal in the dream, it means that we are in authority and have control over our destiny. Breaking the seal denotes a breach of trust or confidence.

Séance

To dream of conducting or being part of a séance indicates our need to get in touch either with our intuition or our spiritual side.

S

Searching

Searching for something or someone in a dream is about being on a quest or mission. What is it that you need to find to give your life more meaning? This dream also indicates a loss of some type. Perhaps you are looking for a lost part of yourself, such as your childhood, or you mourn the loss of someone in your life.

Seasons *see also* individual seasons

Seasons represent periods of our lives. Spring represents our childhood years, summer stands for our youth and young adulthood, autumn suggests maturity and middle age and winter symbolises old age and sterility.

Seed

At a basic level, seeds represent human reproduction, referring to the sperm and the egg. Are you hatching a project or idea? This dream is most likely to be about potential, or how the 'seed' of an idea can grow and become a reality.

Selling

If you dream of selling, it suggests that you are trying to use convincing arguments to win your point. What idea or point of view are you trying to 'sell' someone in real life?

Servant

If you are tired of being at someone's beck and call, whether it's that of your boss or your family, chances are that you are feeling like a servant. This dream can also suggest that you are feeling subservient, that is, subject to constant scrutiny and criticism. Think about whether this is an accurate indication of how you are feeling at present.

S

Seven *see* Numbers

Sewing

Sewing a garment represents the creation of a new idea, theory or set of values. Mending a tear is symbolic of healing a relationship or situation.

Sex

Dreams of a sexual nature serve to make us aware of our basic life force and the need to accept our sexual urges and fears. Take note of the setting in which the sexual encounter takes place, as this can indicate your sense of sexual identity. We often play out sexual fantasies in our dreams. These dreams allow us to explore various possibilities and 'what ifs'. If we dream about homosexual activities it doesn't necessarily mean we have these tendencies but it may indicate that we perceive the qualities within such relationships to be either more intimate or sexually arousing than our own. If we dream about having sex with someone famous or even our next door neighbour, it is often some quality in them that we desire rather than actual sex or intimacy with that person.

Explore the nature of the feelings you experience within the dream. If, while dreaming, you feel disturbed or threatened by the events occurring within it, such as rape or sadism, it suggests that you may be feeling exploited, dominated or abused in some sense in your waking life. If this is the case, then the message of the dream is to take control of your life and move away from the negative influences that are affecting you.

A range of sexual behaviours and identities can be explored in dreams about sex. The key to interpreting such

S

dreams lies in examining your personal attitude towards sex and intimacy.

Bisexuality This dream is about balancing the feminine and masculine aspects of our sexual selves. It may indicate an acceptance of both of these aspects in your sexual nature.

Castration This is to do with fear of impotence and lack of authority. We refer to someone as 'having balls' when they are being assertive.

Clothing Clothing worn during sex suggests that the dreamer feels guilty about indulging in a sexual encounter.

Fetish Fetishes are an indication of fear of being intimate.

Hermaphrodite People who possess both male and female sexual organs indicate a concern with balancing the feminine and the masculine parts of our sexuality.

Homosexuality This often occurs in dreams that highlight the need to find someone who is similar to ourselves, not necessarily in terms of gender, but in other ways as well.

Incest Incest may represent our need to express love (rather than sexuality) more openly with family members.

Intercourse Dreams of intercourse are a reflection of our need to communicate on a deeper and more intimate level with someone.

S

Kissing Kissing someone is a seal of affection or stands for the desire to arouse the partner in your dream so that there is greater intimacy between you, whether it's erotic or simply domestic. It is also a symbol that you have accepted something or somebody.

Masturbation This relates to the need to be comforted and to release sexual tension.

Rape Rape in a dream can reflect the dreamer's feelings of being 'violated' whether sexually or not. Most rape dreams are about the balance of power between men and women and the ways in which it is abused.

Sadism This is an escapist dream. If you are put down or are fairly submissive in your waking life, you may find yourself playing out your frustrations in a dream in which you have the power that is missing from your life.

Sexual activity In general, sexual activity indicates a need for the dreamer to express his or her love and need for intimacy.

Shadow

Seeing a shadow in our dream is associated with our shadowy selves; any part of ourselves we don't like or are unable to express in our waking lives. This shadowy part of ourselves remains hidden in our unconscious and only our dreams are able to express it. Normally in our dreams it follows us and we are inseparable. If it takes on an ominous and frightening aspect you should ask yourself whether you are 'afraid of your own shadow'? Delve deeply to find out what it is about your 'shady' nature that you are so afraid of letting out into the light. It may not be as scary as you think.

S

Shampoo *see also* Soap

Dreaming of shampooing your hair is an indication that you need to clear your head in order to make a decision or take decisive action.

Shapes

Geometric shapes appearing in dreams are abstract representations of our inner world.

Circle The circle symbolises the self and personal identity. It may represent a female or, if the object is a ring, symbolise perfection and eternity.

Crescent This represents the feminine and intuitive.

Cross A cross suggests difficulties in aspects of our lives.

Diamond This symbolises direction and choices.

Square A square is a solid shape representing down-to-earth and practical matters.

Star The points of the star are a reflection of your goals and aspirations.

Triangle The nuclear family—mother, father, child—are suggested by a triangle. It is also a symbol of man's three parts—mind, body and soul.

Shark

S

When we talk of someone being a shark, we mean that they are unscrupulous. Sharks are also perfect predators in the sense that they have no natural enemies of their own.

Dreaming of a shark may suggest that you feel unprotected and vulnerable around people or in situations that are out of your league.

Shave

Shaving is an unmasking of our true selves—usually by removing an unwanted veneer or façade. Men do this by daily facial shaves and women by shaving other parts of their bodies. If you dream of having 'a close shave' take care not to take too many risks.

Sheep *see* Animals

Shell

To avoid getting hurt we crawl into our shells—symbolising our tough exterior. A shell is also home for many marine creatures such as turtles, crabs and other shellfish. Dreaming of collecting shells may be indicative of a search for security or protection against contending forces.

Shelter

Like shells, a shelter represents our search for protection. If we dream of sheltering someone, it may mean that we are really trying to protect parts of ourselves from potential hurt and disappointment. Being sheltered by someone else signifies our belief that we are protected by a divine source.

Ship *see* Journey; Boat

Shirt

A shirt or blouse signifies the state of our emotions. One can be a 'stuffed shirt' who is unable to accept new ideas. At the same time, someone can be so generous that they give you

S

'the shirt off their back'. Think about other symbols in the dream such as the colour, texture and condition of the shirt to arrive at a more precise interpretation.

Shoes

New, shiny shoes give us confidence in a job interview or important social occasion. For this reason they are associated with our position in life. Walking without shoes indicates that you are going through a tough time, while taking shoes off signifies that you are leaving the past behind you. Shoes keep us grounded and are a symbol of moving forward as well as a reminder of our need to be sympathetic to others (to 'be in someone else's shoes').

Shoot *see* Gun; Rifle; Weapon

Shopping

Retail therapy is another term for shopping. Looking at shops or purchasing goods represents our desires and needs. These may be for love, sexual fulfilment, wealth or a career. Pay close attention to what type of store you see in the dream. A clothing store has to do with image, whereas gifts are symbolic of talent and potential. A fun or game store could indicate your need to be more laid back and young at heart.

Shovel

A shovel in a dream is used to dig deeper so as to reveal our innermost selves. You may need to dig into past experiences and pull out memories that will serve you at this time.

Shower

Dreaming of being 'showered with compliments' denotes your desire for success and praise. A shower is also hygienic

S

and cleansing, washing away what is not wanted (grime and dirt). You may wish to be cleansed of (to get rid of) something that is no longer a part of you or your belief system.

Shrinking

If you dream of shrinking in size, you are obviously reverting back to a former state—that of childhood. This dream may not be so much about childhood itself as the fears, anxieties and emotions that go hand in hand with that period of your life. You may be feeling insignificant and helpless in a situation. When other things shrink around you on the other hand, it indicates that parts of your life have become less threatening or less important to you.

Sickness *see also* Illness

To be sick highlights that all is not right with you. On a physical level, this dream may suggest that you need to watch your health. On an emotional one, it may signal that you are 'sick and tired' of something or someone in your life. It may be time to let go and be rid of whatever it is that makes you feel this way.

Sieve

The sieve symbolises the sorting out of the good from the bad. This dream suggests that the dreamer has the resources to make the right decisions and needs to trust his or her own gut instinct.

Signature

Dreaming of signing your name on a document is an indication that you are about to or have just made an agreement. The signature also symbolises being recognised for your individuality, or leaving your mark on the world.

S

Silence

Silence in your dream indicates an absence of something and your inability to voice an emotional state. Just as absolute stillness and silence may proceed a storm, silence may represent this state of expectancy and uneasiness.

Silk

Traditionally, ancient cultures regarded silk as a valuable cloth, which only those in high authority were allowed to wear. Today we still associate silk with things that are precious and sensual. Something that is as 'smooth as silk' is very pleasing to us. Think about what things around you are represented by silk and whether the dream is telling you that you need more indulgence in your life.

Silver

Silver represents something of value. We refer to those who lead privileged lives as being 'born with a silver spoon in their mouths'. Silver is also associated with the qualities of the moon. Is there something that's not within your reach at the moment? As a metal, silver is associated with emotions that are pure. To see silver or to wear silver in a dream can also suggest that the dreamer needs to tap into his or her emotional side.

Singing

If you are singing in a dream, you are expressing your innermost self. Usually, this is a release that allows you to feel uplifted and happy. The dream may be highlighting your need to express yourself in a more natural and authentic way.

S

Sinking

Sinking reflects the dreamer's feelings of desperation and

loss of confidence. If you are sinking in water, it suggests that you feel overwhelmed by some emotional issue. You have to decide to 'sink or swim" in this situation. Sinking in sand is associated with feelings of insecurity (a lack of solid ground beneath). This dream could be warning you to beware of sinking funds into some project or scheme. Seeing someone else sink can make us aware of a problem that requires us to take action.

Siren

Like an alarm, a siren is a warning, usually of danger ahead. Sirens (alluring women) were also mythological sea nymphs whose singing lured sailors to their death. As a result, dreaming of a siren represents temptations that will cause upheaval and chaos.

Six *see* Numbers

Size

Size does matter in a dream. It indicates how important you see someone or something as being. If the object is large, the importance it has to you will be correspondingly great. In a relationship, we sometimes feel threatened if the other person has a 'big' reputation. If the object in our dream is small, on the other hand, it probably has little importance to us. However, it may also be an indication that you as the dreamer are vulnerable or 'feeling small'.

Skating *see* Ice

Skeleton

The idea of a skeleton occurs in many idioms. Thus, this

S

dream may indicate the 'bare bones' of an idea or project. A 'skeleton in the closet', on the other hand, represents something about ourselves that we wish to hide—perhaps a secret of some sort. The skeleton also provides us with an image of death. Is there a part of you that has been worn away? Perhaps you've 'killed' off feelings or aspirations that were once your driving force.

Skip

Skipping is a childhood activity associated with that period's state of happiness and innocence. Your dream may be trying to recapture the emotions you felt during these carefree and playful years.

Skull

Dreaming of a skull was once interpreted as a sign of the need for repentance. It was also the Christian symbol of life after death. If you dream of speaking with a skull, you may need to contact people you haven't seen for a while. If a skull is talking to you, it may be the part of yourself that you have 'killed off' or ignored and that is now showing up again.

Sky

We associate the sky with peace (heaven) and limitless expanse. We also see it as a reflection of our moods. If the sky is dark, it indicates our own anxiety, whereas if it's blue and clear, it reflects our sunny disposition. On a psychological level, the sky represents the mind and our potential ('the sky's the limit') and our tendency to dream or fantasise ('a pie in the sky'). A dream in which you are floating in the sky suggests that you are escaping into daydreaming in an attempt to avoid reality.

S

Smell *see also* Odour

A smell can remind us of a particular situation, emotion or person. Smell is the strongest stimulus for recognition—a baby, for example, recognises its mother by the smell of her milk and not by her visual image. Think about what the smell in your dream is associated with. Is the smell of anti-septic disagreeable to you? Perhaps it reminds you of a time when you hurt yourself as a child.

Smoke

If you agree that where there's smoke there's fire, this dream is a warning of danger ahead. Smoke is also a camouflage (smoke screen). Is there a situation in your life that is not as clear as it should be? If you dream that you are smoking, it indicates that you are feeling anxious.

Snail

The latest use for this word is 'snail mail', meaning postal mail, which is slow in comparison to e-mail. However, if you dream of a snail, chances are that you associate it with some aspect of your life that is slow in moving along. On the positive side, the snail leaves a trail and you can follow its progress.

Snake *see* Animals; Reptiles

Snow *see also* Ice

If you are 'snowed under' it means that you are over-whelmed by your present circumstances. Emotionally, snow indicates coldness and in this context the dream may be pointing out the need for you to thaw out a little. Snow is also associated with purity, beauty and a soft texture, while its presence can give a new perspective to something ordi-

S

nary. If you dream of snow sports, you may be longing for relaxation and freedom. Take note of the other symbols in this dream when seeking to discover its significance. Sometimes snow can be associated with romance, so it is important to find the right meaning.

Soap

An obvious interpretation for soap is the need for cleansing or freshening up. 'Cleaning up one's act' or 'coming clean' are phrases we use to describe changing our negative habits and actions. Your dream may be highlighting the need for this cleansing process to occur.

Soldiers

Dreaming of soldiers may express a need for discipline or a concern about a lack of it in your life. On a deeper level it may indicate an inner conflict as the dream highlights the ways in which we are at war with ourselves. If the dream is accompanied by negative emotions, however, it may be indicating that the dreamer's waking life is too regimented and predictable.

Solicitor *see* Lawyer

Space

If you dream of space around you or in a building, this space may represent your untapped potential. The dream may also express your need for space so that you can achieve your goals without being 'cramped' by any external pressures. Dreaming of 'outer space' in the sense of that which lies beyond the earth's atmosphere suggests that that you are searching for greater meaning or something bigger. This dream may be indicating that it's time for you to look for some sort of spiritual connection to provide that meaning.

S

Spear

The spear is a masculine symbol of power. It is associated with the dreamer's own assertiveness and dominance over a situation. Do you need to get straight to the point?

Speed

In dreams there are no limitations on speed, as we are filled with a notion of fast movement and sometimes a lack of control over that movement. This dream may be highlighting the dreamer's real-life feelings of intensity and lack of ability to cope. If you feel exhilarated with the speed in your dream, you may be experiencing the 'high' of the trip, but not necessarily the responsibility that comes with it. Many drivers concentrate on the end result of getting to a destination, but don't accept the consequences of their speed.

Spice

Spice is usually associated with zest and pleasure ('spice of life'). Does your life need spicing up?

Spider *see* Insects

Spirits *see also* Ghosts

Spirits in your dream reflect your fears and anxiety about death. If you see spirits of dead people, you are searching for reassurance. If they are kindly spirits, you will feel more positive about your life or sense that you are being 'looked after'. Spirits are also associated with messages from the 'other side' or with the gaining of an insight. This is a common interpretation in practically all cultures. If the dreamer is looking for an answer to some problem in waking life the message from the spirit world may provide the answer to his or her question.

S

Spittle

Spittle has two possible interpretations—as something we hold in disgust and as a sign of good faith. When people have a verbal agreement, they spit on their palms and shake on it to seal their word. However, we have often seen the use of spittle to express the opposite meaning in movies in which the victim is held down and has no other means of expressing his or her disgust and defiance. When we say 'spit it out' we are talking about getting rid of something— such as a piece of information or unpleasant fact. Perhaps there is something that you need to 'spit' or get out of your system in real life.

Splinter

A splinter is a minor irritation that causes discomfort until it is removed. Words can also be hurtful and cause negativity and pain. Dreaming of having a splinter suggests that you are hurt and irritated by someone's opinion of you. However, if you are labelled as belonging to a splinter group, the dream is showing you that it is fine to break away from the mainstream if that makes you happy.

Sport *see* Race

Spring *see also* Seasons

Spring symbolises new growth and new opportunities. Make the most of them.

Squirrel *see* Animals

Stab *see also* Knife

A dream in which you are stabbed suggests that you are open to or 'wounded' by someone else's remarks or criticism. A 'stab in the back' is a betrayal, whereas a 'stab in the dark' is a wild guess. Generally, this dream indicates decisive action associated with some pain.

Stage *see also* Play

If, as Shakespeare says, 'all the world's a stage' and we are all actors merely playing parts, consider what part you are playing. What type of a performance is it? If you are looking at a stage you are probably looking inside yourself for future direction. Being on stage performing suggests that you have certain expectations of yourself and that you want your talents to be recognised publicly. On the other hand, you may be just going through a 'stage' in your life, in which case this act is only temporary. This dream may also be an indication that if life is just a stage for you, you are going through the motions without a sense of meaning or any real purpose. If this is the case, the dream may be trying to tell you that you need to find some meaning to life.

Stairs *see* Buildings, parts of

Stars

We associate the stars with ambition ('starry-eyed') and destiny ('it's written in the stars'). To look up at the stars is to indulge in wishful thinking. It is no wonder that movie idols and celebrities are referred to as 'stars'. They are so far removed from reality that they are out of our reach. This dream encourages you to focus on what you are wishing for. Your aspirations may not be wishful thinking, but a wish that can come true. Such a dream may indicate that the dreamer is not aiming high enough in real life. Why aim for the moon when you can have the stars? If your goals and ambitions are realistic perhaps you should aim a little higher.

S

Starving

If you dream of starvation it may be a sign that you are ignoring your needs or not taking care of yourself. The starvation in your dream stands for a lack of something that is vital for your life and suggests that your body is being denied necessary nourishment. In medical conditions such as anorexia, the mind prevents the body from feeding itself, by holding onto a distorted image of that body. If you dream of starving, think about what you may be denying yourself, and why. There may be other options than neglect and punishment, which would help you overcome your anxious state.

Statue *see also* Sculpture

When someone is said to be as 'cold as a statue', they are accused of emotional coldness or lack of animation. Seeing a statue in your dream suggests that you are being presented with the unresponsive side of human nature. This may represent parts of yourself or of the people around you. A statue can be a perfect reproduction of a person (as in the case of Michelangelo's David) so perhaps the dream is trying to tell you that no human person is ideal and that no-one should be put on a pedestal. If a figure is being 'shaped' and 'chiselled', it suggests that the dreamer is influenced by someone, such as a parent or other early authority figure. If the statue is distorted or has become tarnished in some way, it may mean that the dreamer's own morals, ideals or idealised persons no longer live up to their faultless image. If someone you know appears as a statue, particularly if that statue is gilded, it may mean that his or her perfect image is just a projection. They are purposely trying to cover up their flaws and can't be trusted.

S

Stealing *see also* Thief

In every culture stealing goods is an offence that results in some form of punishment. If you dream of stealing something, observe carefully what it is that you are taking. If you are 'needy' and are stealing to survive, you may feel justified in this behaviour. If, on the other hand, you are taking something without permission, it may be a sign that you feel undeserving and unloved and that this is the only way of getting what you want. If something has been stolen from you, it's possible that you feel cheated or not respected. You should also consider the expressions, 'steal someone's heart', 'steal the show' or 'steal someone's thunder'. These sayings may hold the key to your dream's message.

Steam

Getting steamed up refers to extreme emotions that are held under pressure. What is making you feel this way and can you see a way to solve this problem? On the positive side, steam is also associated with steam rooms, spas and saunas. In this context the dream may be suggesting that you need to relax.

Steel

Steel is associated with strength, durability and inflexibility. When we say that someone has 'nerves of steel' we mean that he or she is a person of great determination who doesn't let his or her emotions get in the way. Depending on the context of the dream, it may indicate that you wish to possess some steel-like qualities. It could also be showing you parts of your self that are steely or impenetrable.

S

Steeple

A steeple is associated with the mind and with our spirituality.

Steps *see also* Buildings, parts of

To get somewhere 'step by step' is to make progress with effort and consistency. Are the steps hard to reach in your dream? If you are climbing up the steps, it means that you will make steady progress in your present situation. Going down steps symbolises descent into your subconscious. It also represents your past (you've already been up these steps before).

Stiffness

Feeling uneasy and being inflexible are both causes of stiffness. Therefore, to dream of being stiff highlights your feelings of anxiety or tension. It also suggests that these feelings are mainly due to your rigid attitudes and lack of flexibility. You may not be able to move forward unless you adopt a more relaxed approach.

Stomach *see also* Body

If you are 'sick to your stomach' about something, or you 'can't stomach' any more, it indicates that you are no longer willing to cope with an unpleasant situation. If your stomach is swollen, it may suggest that you need to change your dietary habits and adopt a more balanced diet. As with any dreams about the body, you should consider having your health checked for any potential problems in those areas.

Stone

Stone has various emotional associations. To have a heart as 'cold as stone' is to be unfeeling. Being greeted with a 'stony silence' indicates that you are unable to move people. If you have this dream it may suggest that you need to work on the emotional side of your life. If you dream of being turned to

S

stone, it indicates that something that was once alive for you is now a dead memory. In other words, you have hardened yourself against something or someone. On the other hand, to be stoned is to be punished.

Stork *see* Birds

Storm

Storms represent outbursts of emotion, particularly anger. When someone is in a 'stormy relationship' it means that his or her relationship is filled with negative emotional energies. Violent storms suggest violent passions, while the way in which we 'weather the storm' reflects our ability to cope with life's hardships. Storms also clear the air and can give the dreamer a feeling of release after the storm (or argument) has cleared. Generally, a storm is symbolic of any type of conflict, whether it takes place on a personal or emotional level, or in the public arena. The conflict will usually cause emotional stress but once it is released the dreamer will feel calmer as a result.

Strangling

Dreaming of being strangled suggests that you feel stifled. Your emotions and self-expression are probably being suppressed or 'killed off'. Because we are generally conscious while being strangled in a dream, the dream is a wake-up call that is telling the more assertive part of ourselves not to let this activity go on for too long. Normally this dream makes us feel so uncomfortable that we either push away our attacker or wake up.

Straw

Straw is traditionally associated with poverty. Humans are

S

reduced to a minimal level of survival when they need to use straw for warmth and bedding. In modern times, straw implies that something lacks stability or permanence. You need to work out what is permanent in your life and make it work for you.

Strawberries *see* Fruit

Stream *see* River

String

Do you hold the 'purse strings' in your family? Are you holding onto the 'apron strings'? Perhaps you are 'stringing someone along'? Like these sayings, your dream can have a variety of meanings. String not only holds things together (whether a relationship or a business), but is also a metaphor for controlling the family finances, connecting with others and not being fully honest.

Study

To study is to focus on a certain subject with the aim of expanding your knowledge. Pay attention to what you are studying in your dream. The dream may be suggesting that you need to acquire a more in-depth understanding of an issue before you go ahead with a plan of action. If you have always longed to go back to study, this dream may be encouraging you to follow your desire (on the principle that it's never too late to learn).

Submarine

A submarine is a more positive dream image than any other sea-going vessel. That is because it represents our ability to delve deeply into our subconscious while also functioning in the real world. Moreover, because the dreamer has the

S

protection of the submarine, he or she will feel safe about delving more deeply into the subconscious mind.

Success

Dreaming of success is usually wishful thinking. It is a compensatory dream in which we try to make up for our feelings of failure and lack of importance in waking life.

Sucking

Sucking suggests a draining of resources, either emotionally or physically. We normally associate sucking with babyhood and our dependence on our mothers for nourishment. As a result, a dream of sucking can suggest either emotional hunger or the feeling that one's energy is being drained. 'Sucking up' to someone, on the other hand, implies being dishonest in your feelings towards a person for your advantage—usually in a business context. When we label someone a 'bloodsucker' we mean that the person is parasitic—that is, that they feed off others for free. Your dream could relate to any of these meanings, so it is up to you as an individual to work out what is happening in your waking life to cause this dream.

Suffocating

Suffocating in a dream is an indication that we feel overwhelmed by external forces. As a result, this dream makes us aware of our lack of control in our environment. If someone is suffocating us, it suggests that we are being emotionally pressured by their demands, and this may include an overdose of love and possessiveness. Because suffocating implies an absence of oxygen, this dream may also indicate that we feel restricted and unable to 'live' our own lives. If you are feeling pressured and life is no longer fun, think why you are experiencing this dream. You may also want to

S

get your health checked, as the dream could be alerting you to a physical problem.

Sugar

As sugar is both pleasurable to our palate and a cause of tooth decay, interpreting its symbolic meaning requires you to understand its dual nature ('sickly sweet'). Sweets suggest rewards, while to be 'sweet on someone' is to have romantic feelings towards them. Is your life lacking in 'sweetness and light'? If so, inject some pleasure into it and treat yourself to some sweet outcomes. Putting sugar on something bitter can also make it easier to swallow. To dream of sugar can be an indication that something in your life is not pleasing to your palate—in other words, that it is not good.

Suicide

Is something in your life ending abruptly? (This may be a relationship or a work-related issue.) Dreaming of suicide generally reflects the anger we feel towards ourselves. What parts of yourself are you trying to destroy? Perhaps you feel that you have little to live for in your life and that you and everyone else would be better off without you. In this case, the dream is an emotional plea from your subconscious to acknowledge that you can no longer cope with a situation on your own. If you see someone else committing suicide it could be that you wish this person would disappear from your life. Sometimes, however, the person in your dream can represent a quality in yourself that you wish were destroyed.

Suitcase *see also* Bag/Basket; Luggage

A suitcase is a symbol of travel and adventure. Wherever we

go we take parts of ourselves with us, and these things are the contents of the suitcase. Fears, insecurities, longings, ambitions, values and social status are just some of what may be in your suitcase. As a result, dreaming of a suitcase can represent either your need for independence, or your need to let go of some of the contents in your 'suitcase' (your 'emotional baggage') before venturing forward on the next phase of your life.

Summer *see also* Seasons

Summer represents pleasure, warmth and fertility. It is a positive time of your life in which the sun is shining down on you, so go ahead with your plans.

Sun

Traditionally, to dream of the sun was associated with achieving success. Today we tend to interpret the sun as representing our intellect and awareness of what is going on around us. It is also an image of vitality, warmth and creative energy. Being in the sunlight arouses feelings of well-being and relaxation.

Sunrise

Sunrise implies new beginnings, youth, hope and new realisations. We also describe a new awareness as something 'dawning on us'.

Sunset

Sunset is the opposite of sunrise. It represents an ending of the creative energy we had in our youth and, as a result, is associated with old age. To dream of a sunset denotes a need for closure in some aspect of your life. On the positive side, the ending of something can also be a release.

S

Surgery

Dreaming of undergoing surgery suggests that you feel as if some aspect of your individuality—whether it's your way of life, values or ideals—is being interfered with. If you are due for surgery, this dream may be an anxiety dream that reflects your fears of the procedure. If not, you should still take note of what part of the body the surgery was performed on and the subsequent result. Generally, if the surgery was associated with the heart, it's an emotional issue that is troubling you, whereas if the surgery was on a limb it may indicate your inability for flexible movement. As with all dreams relating to health, consider getting a medical check-up. Your dream may be prophetic or a reflection of something that the subconscious has picked up on but that your consciousness hasn't yet acknowledged.

Surroundings

Surroundings in dreams are important indicators of our feelings and attitudes. If you are in a dreary setting, it probably reflects your feelings of depression, while bright and airy places suggest contentment and security. Chill surroundings tend to represent emotional coldness while a warm and relaxed environment indicates that the dreamer feels safe and sheltered. See the entries on individual settings and climates for more specific examples.

Swallowing

In a dream context swallowing suggests the holding back of emotions. We refer to 'swallowing our pride' or finding something 'difficult to swallow'. As swallowing is a natural function such as breathing, for it to be highlighted in your dream normally suggests some sort of blockage. What is it that you can't swallow?

S

Swamp

If we are feeling swamped, it means that we have no control over our feelings. To dream of a swamp indicates a need for more control in your life so that confidence can be restored. Swamps are also thought of as dank, mysterious and dangerous places. How does this environment reflect your current life? Are you surrounded by swamp life?

Sweeping

When we dream of sweeping, it suggests that we are clearing away attitudes and ideas that we no longer hold to. Consider these idioms—'making a clean sweep', 'sweep someone off their feet' and 'sweeping something under the carpet'. Which of these sayings best reflects your present situation?

Sweets *see* Sugar

Swimming *see also* Water

Swimming upstream with your head above water denotes success and confidence. Personal survival is important to you and swimming to your destination means that you will achieve your goals. Swimming against the tide indicates that you will meet with an opposing force or move against the general consensus. Swimming with others suggests that you have things in common with others—you are all swimming in the same pond. It indicates that you feel accepted at a social level. Swimming underwater suggest going deep within yourself over some issue, particularly an emotional one, in order to see the whole picture. Diving into water stands for 'taking a plunge' or a risk. Clear water indicates that you are feeling positive, while muddy water could be a reflection of your gloomy state of mind. Again, this type of

S

dream depends largely on the feelings you experience while dreaming. If you are swimming underwater, for example, and feel as if it is a struggle or even scary, then you are not ready to face the deep emotional issues surrounding you.

Swimming pool

A swimming pool represents our innermost thoughts and feelings. These feelings are more contained than those represented in dreams of a lake or the sea.

Swing/Swinging *see also* Rocking

The backwards and forwards motion of swinging reminds us of the cradle and the motions of the swings of childhood. Dreaming of swinging indicates a desire to go back to the carefree feelings of childhood when swinging allowed us to be playful and relaxed. 'Going with the swing' and 'getting into the swing of things' are sayings that highlight the need to let go of adult limitations. This dream may be showing you that the best way to be at ease is to adopt this childlike attitude.

Sword *see also* Weapon

Dreaming of a sword represents our sense of courage and strength. If we take up the sword and fight, it symbolises our desire to fight for what we believe is right. The dream may bring out the warrior in us, whereas in waking life we may not be willing to actively pursue justice and retribution. A sword is also associated with power or authority. The sword has a double edge to remind us that power can either be used as a positive or negative force in our lives.

S

Syringe *see* Injection

T

Table *see also* Furniture

A table is a symbol of social interaction. We eat at the table, either at home or at a restaurant, and at the same time gather around it to socialise with family, friends and colleagues. Dreaming of a table, therefore, is about order, ritual, communal activities and your place in society. Take note of where you are sitting at the table. If you are at the head of the table, this is a positive reflection of your self-image and status. Being at the far end of the table, away from familiar people, indicates that you need to polish up your communication skills.

If the table is bare, you may not be giving much of yourself or you may be lacking in resources, either emotionally or financially. A sumptuous table filled with food implies generosity and prosperity. A table is also a place where decision making takes place and if this applies to you, whether in the meeting room at work or in your home, the dream may be highlighting your anxiety about a decision you need to make. Setting or 'dressing' a table suggests that you are trying to make a good impression. The more elaborate the table, the more anxious you are to promote a successful social image.

Tablet *see* Pill

Tacks

In a dream, tacks represent the many small aggravations and problems in your life. Like pins and needles, tacks are symbolic of the things that annoy us and cause us irritation.

Tadpole

A tadpole denotes new life, and the appearance of one in a dream indicates that a new phase is beginning in your life. This may be a new project, attitude, relationship or lifestyle that has not yet taken shape but is still forming in your mind.

Tail

Dreaming of a tail, either on a person, animal or yourself implies a concern with the things that you carry with you from your past experiences. You may be at the 'tail end' of a stage in your life. Think about the general meaning a tail has for you, and apply this meaning to your dream.

Talisman

A lucky charm is a less serious version of a talisman, yet is used to achieve the same result—protection of the wearer against bad luck. A dream involving a charm or talisman points to a lack of self-confidence in the dreamer and his or her need for external assurance. If you have this dream think about what may be making you feel inadequate and do whatever it takes to make you feel in control.

Talking *see also* Language

Generally, dreaming of talking denotes the dreamer's ability to communicate with others. Most of us dream of being unable to talk or not being understood by others. If you have difficulty speaking in your dream, it is an indication that you have built up emotions that you find difficult

T

to express in speech. Speaking without being understood is frustrating both in dreams and real life. Sometimes the only sounds coming from the dreamer are babble. Do you have a communication problem? Are you frustrated that people aren't listening to you? Perhaps this dream is telling you to employ a new communication strategy. The dream may also indicate that you feel emotionally cut off from people around you.

Tame

To dream of taming a wild animal symbolises the need for more restraint in our lives. Our animal self can get out of hand, craving excitement and recklessness. Sometimes self-discipline and self-control are better in the long run, even if they do appear to be dull and predictable. However, if a negative feeling accompanies this dream, it may mean that the dreamer needs to break loose a little.

Tan

If you dream of acquiring a stunning tan despite your natural colour, it may be a sign that you are changing yourself in obedience to fashion trends. This implies a degree of vanity as well as a need for approval from others. Focus on why image is so important to you and why you need to 'show' your eagerness to be accepted through the colour of your skin.

Tangled

Being tangled in a dream indicates confusion. Possibly one object is tangled with another and you need to untangle it before you can make use of it. Take note of how you eventually get the object untangled, as this will show you how well you will succeed in undoing a difficult situation in real

T

life. Tangled hair is a symbol of the image you portray to others. If ties are being tangled in your dream, the dream is about relationship ties and the difficulties you may be facing in this area of your life.

Tank (war)

To dream of a war tank denotes a need to defend yourself from a position of safety, represented by armour. If you have this dream you should ask yourself whether you feel threatened at the moment and why you need to employ such drastic measures to fight for your beliefs.

Tank (water)

A water tank in a dream is a symbol of the dreamer's desire to get in touch with his or her emotional self. If the tank is full it indicates good times ahead. If on the other hand it is empty or leaking, you can expect to experience loss or to need help from outside sources.

Tap

Dreaming of a tap has connotations of turning our emotions on and off. How we do this usually depends on whether our needs are being met. An inability to turn off a tap indicates that we lack control over the things we take for granted as belonging to us. 'Tapping into' something suggests that you are gaining a new understanding, while tapping on a door means that you need to pay attention to some aspect of your life.

Tape

If you dream of taping together something that is broken, it implies that you will be required to mend a friendship or a relationship. Dreaming of a tape measure suggests our need

T

to perform. How do we measure up to others or our own expectations? A recording tape is associated with self-expression and communication, while red tape symbolises bureaucratic issues.

Tapestry *see also* Weaving

A rich tapestry represents the tapestry of life—that is our history and our experiences. To be weaving a tapestry is a symbol that you have control over your life's direction. If the tapestry is complex and full of detail it is indicative of the way in which the dreamer conducts his or her life. The message here is of the need to find balance in life and to take control of its direction (symbolised by the tapestry's pattern and the way it takes shape). Examine the tapestry in the dream carefully and try to interpret all the surrounding symbols in it so that you can gain a fuller understanding of the message of your dream.

Tar

Dreaming of road tar indicates movement or travel. If the tar is fresh and sticky, you may be feeling stuck and unable to move on to your journey. Tar can also be repaired, so despite its black colour, its appearance in a dream can be a positive sign that all is not lost.

Target

If we dream of a target, it shows that we are 'on the mark' as far as achieving our goal is concerned. To be taking aim at someone else (in other words, using them as a target) may be a sign that you dislike them. Alternatively, they may reflect parts of yourself that you have trouble accepting. If you are the target, it suggests your awareness of being singled out or victimised in your waking life.

T

Tattoo

A tattoo represents individuality, identity, adornment or the desire to make a statement through artistic expression. If you can see the tattoo in the dream, regardless of whether it is on your body or someone else's, it probably holds a special significance for you. Initials, shapes, words, patterns or animals all represent things that you may want to incorporate in your life. As a tattoo is permanent, it may be a reminder of a past experience, memory or relationship which may have been painful to the dreamer.

Tax

Taxes are associated with paying one's dues. Most of us regard taxes as a penalty fee for our standard of living or chosen lifestyles. Dreaming of a tax can suggest that you are feeling 'taxed' and unwilling to give a great deal of yourself to others. Perhaps you feel as if you are already giving enough and don't need to hand out more of your emotions and time.

Taxi *see also* Cab

A taxi represents the help that you receive but have to pay for. Because a taxi is a means of transport, dreaming of being in one indicates that you are going places or being taken somewhere. Just be careful that you aren't being taken for a ride.

Tea

A dream in which you are sipping tea symbolises your ability to socialise. It is also a symbol of time out, in which the people and things around you uplift you. Do you need to include more relaxation and good conversation in your life?

T

Teacher

If you dream of a teacher who taught you in your school years, it may mean that something has resurfaced around the experience. Usually teachers are authority figures whom we are taught to respect. Did you clash with the teacher? Were your individuality and creativity repressed? Did the teacher embarrass you or expect you not to perform? These same fears may be revisiting you at a stage in your life when you are vulnerable and feeling more like a student than an authority figure. On the positive side, dreaming of being a teacher or being taught could be a sign that you are looking for more sophisticated knowledge and guidance on some issue.

Tears

Have you ever woken up from a dream in tears? If you have, it suggests that some hurt has been brought to the conscious level while you've been asleep. For this to happen, the hurt or strong emotion must have been quite intense. Often we cry in dreams because of our tendency to cover up our real feelings in our daily life.

Teeth *see also* Body

Dreaming of teeth is a very common dream. Teeth represent our 'bite' or our aggressive nature. When we can't get our teeth into something, it suggests that we have little control. If you dream of losing your teeth, it has to do with 'loss' in general such as loss of youth and all things associated with our anxiety of getting older. A rotten tooth is a symbol of our painful feelings that keep 'aching' until we find relief. Could it be that your relationship or 'bond' with someone is hurting? Perhaps you've said hurtful words that you now regret? Bleeding gums indicate a loss of blood (loss of life force) through lack of support from those around you. False

T

teeth clearly indicate fear of losing one's sense of true self; that is, of honesty and integrity. Look at all the images in the dream, such as grinding teeth or teething troubles, to determine the correct meaning.

Telephone

We tell people to 'stay in touch' and 'keep in contact' and the most efficient and accessible way for most people to do this is by telephone. A dream in which you are calling someone up or answering the phone reflects your need to communicate and connect with others. Sometimes it can symbolise your desire to get in touch with various aspects of yourself. If you don't answer the phone in your dream it suggests that you may not want to hear something. Is someone trying to get through to you? Calling an emergency number indicates that you need assistance with an emotional issue that is causing you stress or has placed you in a dilemma. If you recognise the number that you are calling, you may need to contact that person. Perhaps he or she has been on your mind during your waking hours. Being unable to get through, either because the telephone line is out of order or the number is busy, indicates your frustration with not being able to get your message across to someone.

Telescope

If you are using a telescope in a dream, it means that you are taking a closer look at something. Because a telescope enlarges and enhances the object, this dream can also be a warning not to make something bigger than it is.

Television

Dreaming of watching television reflects a desire for escapism and distraction from your present situation. If you

T

are watching the news, listen carefully to what is being broadcast. It may have a specific meaning for you.

Temple *see* Religion

Tennis *see* Games

Tent

Seeing a tent in your dream signals your need to find a simpler way of life and escape the hustle and bustle— perhaps by camping out in a natural environment or the great outdoors. A tent symbolises your desire for a nomadic existence; that is, your reluctance to put down roots in one place. You may prefer to wander for a while and to enjoy your freedom from responsibilities that tie you down.

Tests *see also* Exams

If you dream of going for a medical test, the dream reflects a concern about your health. Have it checked out, just in case. Dreaming of tests in general denotes an awareness of being judged by others. Tests represent a competition of abilities in which we are always measuring ourselves against others. A driving test is to do with issues of competence and skill. Any type of written test relates to problems with knowledge and problem solving. It may be that you are anxious about performing and that this anxiety or self-criticism is revealing itself in your sleep.

Thaw

To dream of a thaw is to be aware that our feelings and responses have changed. When our emotions thaw we become warmer and more loving. This dream indicates a desire to 'thaw' some emotional coldness that has been with

T

us for a while. If you have this dream you should work out what it is that you want to 'melt away'. You may also need to consider whether there is someone you wish to forgive.

Theatre *see* Play; Stage

Thermometer

Usually, dreaming of a medical thermometer reflects the dreamer's concern over health matters. Check it out with your doctor. On another level this dream may indicate your emotional levels—hot, indifferent or cold.

Thief *see also* Stealing

Thieving has to do with loss of property, whether of possessions or loved ones. The figure of a thief usually stands for the fear that something is being taken away from you. Thus, people speak of the death of loved ones in terms of their being 'snatched away'. One's heart can also be stolen and the thief may even be the part of ourselves that has stolen our youth, exuberance or beliefs.

Thirst *see also* Drink

If we need to satisfy a thirst it means that we have a desire to satisfy our basic needs. Normally, these are spiritual and emotional needs which, if unsatisfied, will lead to us 'wasting away' in some way. To apply this dream to your everyday life, think about whether you are refusing to satisfy some inner need and how you can be kinder to yourself.

Thorn

A thorn indicates some form of physical suffering. Christ was made to wear a crown of thorns, making thorns the symbol of the Passion. If someone is 'a thorn', it suggests that they

T

are causing you some grief or discomfort. Pricking your finger on a thorny plant, such as a rosebush, means that you are vulnerable and that your defences can be penetrated.

Three *see* Numbers

Threshold

If you are carried over the threshold in a dream, it signals the beginning of a new relationship. In general, the presence in a dream of a threshold indicates new responsibilities in the near future.

Throat *see* Body

Throne

A throne represents absolute power and authority. If you dream that you are sitting on a throne, the dream suggests your right to exercise this power and authority. However, if someone else is on the throne, it is likely that you consider someone else to be more worthy of that position. An empty throne implies that you are not ready to accept a position of responsibility. This may be a position at work or a promotion that you feel inadequately qualified to apply for.

Thunder *see also* Storm

Hearing thunder in the distance provides warning that a storm is about to hit. The storm in the dream usually represents repressed emotions and unleashing it may actually be a relief. Be careful of emotional outbursts and give yourself time to become composed before responding to a situation.

Ticket

A ticket represents the price you pay to get somewhere or to

T

achieve your goals. If you dream of holding a ticket it probably symbolises admission to something. For example, it may represent your desire to be admitted into a new social or professional scene.

Tide *see also* Ocean; Water

The tide in our dreams stands for our need to embrace the 'ebb and flow' of life. In other words the dreamer has to let go of things that cannot be controlled. If you're a control freak, the dream is telling you 'go with the flow'.

Tiger *see* Animals

Timber *see* Wood

Time

Time has no sequence in dreams. It is fluid and can jump from one time zone into another at will. In general, being aware of time in a dream symbolises our age and the passage of time.

Morning This time represents our childhood years, when we are still learning.

Midday Midday suggests our mid-life when we are productive and accumulate wealth.

Afternoon and evening These times stand for old age.

Night Night has various meanings. It may symbolise what is unknown and has not happened yet (the future) or the time when we experienced our darkest fears.

T

Toilet

Dreaming of a toilet is associated with the relieving of physical discomfort in private. In dreams, the room itself reflects the dreamer's need for privacy, in order to release personal feelings and emotions without anyone observing. Dreaming of going to the toilet suggests that you need to flush away what is no longer important to you. If the toilet is blocked it probably means that your emotions are blocked too.

Tomato *see also* Food; Fruit

A tomato represents sexuality and passion. Observe the reaction you have to eating the tomato in your dream. It may actually have something to do with food rather than senses of a sexual nature.

Tomb *see also* Grave

A tomb is a final resting place, so entering one is an exploration of how we feel about death. This may not be an actual death, but an ending of some phase of your life. If there are bodies in the tomb, these may indicate aspects of yourself that you have put to rest. For example, they could be the ambition you gave up on or a world trip you denied yourself because of family responsibilities. In general, anything related to death signifies a renewal or awakening of some sort. As a consequence, this dream is actually related to rebirth and new life.

Tongue *see* Body

Tools

The male organ is often described as a 'tool'. If the tool in your dream is used as a weapon, it may represent sexual violence. Generally, tools appear in our dreams to remind us

T

of resources we have to help us keep things in order. If things in the dream are not in order and you are 'fixing' various items, take a closer look at what is broken and the tool you are using. A hammer, for example, may be telling you to 'hammer home a point'.

Tornado/Cyclone *see also* Storm
To dream of being caught in a tornado indicates that you are struggling against an emotional issue you feel helpless to solve. Just like a tornado, the issue has swept you up and flung you where you don't want to be. This dream can also mean that communications with others in waking life have become unproductive and that the dreamer, instead of really resolving issues, is simply going around in circles.

Torpedo
Like a rocket, a torpedo bears a physical resemblance to the male organ and, as a result, suggests sexual drive. As a weapon, the torpedo suggests how the sexual drive can lead to excessive aggression if not directed in a responsible way.

Tortoise *see* Animals

Torture
If you see someone being tortured in a dream, chances are that the tortures represent past hurts and disappointments, usually emotional ones. Dreaming of being tortured suggests that you are trying to come to some understanding about personal injury—whether it is pride or abandonment—that you haven't yet been able to forgive or forget.

T

Touch

Touch is a means of communication. In the physical arena touch communicates love, tenderness, intimacy or simply contact. This dream may indicate that you are searching for more physical contact. Alternatively, it may be encouraging you to acknowledge that you need others around you to offer support, particularly at times when you feel alienated.

Tourist

To be a tourist in a dream is to see things from an outsider's point of view, or with a fresh perspective. It may also indicate that the dreamer feels unfamiliar with his or her new surroundings. If you are helping a tourist in the dream, it suggests that you will need to explain yourself more clearly and be of greater help to others in your working environment.

Tower *see also* Building

Calling someone 'a tower of strength' implies that they can be of great support during a crisis. To live 'in an ivory tower' on the other hand, is to be removed from the world and immersed in your personal space. Whichever of these two expressions best reflects the meaning of your dream will depend on how you see your role in life. Either way, the tower stands for the things that you have created in your life. Are you a helper of others or do you stand back and not get involved?

In real life, towers can sometimes be built with shoddy materials and symbolise a lack of safety, particularly in the area of building relationships. So, if the feelings accompanying this dream are negative, it may be a sign that you need to tear down the tower and rebuild it on a more positive

T

foundation. At its most extreme, the dream may be telling you that you need to change your attitude towards life.

Town

Towns are places where there is a strong sense of community and a great deal of social interaction going on. Dreaming of your hometown suggests that you feel comfortable with doing things the way you have been since childhood. On the other hand, if you see yourself in a strange town, it may mean that you don't yet feel comfortable in a new environment. The new town may also stand for a side of yourself that you haven't accepted yet. Deserted towns represent past social contacts or values that are no longer of use to you ('ghost towns'). If you are lost in a strange town, it may mean that you are looking for a new direction in life. This dream suggests that you may be forced to rely on the advice and kindness of strangers in order to find your way.

Toy

Toys are associated with childhood and 'childishness'. Do you need to take things more seriously? This dream may also mean that you are 'toying' with people's emotions and need to think carefully about your actions. On the positive side, playing with toys can suggest that you are eager to explore your creative side and that the 'child within' is ready to come out and play.

Track *see* Path

Train *see* Railroad

Trampoline

Jumping on a trampoline in a dream reflects anger (causing

T

400

you to jump up and down) that you have experienced in your waking life. Possibly this anger has not been expressed outwardly, which is why it is resurfacing in your dreams. Images of bouncing and springing up may also suggest that you need to take more of an active role in a situation or relationship.

Transformation

If you've ever dreamed of being able to transform yourself, others or things around you by some magical means, you would have experienced feelings of confusion. This is because you are coping with major changes in your life in which your actions can make an impact on a current situation. You may be entering into a new physical, emotional or psychological state that is making you feel confused about this unfamiliar territory or uncertain about that which has been transformed. The dream is telling you not to be concerned with this change, as it is a natural progression. It suggests that once you accept this as true, you will feel more in control.

Transparent

When someone says that they 'can see right through you', they usually mean that they can see you clearly for what you are. If you dream that you are transparent it may suggest that you feel vulnerable and fear that your thoughts and feelings are exposed for all to see. Accept this feeling and resolve to deal with it more 'clearly' when you are feeling less threatened.

Trap/Trapped *see also* Cell

Being caught in a trap represents the inability to break free of old attitudes, habits and outside influences. We feel trapped because we are afraid to move on. It may be that

T

we feel trapped at work because of a loss of opportunities or that we are trapped in an unhappy relationship. Whatever the situation, it is our fears that keep us in the trapped state. If you are having this dream regularly, you may need to seek outside help to get you out of your predicament. A trap door, on the other hand, is a mysterious or secret place where we hide ourselves when faced with a perceived danger.

Travel *see also* Journey

To travel is to seek a change from our usual environment. We talk about 'travelling through life' to indicate both the process of ageing and our self-development through experience. If you are travelling alone in your dream, it implies that you wish to be more independent. However, it could also suggest that you are solitary or feel alienated from others. Travelling with other people represents sociability and the way we get along with others. If you are going on a business trip, the journey is a symbol of where your career is taking you. Going on a holiday, however, suggests your need to 'get away' from the pressures of daily life and from people who constantly make demands on you. This dream is encouraging you to give yourself 'time out' and recuperate.

Treasure *see also* Jewellery/Jewels

Finding treasure in a dream stands for the discovery of something of value to you, usually a precious part of yourself of which you had not previously been aware. This may be a quality such as the ability to love, create, and forgive or other similar attributes. If the treasure is difficult to reach, it suggests that your highest goals are not easy to attain and that you will be able to appreciate their value only by going through trials and setbacks. A treasure that is being stolen

T

suggests that we don't feel worthy of owning what we consider greatly desirable.

Tree

The tree symbolises all aspects of our life. It represents our growth throughout our lives both emotionally and physically. When we speak of roots, we refer to connections with people and the environment as well as our 'family tree'. The branches of a tree represent different sides of our personalities—the wider they are, the more gregarious and generous you will be. 'Branching out' is another term that describes growth and direction. Buds, leaves and fruits on the tree are symbols of stages of life—from bud to flower to leaf to falling leaves and bare branches. Usually, these are positive images as they give the dreamer faith in his or her future by pointing out that aspirations, hopes and achievements will come to fruition, after which a new stage will come along.

Falling leaves denote the things that we leave behind because we no longer need them. If you dream of bark, the dream may be showing you your protective attributes. However, you may need to shed these a little if you are to absorb new energy and allow people into your life. A dead tree symbolises what was once alive but is no longer with you. This may be of an emotional, spiritual or personal nature. It could also represent a person who once featured in your life but has now moved on. A tree that is in full flower represents fertility and the feminine aspects of ourselves, which we may have been ignoring.

Dreaming of a tree that is about to fall suggests that you are feeling a deep loss over something. The bigger the tree, the greater the loss you are feeling.

T

Trespassing

Finding yourself in a situation in which you are a trespasser denotes that you are intruding and not respecting someone's privacy or boundaries. If someone is trespassing on your space in the dream, think about why you feel that your wishes aren't being considered.

Triangle *see* Shapes

Tribe

If you dream of a tribe, it may represent a social group that you belong to such as a club, religious association, family or other group of people with whom you share common interests. Do you desire acceptance from some group? Do you feel that you don't stand out as an individual? Work out whether the tribe is primitive or not, and what its rules are. Take note of and record in your mind any other symbols that will assist you in interpreting this dream. It may be worth asking yourself if you are feeling alienated in your waking life and, if you are, joining a group with whom you share a common interest, as this dream may suggest a real need for belonging.

Trophy

A trophy is a sign of a well-deserved achievement. Your dream may be pointing out that you wish to be validated for your efforts or that you need to set a goal for yourself that you want to achieve.

Truck

Dreaming of driving or of being a passenger in a truck indicates ambitions that are to do with work and large corporations. The larger the truck, the more ambitious you are and the greater the load (responsibility) that you carry.

T

Trumpet

The trumpet has traditionally been a symbol of triumph. In the Bible, the sounding of the trumpet is associated with joy, news (the Annunciation) and glory (angels with trumpets). However, trumpets are also associated with conflict. In war, the trumpet sounded the retreat or advance as well as playing a final goodbye. Depending on the dreamer's cultural background, age and experience, the sound of a trumpet will arouse various emotions and personal interpretations. It could just be a 'wake-up call' for you.

Trunk

According to traditional dream interpretations, a full trunk denotes that you are careful with investments and make the best use of your resources, while an empty one reveals that you have been extravagant and have no reserves for difficult times ahead.

Tunnel

Seeing a tunnel in a dream indicates a wish to delve deeper into the unconscious and explore the deeper parts of ourselves. Crawling through a tunnel is reminiscent of our birth experience, the tunnel resembling the birth canal. Perhaps you feel a need to crawl back into the safety of the womb and only emerge when you are ready to make contact with those on the outside. The tunnel could also signal a 'fresh start' or a re-birthing of your ambitions and desires. Because a tunnel is a passage with two definite ends, it can also represent our life's journey. Those of us who break through the obstacles and blackness of the tunnel, usually emerge to find a positive outcome (light at the end of the tunnel). On a more punning level, the dream may be pointing out to you your own 'tunnel vision'. It may mean that you need to be more

T

aware of other things that are going on around you, rather than just focusing on the one.

Turtle *see* Animals

Twins

Gemini is the astrological sign of the twins. The twins symbolise our dual natures—the mixture of good and bad in us. If you dream of seeing twins, the dream may be pointing out the two opposing aspects either of yourself or an issue. Often the message of the dream is the dreamer's need to reconcile the two. Search the symbolism of the dream carefully for clues on how this may be done.

Tyre *see* Driving/Driver

T

U

Ugly

To dream of an ugly person or see yourself as ugly means that you are looking at parts of yourself that you find unattractive.

Ulcer

An ulcer is an erosion of tissue that has caused bacteria to come to the surface. Like a boil, the purpose of this eruption is to clear the system. As with all dreams about health, it may be worth making an appointment with your doctor. However, this type of dream usually points us towards the need to heal emotional ruptures or hurts. A mouth ulcer suggests issues to do with communication while a stomach ulcer has more of an emotional significance. Ask yourself if you are going through a stressful time of change in which you need to make decisions that affect your lifestyle. If you are feeling agitated the ulcer could be a symptom of this dilemma and of your high levels of stress.

Umbrella

Dreaming that an open umbrella is covering us relates to our coping mechanisms and need for protection in new situations. If you are fully covered by the umbrella, you probably feel secure in your ability to cope. However, if the umbrella leaks or is not effective, you may have to ask

for help. Carrying an umbrella is a sign that you are prepared for any scenario. The umbrella, in the sense that we
work 'under' a specific boss, also symbolises large compa-
nies or corporations.

Uncle *see also* Family

Unless the dreamer has been recently thinking of or has
visited an uncle, dreaming of this relative usually represents
issues to do with family tradition and values. An uncle is
generally regarded as the male authority figure next in
importance to the father. As such, dreaming of this figure
may reflect your need to be free of a domineering influence.
Examine your relationship with your uncle/s to help you
determine the significance of this dream.

Underground *see also* Tunnel

To dream of being underground signals a withdrawal
from all the aspects of life that cause us to be agitated.
Perhaps we need to stay underground for a while to think
about an issue and should only resurface once the decision
is made. If you dream of building an underground house
or shelter, it is an indication that you lack security in your
life. Being in a subway suggests that you are about to take
a trip inside yourself, to discover who you are and what
you stand for. However, dreaming of an underground is
not necessarily only about withdrawal. It can also indicate
the need to reflect on aspects of life, which are problematic
at a deeper level. The message here is that you need to
take the time to reflect before making a decision. If the
dream is set in an underground house or shelter it is likely
to be about primal fears. This dream suggests that you
don't feel safe, and may be threatened by people or situations in your life.

Underwear *see also* Clothes

Seeing someone in underwear really means that you are catching a glimpse of vulnerable parts of yourself. If you dream of being embarrassed in your underwear, the dream indicates your anxiety of being 'found out'. It could also mean that you are trying hard to conform and be someone that you are not. To be seen in your underwear, is to be seen for what you really are. This dream can also be interpreted as symbolic of the dreamer's feelings regarding his or her sexuality.

Undressing

Undressing is about our need to reveal ourselves to others. It is an honest revelation, suggesting openness, which will enable you to heal past hurts and disappointments by facing up to them. If someone else is undressing, the dream may be suggesting the need for you to be more attentive and receptive to someone else's needs. Someone may be undressing you in the dream and this could be occurring with your permission. But the dream could alternatively be suggesting that someone else is taking control to expose parts of yourself that you are not ready to divulge. Undressing in a dream may also relate to the need to be more open or frank in your communications and situations involving others in your waking life.

Unemployment

Dreaming of being unemployed reflects a fear of inadequacy. If you are employed, this dream may mean that you are concerned about losing your job. If you are unemployed in real life, the dream may be a reinforcement of this real-life situation, which makes you feel as if you are not using all your talent and opportunities. Dreaming of seeking employment and not having luck in finding a job may be a sign of the need to be more active, and to make sure that your future employ-

U

ers are aware of all your skills and experience. Those who are inundated with work can also indulge in a fantasy of being unemployed. This is just wishful thinking that helps us to escape the pressure of constantly performing under our boss's scrutiny. It may be that your subconscious has taken note of comments you've heard at your workplace such as 'shape up or ship out', and this has made you think of being redundant.

Unicorn

The unicorn is an ancient symbol of purity and innocence. Dreaming of this mythical creature suggests your desire to escape from the practical and indulge in the realm of fantasy. This isn't always realistic, of course, and you need to make sure that your life is balanced to include both the innocent and the savvy aspects of yourself. Unicorns are also magical creatures, which are associated with good luck. In a dream they may suggest that the dreamer is wishing for a change of luck or some magic in his or her life. However, as the unicorn belongs to the realm of fantasy, this is not going to happen unless the dreamer takes action in waking life.

Uniform

A uniform, whether it's a school student's, nurse's or soldier's, represents identification with a particular role. For example, if you dream of a soldier, it may be a sign that you feel 'at war' with yourself or others around you. Wearing a school uniform indicates your wish to fit into a group and most likely belong to the 'in' crowd. Think carefully about the type of uniform in your dream and interpret it with the help of other symbols.

University

As a university is a place of 'higher' learning, dreaming of being a student there highlights your need or desire for further education. You may be feeling stuck and bored with the limited knowledge available to you, in which case the university appears as a place where knowledge can be broadened and your potential for learning increased.

Up

Moving upwards suggests a positive change in your life. This dream may indicate that you have a positive mental attitude or are about to adopt one and that life is 'looking up' for you. It is a dream of hope and optimism.

Urine/Urinating

Urination represents the control we have over our bodies and emotions. We may choose to hold our urine in or to release it. Therefore, to urinate is to release tension—particularly sexual tension. A common dream involves trying to go to the toilet, but finding that each one is either locked, blocked or in full view. This dream can be an indication that you actually need to urinate during the night. More symbolically, it may be indicating that whenever you try to express or release your emotions you find obstacles in your way. As a result you are being prevented from releasing whatever it is that you've been 'holding in'.

Urn

Today when we think of an urn, we tend to envisage the urn used for holding the ashes of a loved one. As a result the urn is usually associated with death. Perhaps the urn is a reflection of our attitude towards death—do we visibly keep it around in a place where it can be viewed to remind us of our own mortality, or do we hide it out of sight?

V

Vacation *see* Holiday

Vagina *see* Body

Valley

A dream in which a lush green valley surrounds us represents the nurturing and protective parts of our personalities. If you are safe yet lost in the valley, it may mean that changes around you are occurring that will take you to a more peaceful emotional state. A valley which is barren or marshy points to the parts of your life that need a feminine touch if they are to be brought back to life and made sustainable. In the Bible the valley of darkness is a symbol of death and the valley of tears represents grief about death. You may want to delve deeper into the meaning that holds the most significance for you.

Vampire

This terrifying creature of the night is created by our fears of being drained to the point at which we lose our life. The expression 'to be sucked dry' is an example of how the demands that are made on us can feel as if they are physically 'killing us'. The vampire is associated with evil and anything that is negative in our life, so if we dream of being attacked by one it indicates that we feel seriously weakened by another person's will. On the other hand, if you have this dream over the Halloween period, it may simply mean that the activities and images of your waking state have activated your imagination.

Vampires are associated not only with evil but also with eroticism. Depending on the feelings associated with the dream, you may be either experiencing a need to explore your sexuality or finding that your sexual relationship is sapping your energy and life force. Either way, this dream suggests that you experience these feelings as disturbing.

Vanishing

If you dream of something or someone vanishing in your dreams, you should consider what opportunities you may have lost or whether there are people in your life who are no longer there.

Varnish

What are you covering up? Varnishing furniture either covers up imperfections or adds an external layer to restore and protect the wood. If you are varnishing, ask yourself if you are building layers of protective coating around you, so that the influences of others are unable to penetrate and get to you. If you see others varnishing, take care not to be deceived and be honest about your own intentions.

Vase

A vase is associated with the feminine and with creativity—as the holder or receptacle of what is valued as beautiful. We are frightened of breaking a vase, and consequently take more care than usual around one—especially if it's not in our own home. This may be because we see it as fragile and precious to the owner and therefore to be treated with respect. A vase containing flowers is the item we first think of when we invite guests to our home or need to impress homebuyers. It represents beauty, creativity and growth. Consider whether any of these qualities hit home with you.

Vault *see also* Safe

In a dream a vault that contains valuables, such as a bank vault, represents the place where we house our resources. These may be emotional, physical or practical. The dream may be prompting you to take care of these resources so that they are not stolen. A burial vault, on the other hand, is associated with death and loss. In a dream this loss is most likely to be the loss of something that was once stored in our memories.

Vegetables *see also* Food

If you dream of vegetables, you should make sure that you are getting all the vitamins and other nutrients you need. Sometimes in our conscious state we tend to think that we should eat more vegetables but don't make a regular habit of it. The subconscious picks up on this and we dream about it.

Veil

The veil represents mystery and the hidden. In many cultures women are veiled to hide them from the gaze of men who are not from the family circle. In Western society a bride is veiled before the final wedding vows are sealed with a kiss. This ritual is a reminder of the transition from a single to a wedded state. If you are wearing a veil in your dream, think about whether you are going through a major change—emotionally or physically—or whether you are trying to keep people from seeing parts of you that you would like to keep hidden. Such a dream is usually indicative of something in the dreamer's life that is not predictable. There is an air of uncertainty surrounding recent decisions with the result that the outcome is veiled in mystery.

Velvet

Velvet is one of the richest and most sensuous of fabrics and has been around for centuries. In olden days, only the rich, the powerful and the clergy could afford to wear velvet. Consequently, it represented their status and wealth. Dreaming of wearing or touching velvet is a sign of the sensual and indulgent parts of yourself.

Vet

A vet is a symbol of our need for creature comforts. This dream suggests that our basic (animal) needs are not being met.

Vicar *see also* Priest

A more approachable authority figure than a priest, the vicar in our dreams represents our spiritual quest or progress.

Victim

Seeing yourself as a victim denotes that you have given yourself this role by holding back your potential. Be more proactive in your approach to life, and adopt a more positive attitude. Only you can get yourself out of the role of victim.

Vine

The vine is a traditional symbol of fruitfulness and abundance. Dreaming of a vine reflects the family ties that bind you. It also points to your own growth. A clinging vine, on the other hand, is one who finds it difficult to 'let go' of things.

Violin *see also* Musical instruments

The sound of a violin appeals to our emotions, evoking passion and stirring the strings of our hearts. It is the sound of celebration and of love lost. What feelings are stirred in you when you hear the violin in your dream?

Visit

To have someone visit you in your dream is a sign of news of some sort. This news may refer to an issue you have been trying to solve. Seeing a visitor suggests that your concerns will be alleviated, especially if the visitor is wearing bright colours. If the visitor is wearing black, you need to beware the risks you are about to take. People who have experienced depression sometimes describe it as 'the black visitor'. But if you are visiting someone in your dream it means that you may want to contact that person in real life. If the person is someone you don't know or don't have any kind of relationship with, consider who or what he or she represents. For example, if the person is ill in hospital, the dream may be suggesting that you should make an effort to take care of your health and visit your doctor.

Voices

Hearing voices in your dream, without knowing whom they belong to, can be frightening. In some cases, the voices may be representations of parts of yourself that you've discarded and which no longer sound familiar to you. The voice in your dream could also be your conscience—that little voice inside your head. Take note of what it is saying because it may be telling you what's best for you. To those who believe in the spirit world, the voices may be interpreted as belonging to a higher spiritual self or their spiritual guide. Trying to remember the words and tone of the voice will help you to understand your dream more fully.

Volcano

A volcanic eruption in a dream tells us that we have lost control of our emotions or a particular situation in our life. This violent release can be a healing experience for the dreamer after the build-up that comes from keeping feelings of hurt or anger inside. The lava flow and the damage it causes are a result of this emotional build-up. The more lava there is in your dream, the deeper the feelings that have 'erupted'. If the lava has cooled off, so too have your anger and passion.

Vomiting

Vomit is a release of that which is indigestible to us. How many times have we said that something made us 'sick to the stomach' or made us 'want to vomit'? Dreaming of vomiting is your way of getting rid of (throwing up) what is unacceptable, unethical or poisonous to you. There is a common phobia associated with vomit, and when others are vomiting in a dream it can be associated with this fear, particularly if the dreamer has a strongly negative response to the person vomiting in the dream.

Voting

If you dream of casting a vote, it is a sign of your trust in the cause or political idea that the person stands for. Voting is also a decision-making progress. Ask yourself what you base your decisions on ad why.

Vow *see also* Contract

A vow is more of a spiritual agreement than a contract between two people. Perhaps you have made a vow to your-

V

self about something that involves a stronger obligation than a mere promise. A promise can be broken without incurring the serious consequences that result when one breaks a vow such as a marriage or religious undertaking. If you dream of taking a vow, pay attention to what sort of vow it is. Does it involve others?

Vulture *see also* Birds, Birds of prey

The vulture is a symbol of people 'picking on you' or living 'off you'. Are you having issues with dependants in your life?

Wadding

Wadding is used for protection, so a dream involving this substance is likely to symbolise either a desire to protect yourself emotionally or, if you are removing the wadding in your dream, to come closer to the heart of a matter. Wadding can also be used as 'stuffing', and in this context your dream may represent a concern about overeating.

Wading

We usually wade in water—a symbol of the emotions. But wading, like baptism, also suggests the desire for cleansing or symbolic rebirth in a purified state. Wading through water often suggests that the dreamer, though in touch with his or her emotions, is not really coming to grips with them. Wading in muddy water is a result of not facing up to emotional issues. To interpret this dream you should pay attention to whether the water in your dream is clear or muddy, and take note of whether you are going with the flow or at risk of getting 'bogged down'.

Wafer

Wafers are a delicate form of biscuit used to represent the body of Christ in the Christian service of Communion. These associations suggest that the wafer in your dream is likely to represent something in yourself or your life that is delicate, easily broken, and which demands respect or even has sacred value. The expression 'wafer-thin' reinforces the association of wafers with fragility.

Wager

Dreaming of a wager suggests that you may be preparing to take a gamble in your waking life. If the wager in your dream pays off, you should take it as a positive sign. But if your dream wager causes you a great deal of anxiety, it may be a sign that you fear the risks that your real-life gamble is forcing you to make.

Wages

If you dream that you are underpaid, it is a sign that you feel underappreciated; while a dream of being overpaid suggests that you may be experiencing guilt about failing to act, or not doing enough in a given situation.

Wailing

Traditionally, wailing is a way of releasing emotions at funerals and other painful occasions. If you have a dream involving wailing, it may be serving the same purpose. If you have been suffering from an emotion or grief or unhappiness that you have been unable to express, your dream may be trying to help you acknowledge and release it. The sound of wailing is also associated with sirens, and in this context hearing wailing in a dream can suggest your fear of an impending emergency or disaster.

Waiter

The behaviour of the waiter in your dream will help you assess the way you feel about your treatment by those around you. Thus, a waiter who is slow or rude suggests your belief that those close to you are ot treating you with enough respect or consideration. If you are scolding the waiter, it is a sign either that you are prepared to demand the respect you feel you deserve, or that you feel self-conscious about the demands you are placing on others. Similarly if the dreamer is the waiter they may feel that there are too many demands on them in waking life, particularly by those close to them.

Waiting

A dream in which you are forced to wait for something or someone exaggerates your feelings of impatience. Perhaps you feel unfairly held back at work or in your career and wish you could remove obstacles that stand in the way of your progress. However, this dream may be drawing your attention to the importance of patience or even suggesting that you need to accept a slower approach to your goals.

Wake

A wake is the part of a funeral that allows the mourners to release their emotions. This dream is likely to occur at a period of transition in your life, when you are being forced to give up something in order to move forward. Like a real wake, a dream wake emphasises the need to let go and to accept change.

Walking

The way in which you are walking in your dreams is an indication of where you are in your life journey. If you are walking confidently, with a clear direction, it is likely that you feel confident about your path in life. If you are lost or worried about being late, it's a sign that you are confused about your direction and concerned that you cannot reach your goals. Walking with a limp or a stick indicates a need for support.

Wall *see* Buildings, parts of

Wallet

A wallet can symbolise any aspect of our resources: not only financial, but also emotional, sexual or intellectual. To dream of losing your wallet suggests a concern with inadequacy in one of these areas. To dream of finding one suggests your desire for a windfall or piece of good luck.

Wallpaper

Wallpaper tends to symbolise our surface or façade: the part of ourselves we present to others. If you dream of putting up wallpaper, it could be a sign either of your desire to hide something, or to change the way others see you. Stripping away wallpaper suggests a desire to make a positive change in our lives.

Walrus

The walrus is most famous for its large size. For this reason dreaming of one is likely to signal anxieties about weight. Perhaps you feel like a walrus, or someone else has made you self-conscious about your size.

Waltz *see also* Dance

The waltz is a dance particularly associated with romance and courtship. For this reason a dream in which you are waltzing may represent your romantic situation and concerns. For example, it may be a sign that you would like more romance in your life, or a reflection of your concern that you have either too many or not enough 'partners'.

Wand

Wands are strongly associated with magic and fairytales so

dreaming of one suggests your desire for some kind of 'magical' transformation in your life. Alternatively, this dream may signal your sense that someone close to you wields too much power or influence over your actions. It may be that you are too dependent on the opinions of others whom you consider to be more 'qualified'.

Wandering/Wanderer

A dream in which you are wandering suggests a period of uncertainty and doubt about your goals. Wandering can be a necessary part of the process of self-discovery or making up your mind, so this is not necessarily a negative dream.

War

War symbolises any conflict, often including a loss of the ability to communicate. Dreaming of war may be an expression of feelings of anger you have tried to suppress ('fighting mad') or it may be a sign of an internal conflict ('at war with yourself'). Either way, the damage that is associated with war in real life suggests that you need to try and resolve conflicts before you or those around you get hurt.

Wardrobe *see* Furniture

Warehouse *see* Buildings

Warmth

In dreams, a feeling of warmth is associated with a need for emotional contentment or well-being. This dream could be either compensatory (providing something that is lacking in your waking life) or a reflection of a current situation in your life.

Warning

A dream in which you are either giving or receiving a warning is a sign that something in your life is trying to get your attention. You may need to ask yourself whether something in your life spells danger, or whether an action you are about to undertake may hurt yourself or a person close to you. This dream may also be a warning to you to pay attention to a powerful emotion before it gets out of hand.

Warrant

Dreaming of a warrant symbolises a concern with issues of permission or legality. The meaning of the dream will depend on the type of warrant that appears in it. For example, if you are issued with a search warrant, it is likely that you need to examine your own or somebody else's motives more carefully. A warrant for arrest, on the other hand, suggests the need for either you or someone close to you to stop doing something that may be dangerous or even illegal.

Warts

Like pimples and other blemishes, warts suggest a concern with self-image; especially with the things that we fear will mar or spoil our physical appearance. More symbolically, a wart can also be a negative emotion that we can't seem to get rid of.

Washing

A dream in which washing occurs suggests a desire for purification, whether it is spiritual or emotional. This dream could indicate your desire to cleanse your life of unwelcome or negative attitudes and emotions. It may also suggest that you wish to start some situation over again with a clean slate. The object or body part being washed will help you interpret the aspect of your life the dream applies to. For example, washing your hands implies that you want to get rid of guilty feelings concerning an action you are responsible for, while washing your genitals indicates the desire to get rid of negative sexual feelings, or even to end a relationship that is no longer working. The expression 'washed out' is about tiredness, while 'washing your hands of something' denotes your wish not to take responsibility for the consequence of an action. The biblical reference to this is obvious, as Pontius Pilate washed his hands of Christ's execution.

W

Wasps *see* Insects

Waste *see* Excrement

Watching

If you are conscious of watching something closely in a dream, it suggests that something in your life requires vigilance. Perhaps you are suspicious about the motives and goodwill of someone close to you. Alternatively, you may need to pay more attention to your own actions and motivations.

Watch

Dreaming of a watch or clock usually signals concerns with time issues. The watch in your dream may be prompting you to pay more attention to a deadline or reminding you that you haven't been keeping your eye on the passage of time.

Water

In general, water, which is capable of flowing in many directions and taking many forms, symbolises our emotional lives and energies. The meaning of a dream containing water is likely to depend on the form that water takes. For example, deep water tends to suggest either danger (the risk of 'drowning' in our emotions) or a desire to explore the 'depths' of some feeling or emotional situation, while a dream of entering water may symbolise the beginning of a new relationship or life situation. Flowing water tends to suggest change and movement in our emotional lives, while calm or stagnant water can imply that we have become 'bogged down'.

Wax

Wax is a soft substance that can take many forms. For this reason it can stand for the capacity to adapt to different circumstances or to alter one's attitudes. A dream with wax in it may be prompting you to consider becoming less rigid in your approach to an issue or person. Alternatively, it may suggest that you are too pliable, and that you need to offer some resistance to the attempts made by others to 'mould' you. Dreaming of waxing unwanted hair indicates your concern about beauty and image, while waxing the car or furniture is about pride and the need to 'show off' your best attributes.

Wealth

This dream probably symbolises a desire on your part to improve your status or living standards. The wealth in your dream, however, can also stand for any of the resources that are available to you. In traditional gypsy lore, a dream of wealth was believed to forecast sickness or even death. Dreaming of wealth can also be like a money dream—a feel-good dream—particularly if the dreamer is under financial stress in waking life. Often the subconscious mind will give the dreamer a means of escape through dreams.

Weapon *see also* Gun; Rifle

In a dream, weapons represent the dreamer's aggressive urges. These are not necessarily directed against others, but sometimes at parts of ourselves. If you have trouble making a weapon work, the dream suggests your feelings of impotence or inadequacy. See also under individual weapons.

Weasel *see* Animals

Weather

The weather conditions in your dream probably represent your mood or general attitude towards the topic indicated by the dream. For example, if a storm is building, emotional conflict or anger is indicated, while a bright, sunny day suggests happiness or contentment.

Weaving

Weaving can symbolise any attempt to make something, whether it's an object or a relationship. Weaving can also suggest 'the web of life', and in this respect the woven fabric can represent the patterns or design you are making as a result of your own actions.

Web

As in spider webs, the web in your dream can suggest entrapment or getting caught in a 'sticky situation'. The complexity of a web also symbolises the complexity of your life, where everything is interrelated, and damage to a small part can ruin the whole. The expression 'a web of lies' on the other hand, suggests our potential to become trapped in the complex deceits that we ourselves weave when we fear being honest. The larger the web, the more complex and large is the situation in your life that you need to untangle.

Wedding

Dreaming of a wedding tends to symbolise commitment or relationship issues. For example, it may suggest your desire

to be more involved in a relationship or partnership. If, however, your real-life partner is marrying somebody else in the dream, it is more likely to suggest your feelings of jealousy or insecurity. This dream can also symbolise any new beginning or enterprise, particularly if it involves a public celebration. Perhaps because such new beginnings tend to occur at the cost of the 'death' of a former life or identity, traditional gypsy lore interpreted this dream as the sign that the dreamer would soon be required to attend a funeral.

Wedding ring

The shape of the wedding ring associates it with the idea of eternity, and an encircling love. Dreaming that you give or receive a wedding ring may symbolise your desire for these things. More generally, this dream may represent the making of any kind of commitment or vow.

Wedge

Wedges are something we use to maintain an opening, whether in a door or a window. As a result, dreaming of a wedge may suggest our desire to open ourselves to a new situation or emotion. It may also signal the need for more openness or communication within a relationship. Don't let a wedge come between you and someone you love.

Weeds

In our dreams, as in our gardens, weeds represent the unplanned, unwelcome or obstructive elements in our lives. A dream in which you are digging up weeds suggests the desire to 'weed' out or get rid of your negative emotional baggage. A garden overgrown with weeds suggests that these thoughts or elements may be choking the more positive aspects of your life, to the point of hindering your growth.

Weeping

In waking life weeping is a sign of grief, so a dream in which weeping occurs symbolises your need to express such an emotion. This dream may be reminding you of feelings or sadness or loss that you have kept 'bottled up'. Sometimes this motif is displaced onto a related object, such as a 'weeping willow'.

Weighing

The act of weighing something in a dream may have less to do with its actual weight than with your attempts to assess its value. This dream could also indicate the need to make a decision, as when we 'weigh up our options'. An object you are weighing in a dream may also represent a burden you feel you are forced to carry.

Weight

The weight in your dream could stand for the things that are 'holding you down'. This dream suggests your conscious-ness of being forced to take responsibility for others, or shoulder extra burdens. If, in the dream, you are having trouble moving, you need to think of ways to lighten some of these responsibilities.

Well

A well is a deep space, traditionally a source of water, so the well in your dream may represent your own inner 'depths' of emotion and personality. This dream may signal your desire to access knowledge located in those depths.

However, the double meaning of 'well' can also give this dream a meaning that is to do with health or healing. If the well in your dream is a wishing well, it may be a sign that you have been indulging in 'wishful thinking'.

Werewolf

These imaginary animals were once believed to be able to transform themselves from human to beast-like form. Dreaming of one may indicate your fears about your more primitive or 'animal' instincts getting the upper hand. On the other hand the werewolf's transformation was meant to take place on the full moon, so this dream may be referring to a monthly cycle, such as menstruation. What do you turn into when you experience premenstrual tension?

West

The west is associated with the setting sun and, for this reason, dreaming of this compass direction may symbolise the end of something. The expression 'Go West, young man', associated the West with adventure and exploration, so dreaming of this direction may suggest your desire to explore something new.

Whale

The primary association of these sea mammals is with size. In this respect dreaming of a whale may indicate a concern about your weight, or how you appear to others. More positively, the expression 'a whale of a time' indicates a social event or other situation in which those involved are having a lot of fun. In today's society however, whales are also thought of as an endangered but valuable species so their appearance in a dream may indicate your desire to protect something of value.

Wheat

A dream with wheat or wheat fields in it is likely to symbol-ise the things in your life that you need to grow or cultivate, whether a talent, relationship or career. Wheat also carries associations with harvest: the time of year when we reap the benefits of our experience or hard work.

Wheel

The wheel stands for mobility and the ability to deal with life's challenges. The wheel of fortune also associates this object with the variable fortunes or 'ups and downs' we are likely to encounter in life. If you dream of losing a wheel, it may indicate that you lack energy or motivation for some enterprise.

Whip

A dream in which a whip is being used may indicate your desire to speed up or hasten some process or event. Similarly, the expression 'take the whip hand' denotes a desire to take control. But the whip in your dream may also stand for something that inflicts pain, such as the critical remarks made by others. It may even by a warning to you to think about how your own actions or tendency to 'lash out' may risk hurting others.

Whirlpool

A dream that indicates danger and confusion. If you see a whirlpool in your dream it may be prompting you to think about a situation in which you risk being dragged down or held under. The dreamer might feel that he or she is in a downhill spiral in waking life. There is a definite need for the dreamer to empower himself or herself.

Whistle

A whistle in a dream is a sign to pay attention to some situation, person or feeling. On the other hand, 'whistleblowers' are persons who refuse to remain silent in the face of injustice, but draw public attention to an unfair situation. In this context your dream could be prompting you to think about a situation that is unfair to yourself or to others.

W

Widow/Widower

If you are a married woman and you dream of being a widow, the dream may symbolise either your fears of abandonment, or your desire to escape the constrictions of your relationship. For a married man the situation is reversed. If you are not married and have this dream, it is likely to represent any potential loss.

Wife

Dreaming of a wife signals a concern with issues of family and relationships. This dream could be prompting the dreamer to pay more attention to family members. Alternatively, it could symbolise the dreamer's desire for greater security or closer emotional relationships.

Wig

If you are in danger of losing your hair in your waking life, dreaming of a wig may symbolise your fear about the loss of attractiveness this may result in, and a desire to cover up your baldness. More symbolically dreaming of a wig can represent a desire for any form of 'cover up' or concealment.

Will

A will represents your intentions. This dream could be prompting you to order your priorities or decide on a course of action. Wills are also associated with death, so this dream could also be suggesting that you are about to enter into a new phase of your life. Because wills commonly make provisions for your relatives or offspring, dreaming of one may also reflects your concerns about looking after those close to you, such as children. It is common to have a dream about wills when we are about to take a long trip overseas and are leaving family behind.

W

Wind

Wind is related to breath, the vital force that sustains us. It is also associated with turbulent weather conditions, and in this respect may suggest that you are going through 'stormy' emotional times. The phrase 'long-winded' is used to describe people who talk too much and in this context the dream may express your impatience with someone who seems to be all talk and no action. The wind often changes direction, and therefore it may be symbolic of the dreamer's feelings of restlessness or need for change.

Windmill

The windmill is a traditional device for harnessing the energy of the natural environment. For this reason dreaming of a windmill relates to the way in which you are using your talents or resources. If the vanes of the windmill are turning freely, you probably have a store of creative energy. If, on the other hand, they barely turn at all, it is likely that something has robbed you of your energy or motivation.

Window *see* Buildings, parts of

Wine

A dream involving wine can have several meanings. It can

suggest celebration, enjoyment and social pleasure. In a religious context it can symbolise communion, or the desire for spiritual insight or union. Because wine is often stored before it is opened, it can also stand for the 'maturing' of your own wisdom and experiences. Spilled wine suggests sorrow or loss.

Wings

Dreaming of wings suggests a desire for freedom, independence, and the ability to achieve flight or 'liftoff'. The association of wings with angels also gives them a meaning of protection. If you dream of a broken wing, it suggests that something is preventing an idea or project you are involved with from 'getting off the ground'. It may also stand for the obstacles that prevent you from becoming independent.

Winter *see also* Seasons

Winter is the time of year when the earth lies fallow in preparation for the renewal of spring. Dreaming of winter may suggest that your own creative or emotional life is going through a period of relative inactivity or that you are waiting for more favourable circumstances to arrive and bring your ideas or emotions to life once more.

Witch

The witch is an archetypal figure for the negative aspects of feminine power and the female personality. For that reason, traditional dream interpretation tends to associate the witch with the dreamer's more negative feelings about his or her mother. The witch can also stand for a part of yourself you feel ambivalent about or have trouble accepting, such as your feelings of jealousy or rage. If there is a positive association with this type of dream, the dreamer may be curious about the power of feminine energy and how it relates to natural forces.

Witness

If you dream of being a witness, it suggests that some situation in your life requires careful scrutiny. You may need to pay attention to the actions or motivations of those around you, or even your own. This dream also suggests that you may be required to give evidence of some kind or to testify before a 'higher authority', such as your own conscience.

Wizard

Wizards are magical figures in myth and fairytales, who stand for wisdom and power. This dream could relate to someone in your life, such as a teacher or mentor. Alternatively, it could be drawing your attention to your own untapped skills or powers.

Wolf see Animals

Woman

If the dreamer is a woman, the female figures in her dream may represent aspects of herself, including those aspects that she does not immediately recognise or identify with. By projecting these feelings onto another female figure, the dreamer is able to express herself in a less confronting manner. If the dreamer is a man, the female figures in his dream are likely to represent not only his relationships with the actual women in his life, but his relationship with the part of himself that is more 'feminine' or intuitive. How the woman is dressed or appears in the dream often indicates whether or not the dreamer is happy with that aspect of self.

A well-dressed woman suggests that the dreamer is happy with the aspect of self that they identify with.

Womb

The womb in your dream represents your desire for protection, nurturing, and being free of adult responsibilities. This dream can be a response to a stressful situation, which makes you long to return to the dependency and protected state of infancy. But if the space is stifling or claustrophobic it suggests that you desire more independence or freedom.

Wood *see also* Forest

Wood is an organic substance, and can signal our desire to be in touch with our basic instincts or to enjoy a more 'natural' or simpler lifestyle. More symbolically however, when we describe something as wooden, we usually mean that it lacks expression or life (to have a wooden heart is not to have feelings). In this context, wood can denote a situation or person who seems to be lacking in emotion or warmth.

Wool *see also* Knitting

The use of wool to make blankets and jumpers suggests its symbolic associations with warmth and comfort. This dream may express a desire for the feelings of comfort and protection that we associate with childhood and with our mothers. Expressions such as 'pull the wool over someone's eyes', suggest trickery or sleight of hand while 'being fleeced' indicates financial loss. 'Woolgathering' is associated with a state of daydreaming in which we indulge in 'woolly' or imprecise thinking.

Work

Given the major part that work—or lack of it—plays in our

lives, it's not surprising that it should appear in our dreams. Of course the work you find yourself doing in your dreams may be very different from your actual job. It's probably wise to interpret the meaning of this work symbolically, rather than trying to relate it to your actual occupation. For example, if you are working in a hospital in your dream, it may represent your concerns either with health or looking after others. Similarly, working in a kitchen might stand for a creative endeavour, while working in an office may signal 'official' concerns or activities.

Worm

The metaphorical meaning of a 'worm' is of an insignificant or even contemptible person. Thus, this dream is likely to symbolise your feelings of unimportance or ineffectiveness, or your sense that others are treating you this way. A Freudian interpretation would see the worm as a symbol of the penis, in which case this dream could signal lack of sexual confidence. However the expression 'even a worm will turn' is a reminder of our potential to change and to grow. Similarly, the worm is recognised today as a crucial part of a healthy garden and is associated with recycling and growth. Calling someone a 'bookworm' isn't necessarily an insult either, but indicates that they are studious.

Worship

If you dream of being worshipped, perhaps you have an over-inflated ego! On the other hand, this dream could be compensatory, enabling you to experience feelings of self-worth that are lacking in your current situation. A dream in which you are the worshipper suggests your openness to being influenced by a powerful person or idea. We all look up to and admire others. However, this dream may be alerting you to the possibility that you are at risk of putting too much value or importance on another person or thing. This is especially common if you are feeling a little empty in your waking life. This feeling usually leads to a search for meaning and hence the need to worship.

Wound

The physical wound in your dream is probably a graphic representation of the more invisible 'wound' or hurt caused to your feelings. The other symbols in the dream will help you to interpret the source of this hurt. However, a wound doesn't always have to be interpreted negatively. As an opening in your body it can also symbolise your openness to an outside influence or emotion such as love or friendship.

Wreath

Traditionally, wreaths were symbols of triumph and were bestowed on emperors or successful athletes. Today we are more likely to associate wreaths with funerals. The wreath in your dream may refer to the ending of a relationship or episode in your life, but it may also suggest a tribute. The expression 'being wreathed in smiles' plays on this association of the wreath with abundance or plenty.

Wreck

A wreck is a traditional symbol of misfortune or failure. If you dream of one, it suggests that you fear the failure of some enterprise or project, possibly due to circumstances beyond your control. This dream warns you to be prepared for trouble ahead.

Wrinkles

A dream in which you are conscious of wrinkles reflects your anxieties about age and the passage of time. However, the wrinkles in your dream can also signal the wisdom that comes with age and experience. If you see your face with premature wrinkles it may suggest that you are overburdened and feeling 'old'. In this case, take some time off to relax.

Wrist *see* Body

Writing

A dream in which you are writing symbolises communication—whether with others, or between the different parts of yourself. Perhaps there is a part of you that you are struggling to express to those around you. What the dreamer needs to communicate depends on the type of writing. Such a dream is often indicative of the dreamer's need to communicate the creative side of self in waking life. This dream can also represent your desire to order your thoughts, to make an impression on others, or to leave your mark in the form of a permanent record.

X

Remember the adventure stories you read as a child, in which 'X marked the spot' of the pirate's treasure? Dreaming of an X may signal something similar. This shape could be trying to draw your attention to what lies beneath it. But because the X shape forms a kind of cross, it can also symbolise ideas of sacrifice or even torture.

X-rays

Because x-rays are invisible, they tend to stand for the things that influence us without our being conscious of it. This dream could be pompting you to try and bring these influences into the light. But because x-rays are also associated with sickness and healing this dream can also represent your anxieties about your health, possibly even fear of some illness that has not yet become visible or whose effects have not reached your full awareness. An x-ray also represents something that is not available through normal vision, so the dreamer may wish to see what is not exposed to everyone in his or her waking life.

Y

This letter resembles the shape of a person standing with outstretched arms. For that reason it is believed to symbolise striving, especially of a spiritual nature.

Yacht *see* Boat; Sailing

Yard
The yard is the outside part of a dwelling that divides the inside of the house from the street or neighbours. For that reason it tends to symbolise the parts of your life that exist between the private and public arenas. A dream in which you are sweeping or tidying a yard suggests your desire to present a favourable image to the world. It may relate somehow to the saying, 'clean up your own backyard', indicating that before you comment on how others lead their lives, you should make sure that your own is in order.

Yardstick
A yardstick is an instrument for taking measurements, and therefore it can symbolise our desire to 'measure up' to the expectations of others. Its shape also carries associations of correctness and 'upright' behaviour.

Yarn *see also* Tapestry

In its meaning of tale or story, a yarn suggests our sense of continuity or place in family history. As the thread or wool we use in knitting, yarn symbolises our ability to make things. Whichever meaning is relevant to your dream, yarn represents your ability to fashion yourself out of the raw materials you are given.

Yawn

Yawning is an involuntary act, and so our subconscious is trying to get our attention. But yawning also signals boredom or tiredness, so a dream in which you are conscious of yawning may symbolise either your desire for more interest in your life, or your sense of being overworked.

Year

If something in your dream draws your attention to a particular year it may be reminding you of an event that took place at that time. But this kind of dream could also be prompting you to think of an anniversary, or to assess the progress you have made recently.

Yeast

Yeast is used as a raising or lightening agent in bread, and as such symbolises the forces in our lives—such as ideas or the influences of others—that can change our personalities or situations, usually for the better.

Yell

Sometimes our dreams frighten us so much that we wake ourselves up by shouting aloud. In this situation our shout is a response to the overwhelming emotions generated by the events of the dream. More generally, if you dream of yelling, or hear someone else crying aloud in your dream, it symbolises the need to express powerful emotions.

Yew

Traditionally these trees were planted in graveyards and were symbols of mourning, a meaning that may be reflected in your dream. The dream may express your worries about the health of someone close to you, or it may commemorate the death of a friend or family member. However, because 'yew' sounds like 'you', the presence of these trees may also be an indication that the object of concern in your dream is yourself.

Y

Yin-Yang

The traditional Chinese symbol of Yin and Yang stands for an ideal balance or harmony between the different potentials and parts of the self: between the intuitive or instinctive and the rational, 'masculine' and 'feminine', or active and receptive. If you dream of this symbol it is likely that you feel the desire or need for more balance in your life or personality.

Youth

Youth stands for potential, growth and the possibility of transformation. The youth in your dream may stand for yourself at that age. Alternatively, he or she may represent the qualities symbolised by the idea of youth. This dream could indicate a period of stocktaking on the part of the dreamer: an attempt to recall and evaluate the decisions made at a crucial period of life. However, it could also signal a general openness to change, growth and transformation.

Z

Zebra *see* Animals

Zeppelin

A zeppelin is basically a balloon filled with gas, so if you dream of one it probably symbolises something or someone in your life who is 'full of hot air'—possibly even 'a gasbag'. Because zeppelins are also associated with disaster and accident, due to events such as the Hindenburg tragedy, this dream could also express your fears of an accident, or anxiety that a situation may be about to 'go up in flames'.

Zero

Because the figure of zero stands for nothing, this dream suggests an anxiety that a situation or relationship you are involved in is likely to bring you no profit, or will amount to 'nothing'.

Zigzag

When we travel in a zigzag we take an indirect, meandering approach to a destination, usually to avoid obstacles or to make the most of the view along the way. It's possible that your path through life may be 'zigzagging', or that you are required to solve a problem that can't be approached by a more straightforward path. More dramatically, the zigzag is associated with the path made by a lightning bolt. In this case the zigzag shape represents a powerful release of energy.

Zinc

In traditional gypsy lore dreaming of this mineral signified the dreamer's lack of trust of his or her friends. Today, it may indicate our need to apply zinc cream to our faces for sun protection.

Zip

Z

Dreaming of a zip symbolises your relationship or connection with others, especially the degree to which you feel able to be 'open' with them. The state of the zipper in your dream—that is, whether it is open or closed—may represent how open or closed you are with your friends. However, if the zip is broken or stuck, this dream (like those in which we appear naked) is more likely to express a fear of social embarrassment or exposure.

Zodiac

The zodiac was devised by the ancient Babylonians who, through observation of the stars and planets, sought to explain the influence of these heavenly bodies on the personalities and lives of those born under particular constellations. Because the animals or figures of signs and their meanings are still so widely known today, it is possible that they may appear in your dreams as symbols either of your own personality traits, or of others. For example, if you dream of a lion, it may represent someone in your life born under the sign of Leo, or the parts of yourself that are courageous or exhibitionist (two of the traits said to be characteristic of this zodiac sign). If the lion is interacting with a goat, the dream may signal the need to be courageous in pursuing your ambitions (represented by the sign of Capricorn or the goat). The different zodiac signs are also traditionally believed to govern or relate to different parts of the body, and these associations may also appear in your dreams. The twelve zodiac signs and the parts of the body with which they are associated are as follows:

Aries Aries, or the ram, is associated with the head.

Taurus Taurus, or the bull, is associated with the throat.

Gemini Gemini, or the twins, is associated with the shoulders, arms and hands.

Cancer Cancer, or the crab, is associated with the stomach and digestive organs.

Leo Leo, or the lion, is associated with the heart, lungs and liver.

Virgo Virgo, or the virgin, is associated with the abdomen and intestines.

Libra Libra, or the scales, is associated with the lumbar region, kidneys and skin.

Scorpio Scorpio, or the scorpion, is associated with the genitals.

Sagittarius Sagittarius, or the archer, is associated with the hips, thighs and nervous system.

Capricorn Capricorn, or the goat, is associated with the knees

Aquarius Aquarius, or the water-bearer, is associated with the circulation and ankles.

Pisces Pisces, or the fish, is associated with the feet and toes.

Zoo

This dream suggests your attitudes toward the more natural or instinctive parts of your own personality. Dreaming that you are in a zoo may signal your desire to understand your natural urges or instincts as they relate to issues such as sexuality, family relationships or social interactions. This dream may also suggest the need to integrate these basic needs into your present life and activities. If you feel trapped or imprisoned in a zoo, it may be that you are not coping well with your artificial environment and need a more open and natural space for your well-being.

Z

Appendices

Dreams interpreted

I dreamed that I was lying on a bed and that my head was in a vice. Someone was turning the handle of the vice and my head was getting longer and longer, though I felt no pain. I could see myself from above, looking most peculiar with this long face. There was a row of red roses there too, and one that I was holding between my teeth. I asked the person what would happen, because I could tell that the squeezing of my head couldn't carry on indefinitely. He said not to worry; that I would be dead by the time the last rose disappeared. And I could see, then, that the roses were indeed disappearing one by one. I felt relieved when he said this, and relaxed immediately.

Symbol	Meanings
Head	The head is the thinking organ and therefore symbolises intellect, wisdom and power.
A vice	Represents some sort of constraint that has the dreamer in its grip.
Red	Has the positive qualities of passion, vitality and strength but also the negative traits of force, aggression, danger and conflict. It is a colour that cannot be ignored.

Roses	Traditionally associated with love, romance and the feminine.
Teeth	Symbolise aggression and the ability to withstand pain (grit your teeth).

What was happening at the time of your dream?

At the time of this dream I was at uni doing my honors thesis and I was under a lot of stress.

Interpretation

I probably felt that my brain was being squeezed and compressed. And the thought of dying (being relieved of this stress) was very attractive. The roses disappearing one by one meant that I was getting closer to the end (death) of my thesis. They were a symbol of congratulations and that I would succeed (which I did).

I was inside a house made with sand flooring and sand walls. It began to flood. I panicked and wanted to leave. It was obvious the whole house would cave in on me if I stayed. It wasn't stable. The neighbours advised me to stay, trying to convince me that it wouldn't be ages until it collapsed and there was no immediate danger. I felt trapped and knew that I wanted to leave for my own good. An older man appeared at the door. I ran to him and cried on his shoulder. He listened and let me sit on his lap.

Symbol	Meanings
House	The house represents the dreamer and the soul. Being inside the house means going inside your-

self and delving into your authentic self.

Sand	Shifts with the wind and as such is not stable or secure.
Wall	Indicates restriction and feelings of being trapped. It also suggests a blockage so that we can't progress or move on with our lives.
Flood	Symbolises a 'welling up' of emotion that needs to be released. It's uncontrollable and destructive. In the end, it can be cleansing and we can begin life again.
Older man	Jung's Wise Old Man archetype who is said to represent a combination of positive masculine qualities such as strength, leadership and courage. He appears in dreams when the dreamer becomes aware that the only true guidance comes from within.

What was happening at the time of your dream?

I was going through a crisis in my marriage at the time of the dream. I wanted to leave, but I felt trapped—I had two young children and a traditional family. I managed to pretend to be happily married, but in my heart I'd planned to wait till the children were older and then leave.

Interpretation

I knew that the marriage was unstable (sand), and that it was overwhelming me (flood). Others around me only saw the 'façade' of the public image as a happy couple and didn't believe me (neighbours in the dream). I stayed in the house (marriage) but planned a future escape through the wisdom and help of the older man (my conviction and the legal system that would allow me divorce).

I was driving along a road in my car, with the ocean on my left side. The water was coming dangerously close to the road, sending a spray of water. I was afraid of veering off. All at once I lost control of the car. I couldn't break or steer. Instead it led me to the water's edge. The car drove into the water and I struggled to get out and save myself. I woke up frightened.

Symbol	Meanings
Car	The car is a means of transport and as such is a symbol of where we are going on our life journey.
Driving	Indicates our motivation and need for achieving our goal. Being the driver suggests independence and self confidence. Unable to control the car points to not having control over your direction in life.
Ocean	Symbolic of our emotional state. Being afraid of drowning in an ocean suggests a feeling of help-lessness and fear of the unknown.
Road	Like driving, a road indicates a sense of direction.

What was happening at the time of your dream?
I was feeling a low sense of self esteem at the time of this dream. I couldn't decide on what career path to follow and whatever came up as a suggestion seemed out of my depth. I felt inadequate.

Interpretation

The car and drive reflected my ambition, but the fact that I was veering into the ocean (unknown) was frightening. I felt that I had no control in which direction I was heading as it all led to having to do further study or gaining more experience in a new field. This was out of my comfort zone (ocean) and I was feeling overwhelmed (fear of drowning). The dream was a mirror image of what I was feeling in real life.

There was a lion in my backyard. Obviously the fence was low enough for it to jump over. I scolded my husband for not making a higher fence. I wanted the lion to go as I was afraid of it. The lion began to stalk me and tried to attack me. I defended myself, still unharmed, but the fear woke me up.

Symbol	Meanings
A lion	Symbolises pride and courage. Pride can be interpreted in a negative way, that is, that our pride is blocking us from expressing our animal (or basic) feelings.
Low fence	Any fence suggests boundaries and enclosure for safety.

What was happening at the time of your dream?

I enrolled to go back to university and gain another qualification in a field I was new at. My husband told me it would be too much for me to handle with full time work, study and taking care of the family. He was unwilling to help and I felt vulnerable and at conflict wanting to achieve my goal but not allowing it to consume me so that my family wouldn't suffer in any way.

Interpretation

The lion represented the ego (I wanted to achieve a new level of qualification) but at the same time I needed courage to do it on my own. The fact that I blamed my husband that the fence was too low, meant that I wasn't taking responsibility for my action. I was happier to blame him if things went wrong, as he 'neglected' my needs (the low fence). The dream showed me that I needed to measure my courage and rely on my own instincts to reach my goals. The lion attacking me meant that I had a conflict to resolve and my ability to defend myself was a good indication that I would at least be responsible for my future direction.

I was going through a tunnel made from dirt. It was narrow and low. I had to go through it, driving a jeep. A voice said, 'You can't do it. It's too low'. I replied, 'Yes, I can'. Frightened, but determined, I accelerated and lying flat on the jeep so that I wouldn't hurt myself, I drove through the tunnel. I scraped the top of my head, but I wasn't seriously hurt. Getting out of the tunnel, I said to the voice, 'Told you I could do it'.

Symbol	Meanings
A tunnel	Represents the journey one takes through life (emerging from the darkness of the womb). It could also be a journey of discovery that you need to explore at an unconscious level.

Jeep	Driving the jeep varies from driving a car as it is not as protected. It represents our ambition and that it may require a more detailed plan.
Head	The head symbolises our thinking and power. Scraping it means that the action of driving through a narrow tunnel was risky.
Voice	Voice in dreams can indicate that you are not alone in your life quest. Usually it suggests that other parts of your personality are voicing your repressed thoughts.

What was happening at the time of your dream?

I was going on a trip alone overseas for the first time. I was afraid, but felt a sense of freedom and excitement.

Interpretation

The dream mirrored my feelings at the time of the trip. It was an adventurous thing to do, as nobody in our family circle had done this, but I couldn't help feeling afraid. Well meaning advice about women travelling solo meant that my fears were increased (you can't do it). However, I had to prove more to myself than to them that I was now an adult (driving a jeep in a narrow tunnel) and I could do it at minimal risk (scraping my head). I was confident that I would succeed (telling the voice that I could so).

My son was running away from me through a dark forest. I asked a group of people to help me, but they just looked on with blank faces. I ran on, out of the wood and saw a narrow pier stretching out to a calm grey sea. The landscape was very wintry and desolate. My son was running along the pier. I saw my husband there. He told me that our son was fine, that he was looking after him. Then we both turned and in the distance saw our son jump off the pier.

I ran to where I thought my son had gone over and jumped straight in, feet first, and went down, down through the greenish water very fast. I thought I wouldn't find him, that he was lost forever. But on my way down I passed him coming up, paddling carefully. Bubbles were coming out of his mouth and he seemed quite relaxed. I was still going down when the dream ended. But I remember flapping my arms wildly to try and slow down, and feeling horribly embarrassed.

Symbol	Meanings
Forest	A dark forest represents our intuition.
Running	Suggests urgency to reach a destination or purpose.
Blank faces	Represent an awareness of people around you who are emotionally removed from your purpose or problem.
Pier	A narrow pier is a symbol of the end of a journey.
Grey sea	Points to our present emotional state. Although the sea is calm, it is grey, rather than a clear blue. This indicates that it is deep and perhaps dangerous, making us aware of our fear of the 'deep' and the unknown.

Landscape	A wintry landscape is desolate and lonely and mirrors our emotionally cold, distant and unproductive state.
Water	Jumping into the water symbolises an urgent need to delve into the subconscious with the aim of renewal of strength and conviction.
Going down	Feet first suggests a cautious approach (jumping in feet first, rather than head first). However, going down too fast indicates a lack of control over a situation.
Bubbles	In this instance indicates a sign of life.

What was happening at the time of your dream?

My son was finding school very stressful, so I marched off to school to sort out the problem. He and I have a very close relationship and I think I don't distance myself enough from him. My husband is inclined to say, 'No, he's okay, he's managing. Give him some credit for coping'.

Interpretation 1

My response was actually an over-response. I jumped in to help him, but jumped in way too far. I was so caught up in what I thought was the right thing to do that I wasn't really thinking about the best way to help him. He was doing better than I thought (not sinking, but holding his own).

The wintry landscape is to do with the slight emotional distance that developed between my husband's rational approach versus my emotional one over this issue. It could also reflect my son's feelings of alienation in a barren, wintry landscape.

The people in the forest are probably the teachers in my son's life who didn't seem to help much at the time.

Interpretation 2

The dream could really have been about me, and the stresses I was experiencing at the time. I could have been using my son as a symbol for this stress because I identify with him. I felt that I wasn't coping very well, but that dream suggests that I was coping better than I thought.

My brother was playing 'dare' with a huge snake-like dragon. It looked like half-snake and half-komodo dragon with scaly skin and purple puce in colour. He opened the dragon-snake's mouth wide and put his head between its jaws. I was alarmed. I knew that the creature was poisonous. He just smiled and said, 'It's okay. I know what I'm doing'.

He then released the dragon-snake's head and made me look at its tail. It was sitting in a bowl of ice cream. It had a few white suction caps with openings and was sucking the melted ice cream through these on its tail.

Symbol	Meanings
Brother	Represents aspects of the dreamer's personality.
Snake/dragon	As a combination this creature becomes a powerful force in the dream. It represents trickery (snake) and wild (dragon) aspects of ourselves which are kept in check.

| Ice cream | A reminder of childhood pleasures that we may have forgotten or have 'melted' over the years. |

What was happening at the time of your dream?

I was having difficulty with my boss. He was undermining my authority and elevating himself as the only one responsible for the company's profits.

Interpretation

In real life, my boss put me on the defensive (my head in the creatures' jaws) on most issues. I felt that I had to prove myself all the time. This could be why the creature looked like a dragon. I felt I had to be a knight and slay the dragon to prove that I was worthy and brave. The snake (cunning) put me on guard that I should not trust my boss' motives. The fact that it was my brother that I saw meant that I had to access another part of my personality to overcome my fear and distrust of my boss.

When my brother showed no fear in the jaws of the creature, I was supposed to understand that once I took a stand, my boss would back down. He could see that I wasn't afraid of him and therefore not be threatened. Interestingly, the ice cream took me back to the time when I was younger and reminded me that everyone was young once. Perhaps my boss wasn't so bad after all if I could connect with him on some other level. Perhaps on a more personal or leisure-based level? He could be 'fed' through the suckers and not the mouth. That is, he could show his vulnerability or human aspects in other ways, rather than the jaws, which represent his verbal prowess (venom).

After the dream, I tried to communicate on a more personal level and was less defensive. It worked.

I was climbing a hill, but the higher up I went, the more I couldn't see below. It wasn't just smaller; it was blurry. It felt as if there were fine silken sheets drawn like curtains below me. Looking from above I could see balloons sitting just on top of the sheets. The colours of the balloons were gold, yellow and orange.

Symbol	Meanings
Hill	Climbing a hill means that you are making an effort to overcome difficulties or achieve your goal.
Curtains	Sheet-like curtains represent new ideas brewing in your mind and an expansion of vision.
Balloons	A search for the spiritual and doing what makes us feel uplifted.
Gold	Associated with wealth, but can also mean the valuable part of us.
Orange	A spiritual colour and enhances one's feelings of inner peace.
Yellow	The colour of the sun and seen as a positive colour. It is associated with the emotional self and with life as well as the intellect.

What was happening at the time of your dream?

I was searching for guidance on how I could advance with a career in writing. I was told that it didn't make money and that very few succeeded.

Interpretation

The hill required me to move upwards no matter what the effort. I was determined to follow my ambition to become a writer. The curtains were telling me not to look below where there was negativity. I was savvy enough to know the pitfalls of a writing career, but the sheer fabric of the sheets suggested that I not dwell too much on the negatives or I wouldn't keep climbing.

The balloons were a sign that my higher self required me to pursue a creative career, so that my perspective could be challenged and new experiences learnt. Gold was the colour of my potential, orange was my search for inner peace and yellow was my mental power and positive attitude.

I felt encouraged by the dream to go on further with my writing career despite the rejections and the instability of employment. The dream suggested that if I looked ahead, worked hard, followed my dreams and focused on the positive, the universe would take care of the rest.

I have a recurring dream about being lost in a hotel. I usually lose the key, forget the room number, take the wrong elevator or stairs, or go into the wrong room. This is frustrating as I try so hard to remember where my room is located. Sometimes I end up sharing with strangers, other times when I've gone on tours the cab driver can't seem to find the hotel. As well as the actual room, I get lost in the car park and can't find my car to drive home.

Symbol	Meanings
Hotel	Dreaming of a hotel indicates a short-term situation.
Key	The key in your dream may symbolise your attempt to find a solution to a problem or situation that has been bothering you.
Elevator/lift	Can suggest the aspect of ourselves we are most in tune with.
Strangers	Unfamiliar faces are those whom we are not 'at home' or 'comfortable' with.
Tourist	To be a tourist in a dream is to see things from an outsider's point of view, or with a fresh perspective. It may also indicate that the dreamer feels unfamiliar with his or her new surroundings.
Cab	A means of transport, indicates that you are going places or being taken somewhere.
Car park	Like the hotel, is a temporary place where the car (your means of moving forward) is stored, but is usually underground (intuition).

What was happening at the time of your dream?

As it's a recurring dream, it usually comes up when I have to make new decisions and I have no precedent to help me make them.

Interpretation

The fact that the dream is set around the hotel reinforces that whatever state I'm in (when I'm making new decisions) it's only temporary. I always seem lost as I can't remember where places are (wrong floor, wrong room). This indicates that I am searching for guidance from a previous experience or a precedent so that I can make a good decision, but the problem is that these are new decisions to me. The 'newness' is emphasised by the image of the tourist and the cab. It is a foreign place (my decision making process) and I am looking for someone (cab) help to get me there (making a good decision). Once again, the problem has not existed before and therefore the cab driver can't 'find' the hotel. Where is the answer (key?). I look for clues so that I will be valued as a decision-maker (ambition/carpark) but even there I am not certain of my direction.

I was walking in a large group towards a town. It looked like an earthquake had hit it. People there didn't seem to notice. I noticed that they were robots in human form. I warned the others not to arouse suspicion. I made the robots believe that my group had been brainwashed and that we were allies. Then I became careless. I looked down and I saw that I was carrying a book without the emblem of approval. The robots began to chase me.

Symbol	Meanings
Town	Towns are places where there is a strong sense of community and a great deal of social interaction going on. If you see yourself in a strange town, it

	may mean that you don't yet feel comfortable in a new environment. The new town may also stand for a side of yourself that you haven't accepted yet or that others find hard to accept.
Robots	Symbol of efficiency, emotional detachment and control.
Book	Associated with wisdom and a desire to find something out. It can also indicate a need to be recognised (published).
Emblems	Similar to labels and uniforms. They can appear in dreams for identification and sense of identity.

What was happening at the time of the dream?

The school council made a decision that I didn't agree with. I felt that I was powerless to protest against the majority. I also felt that I had less respect for the school council as a group who were supposed to have the children's best interests at heart.

Interpretation

The town is the small mindedness—a closing of ranks and a definite pecking order. I may represent the silent majority (large group following) but they don't offer solid support. The council is represented by the robots—machine-like and de-humanised. They are perceived to go through the motions as if programmed, but do not have the community spirit to make choices that are beneficial to all. As I was part of the school council, I 'pretended' to be one of them, but really in my heart I was not part of their system (no emblem on the book). I didn't have the seal of approval, as I wasn't in agreement with their philosophy. Hence, the chase and my need to get away (fear of being found out or being 'brainwashed' into agreeing with the decision).

Dream charms and recipes for a good night's sleep

To charm something refers to enchanting something or someone. Words are spoken or sung in order to provoke an action of some sort. The words become a chant and are repeated until the desired result is achieved. When the object becomes charmed it then possesses magical qualities and is recognised as enchanted. The objects can be as ordinary as a horseshoe or a four leaf clover to bring luck.

The North American Indians used a 'dream catcher' made from a net woven on a round frame which was decorated with feathers and beads. It resembled a man made spider web and was hung over the bed. The net was believed to catch the 'bad' dreams, which then disappeared when hit by the early morning sun rays. The 'good' dreams were allowed to drift below to enter the sleeper's mind. This is a popular charm used today in children's bedrooms.

Herbs and flowers

Herbs have been used over time to induce dreams, inspire you to dream, and have your wishes fulfilled through a dream. Before going to sleep, relax and repeat this affirmation:

'May my dreams bring me peace, happiness and success.'

By putting these herbs in a small sachet under the pillow, you will influence the types of dreams you wish to have.

Rosemary Wards off nightmares and brings restful sleep. Rosemary is excellent for dream recall and answering a particular question you wish answered.

Holly Nine holly leaves tied with nine knots in a scarf under your pillow allows you to have prophetic dreams.

Mugwort Promotes psychic ability and is useful in inducing prophetic dreams.

Cowslip Is supposed to bring luck and encourages contact with departed loved ones whilst dreaming.

Rosemary Improves memory and produces sleep.

St John's Wort Protects against nightmares and bad dreams.

Valerian A great sleep enhancer. It will help you have a peaceful sleep.

Dried flowers If you want to be lulled to sleep with dreams of all things beautiful, this country garden mix will do the trick. Fill a small linen/cotton bag and leave it under your pillow. This is for a large quantity.

1   cup dried rose petals
1   cup any other dried and fragrant flower petals such as
     jasmine and lilac

1 cup dried lavender

1 cup dried lemon verbena

1 cup dried rosemary

Six drops of bergamot essential oil

Dream crystals

Crystals, healing stones and charmed stones have also been known to contain healing properties and have their own inherent energies. Firstly, cleanse the crystal and dedicate it to whatever the intended purpose is. You must hold the thought for the purpose in your mind, while holding the crystal at the same time. If you wish to think on it, put the crystal by your bedside during the night.

Jade Jade is regarded as a dream stone, as it is believed to release built-up or suppressed emotions whilst dreaming. By unburdening oneself, it is believed to manifest your dreams in waking life, allowing you to be more confident and achieve your goals.

Lapis Lapis is highly spiritual stone, once held sacred by the ancient Egyptians. It will help to give you spiritual insight into your dreams.

Opal This stone is said to induce happy dreams and boost self-confidence.

Ruby As a shielding stone, ruby protects you against nightmares.

Green sapphire Your dreams can be more easily remembered with the help of a green sapphire.

Star garnet Stronger than green sapphire, it is used to recall distressing dreams, with the aim that the dreamer will be able to solve the conflict once it becomes conscious.

Tunnellite Tunnellite is believed to stimulate creativity whilst dreaming.

Dream potions

Only with a calming environment can you best achieve a good night's uninterrupted sleep. It's best to take a warm bath before-hand, keep the lighting and colours in your bedroom warm and soft and tidy up any clutter. Avoid caffeine at least an hour before going to bed and have a soothing sleeping potion instead. Hot milk with honey is relaxing. Camomile tea or lemon balm unwind and restore the nervous system.

Aromatherapy essential oils are concentrated and only a few drops in a vaporiser or an oil burner are needed to evoke an ideal environment for sleep and dreams. Burn the oils an hour or two before sleeping and make sure the candle is out before you go to bed. The following oils are known to be ideal for sleep and sweet dreams:

Bergamot (*Citrus bergamia*) Can help to radiate happiness particularly in times of grief. Its green colour has a calming and comforting affect. It is particularly good to use as a healing oil in times of agitation and unhappiness.

Camomile (*Matricaria chamomila*) Calming and soothing properties particularly if one is feeling overwhelmed with negative emotions such as anger or bitterness.

Clary sage *(Salvia sclarea)* Ideal for connecting with the dreamworld, which can help us to gain insight into ourselves. It encourages vivid dreams and dream recall. Before falling asleep, think on any problem or issue that you wish to clear up and repeat an affirmation such as 'I will remember my dream. My dream will have the answer. Its association with predicting the future comes from its old name, 'Clear-eye', and it may be this meaning of having a 'clear eye' or 'inner eye', which helps us see the future more clearly.

Cypress *(Cupressus sempervirens)* Refers to the evergreen leaves of the tree and has been used widely in cemeteries as a reminder of afterlife. As oil, it has comforting, warming and soothing properties and is particularly good at times of change and transition.

Jasmine *(Jasminium officinalis)* Believed to have spiritual properties. It is also thought to develop creativity and to stimulate appreciation for visual arts, music and beauty in general. Jasmine is good for meditation. It relieves stress and tiredness and is an ideal oil to unwind with before going to sleep.

Juniper *(Juniperus communis)* An ancient oil used by old civilisations world wide. It has cleansing properties that are useful to detoxify the body and mental state. Negative energies that have accumulated may be cleared by juniper oil, whether one is moving into a new home or a new work place.

Lavender *(Lavandula officinalis, Lavandula vera)* Helps with insomnia, tension and tiredness. It has balancing and healing properties, which will help guard against negative emotions. Both calming and energizing, lavender oil has many uses—as a sedative, antiseptic, and even anti-depressant. When used in an oil burner, it cleanses the room of negative energy and induces calm. You may massage some oil into the soles of your feet or sprinkle some drops on you pillow.

Neroli *(Citrus aurantium)* Induces peaceful sleep and is known for its purity, due to its white flowers derived from the orange-blossom. It de-stresses the mind and calms the body, and can enhance creativity when used with music and writing activities.

Rose *(Rosa centifolia, Rosa officinalis)* Renowned for its association with love. It is regarded as a soul fragrance, allowing us to connect with our spiritual energy. To induce dreams of romance, rose oil is ideal, as its own unique unfolding from bud to flower is similar to the unfolding of love.

Rosemary *(Rosmarinus officinalis)* Assists us with our sense of purpose and understanding of wisdom. It is known as a psychic protector, as it is best used in the morning in full strength. In an oil blend, use sparingly, as it is a stimulant. It was used in mediaeval Europe to drive away evil spirits from houses, and is widely regarded today as mind stimu-lant. It can help with increasing the level of clairvoyance and intuition. Like clary sage, its properties are associated with clear-sightedness.

Sandalwood *(Santalum album)* Warming and soothing with purifying properties. It has been used as an incense for med-itation for thousands of years because of its ability to quieten the conscious mind so that one can move into a deeper state of meditation. This action clarifies our thoughts and enables us to focus on inducing dreams, particularly if we are looking for direction or answers to some dilemma in our waking life.

Ylang ylang *(Canaga odorata)* A very sweet oil, balancing our physical and spiritual natures together. It is known as a sensual oil, due to its fragrance and its relaxing properties.

Blends for specific types of dreams

Make a blend, mixing the various oils to promote specific dreams. Use a few drops of each oil, depending on your personal preference, and use in an oil burner. Some oils may be harmful if you are pregnant.

Caution: Do not use oils if you are pregnant. Some people may develop a reaction when oils are used directly on skin. Generally, it is best to use oils in an oil burner rather than on skin or in a bath.

Dreams of love	Rose	heart warming
	Basil	healing
	Bergamot	comforting
	Ylang ylang	sensual
Dreams for good luck	Juniper	cleansing
	Sandalwood	clarifying

Restful dreams	Lavender	relaxing
	Camomile	soothing
	Neroli	peaceful
Dreams for creativity and inspiration	Coriander	warming
	Rosemary	clarifying
	Cypress	cleansing
	Lemon	stimulating
Dreams to predict the future	Basil	healing
	Clary sage	uplifting
	Bergamot	comforting
	Jasmine	invigorating

General blend for dream enhancing

10 drops jasmine oil
10 drops nutmeg oil
3 drops clary sage

This is best burnt in an oil burner to promote a dream-inducing atmosphere in your bedroom.

Glossary

Anxiety dreams Dreams that reflect the person's waking anxieties. Being chased, not turning up ready for an exam, roadblocks and other such frustrating dreams indicate that one's insecurities are manifesting themselves in dreams.

Archetypes Symbols and characters that are commonly understood by everyone because they represent universal themes of life.

Collective unconscious Archetypal images/symbols/emotions shared by all people around the world.

Delta sleep This is a deep sleep stage where long brainwaves produce a deep, dreamless sleep.

Dream recall Being able to remember the entire dream, usually in sequence.

Incubation dreams A dream in which you ask the dream for guidance in solving an actual problem in your waking life.

Lucid dreaming Being aware that you are dreaming while still asleep in the dream. The lucid dreamer can learn to manipulate the dream to suit his or her wishes.

Night terrors A series of screaming and agitation that usually occur in young children during a terrifying dream.

Nightmares A distressing dream which causes the dreamer to partially wake.

Parasomnias Disorders of arousal of sleep, including sleep walking, nightmares, night terrors and sleep talking.

Prophetic/precognitive dreams Accurate dreams predicting future events.

Psyche Our total personality.

Recurring dreams Dreams that are repeated.

REM sleep Rapid Eye Movement sleep, known also as dreaming sleep. The brain is in an active state like when we're awake, yet the movements are stilled so that we experience vivid dreams but can't move.

Bibliography

Pamela Ball, *The Complete Dream Dictionary*, Prospero Books, Canada, 1999.

Gregory J. Berry, *Dream Analysis: Thinking Beyond Jung*, Cranset, Hunter's Hill, NSW, 1995.

Tony Crisp, *The New Dream Dictionary*, Optima, London, 1990.

Russell Grant & Vicky Emptage, *The Illustrated Dream Dictionary*, Sterling, New York, 1996.

Geddes & Grosset, *Dictionary of Dreams*, 1997.

Georg Fink, *Dream Symbols A to Z*, Sterling, New York, 1999.

Sigmund Freud, *The Interpretation of Dreams*, Wordsworth, Hertfordshire, 1997.

Carl Jung, *Man and His Symbols*, Aldus, London, 1964.

Carl Jung, *Dreams*, Ark, London, 1986.

Jack Kerouac, *Book of Dreams*, City Light Books, San Francisco, 2001.

Peter Malone, *The Secret Language of Dreams: A Visual Key to Dreams and Their Meanings,* Pavilion, London, 1994.

Sandra A. Torson, *Cloud Nine: A Dreamer's Dictionary,* Avon, New York, 1994.

Kevin J. Trodeshi, *The Encyclopedia of Symbolism,* Berkley Publishing Group, New York, 1995.

Zolar, *Zolar's Encyclopedia and Dictionary of Dreams,* Fireside, New York, 1992.

F. & J. Zucker, *Dream Decoder: Reveal Your Unconscious Desires,* Simon & Schuster, NSW, 2000.

Web Sites

http://www.dreamcoach.com.au

http://www.sleeps.com/dictionary

http://www.lifetreks.com

http://www.sleepdisorderchannel.com/stages

http://www.dreamresearch.net

Index